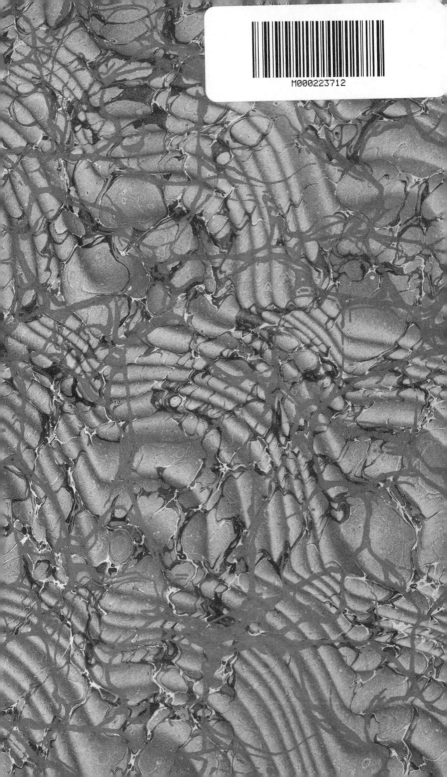

M000223712

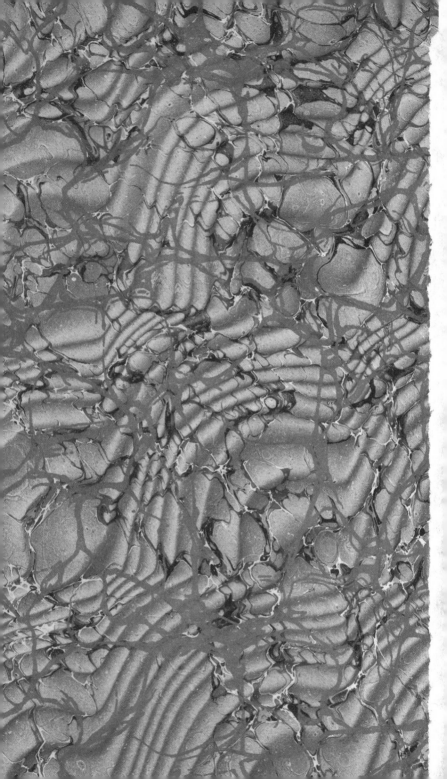

FOR EVERY SEASON,

VOLUME 3

FOR EVERY SEASON, VOL. 3

by Greg Laurie

ALLENDAVID™
PUBLISHERS Dana Point, California

FOR EVERY SEASON

ISBN 978-0-9801831-3-9

Printed in Canada.

Published by: Allen David Publishers—Dana Point, California
Coordination: FM Management, Ltd.
Cover photo: Trever Hoehne
Editor: Larry Libby
Cover Design: Christopher Laurie
Design: Highgate Cross+Cathey, Ltd.

*This book is dedicated to my son, Christopher David Laurie,
who was called suddenly to heaven this year.*

*My heart is broken, but healing by the hand of the One who said He
came to "Heal the brokenhearted." Christopher was a wonderful son
to Cathe and me, brother to Jonathan, husband to Brittany, and father
to Stella and Lucy. He also was a talented artist, designing this and
most of my other books. We miss him so very much,
but we know we will see him again in Heaven.*

Thank God for that hope.

Greg Laurie

Your words were found, and I ate them,

And Your word was to me the joy and rejoicing of my heart;

For I am called by Your name,

O Lord God of hosts.

Jeremiah 15:16 (NKJV)

PREFACE

Storms are an inevitable part of life on this broken planet. The fact is, you and I never know when the next tempest will come rushing over the horizon, and we'll find ourselves engulfed. The key isn't avoiding those storms—no one does that. The key is in being ready for the storms.

In the gospel of Matthew, Jesus painted a clear and unforgettable picture of two contrasting lives.

> *"Therefore, whoever hears these sayings of Mine, and does them, I will liken him to a wise man who built his house on the rock: and the rain descended, the floods came, and the winds blew and beat on that house; and it did not fall, for it was founded on the rock.*
> *But everyone who hears these sayings of Mine, and does not do them, will be like a foolish man who built his house on the sand: and the rain descended, the floods came, and the winds blew and beat on that house; and it fell. And great was its fall."*
> *(Matthew 7:24-27)*

It's interesting to me that both men in this parable heard the teachings of Jesus—but they heard it in two different ways. The first man heard, and took the teaching to heart; he not only paid attention to the words, he put them into practice, and built his life on them. Did he dodge the storm as a result?

No, he didn't.

But when the storm came, when the rain hammered and the violent winds clawed at his home, he and his family stayed safe.

The second man also heard. He may have even said, "Well, that's nice. That's very inspiring. Everyone needs a little spirituality." But then he went on with his life and his preoccupations, not putting any of those words into practice. When the same storm came thundering into his world, however, he had no defense at all. In fact, his whole life caved in.

Books like the one you hold in your hands right now can be a major source of strength in your life, as you carve time out of your day to study and consider the promises and the warnings of the Word of God. And if you will allow these pages to spur you on into a deeper study of the Word and a more faithful walk with Jesus Christ—if you put these concepts to work in the details of your life—you'll find yourself a stronger man, a stronger woman.

No, you won't escape the dark times. You won't avoid the perplexities, dodge the setbacks, or shield yourself from the occasional heartbreaks. Jesus never said that you would. In fact, He clearly stated that "In this world you *will* have tribulation" (John 16:33). But when the storms come, they won't sweep you away. The violent weather may assault you, it may push and pull you, it may even make you weep.

But it will never defeat you.

You have the Lord's own word on that.

Greg Laurie

A FRESH START

You crown the year with Your goodness, and Your paths drip with abundance.
(Psalm 65:11)

As we come to the beginning of a new year and the ending of an old one, we often wish we could turn over a new leaf or have a fresh start. No doubt about it, there have been certain things we've said or done in this past year that we have come to regret.

Wouldn't it be great to just start over again? In reality, as a Christian you can have a fresh start. The new year is still a blank slate, and opportunities lay ahead of you which you can't even imagine right now. But you are the one who must decide which path you will walk in this coming year. "Thus says the LORD: 'Stand in the ways and see, and ask for the old paths, where the good way is, and walk in it; then you will find rest for your souls'" (Jeremiah 6:16). You decide what your priorities will be. You decide which direction you will take, each and every day.

Maybe some of us need a fresh start in this coming year. What better time than now to make a new commitment? We don't know what the year ahead of us holds. We don't know what problems we may encounter or what changes will come. We don't know what blessings the Lord has in store for us. But whatever the new year brings, we don't have to be afraid, because Jesus Christ will be waiting there for us.

I like the words of that wonderful woman of God, Corrie ten Boom, who said, "Never be afraid to trust an unknown future to a known God."

God is in control of your future. He stands ready to bless you in this coming year. And He will... if You stay on His path and walk with Him every day.

Tuesday

ASTRAY OR ON TRACK?

Whether you turn to the right or to the left, your ears will hear a voice behind you, saying, "This is the way, walk in it." (Isaiah 30:21, NIV)

As you look back over the year just gone by, can you say it was a year when you progressed spiritually? Was it a year when you found yourself becoming a bit more like Jesus Christ? Or would you honestly have to say that you have drifted from the best path and now feel "off track"?

Today is a good day to make a change! Right now, people are making their New Year's resolutions. Some will swear off alcohol or smoking or television or overeating. Others will try to mend character flaws, or change destructive habits like gossip or worry or losing their temper. Others will seek to start new habits—like getting in shape physically. The truth is, we can also develop disciplines in our lives that will build us up spiritually. This year can be an opportunity for a fresh start for us all.

As the years go by, we realize how far we still have to go. We realize how much there is to learn, and how we're just beginning to scratch the surface. So much of our lives need to change. We need to be renewed and transformed and revived over and over again. We all have a natural tendency to stray and walk in wrong directions.

It's no coincidence that the Bible compares us to sheep, saying that we all like sheep have gone astray and we have turned every one to his own way (Isaiah 53:6). Every day of our lives, we need to be aware that we still have a sinful nature trying to rise up within us and make us stumble. We all have the potential to fall.

This could be a year of spiritual calamity if you stop moving forward. But on the other hand, it could be your greatest year yet if you make a commitment to walk with Christ like never before.

MY DETERMINED PURPOSE

Don't let the world around you squeeze you into its own mold, but let God remold your minds from within, so that you may prove in practice that the plan of God for you is good, meets all his demands and moves toward the goal of true maturity. (Romans 12:2, PHILLIPS)

With the world the way it is today, with things getting darker and darker and going from bad to worse, it seems to me the only way to live these days is as a completely sold–out Christian. Not as a fence sitter trying to blend in, but saying *I want to walk with God and live a real Christian life.*

Paul said that his determined purpose in life was to know Christ (see Philippians 3:10-14). What is your determined purpose in life? When you get up in the morning, what do you live for? What are your goals? What are your priorities?

If you don't have a goal, you're in serious trouble because, as it has been said, "If you aim at nothing, you're bound to hit it." Can you say with Paul, "My determined purpose in life is to know Him"? I hope so.

Think of the way that God used Paul. He had led countless people to faith, established churches out on the frontiers of his world, and wrote letters that we regard today as the very inspired Word of God. Yet Paul realized he had so much to learn and so far to go.

It's hard for us to think that someone like Paul would face the struggles and temptations we all face. But indeed he did. How much more should we be saying that we need to change radically in this coming year? We need to become more like Christ in this coming year, and don't let anyone pull the wool over your eyes…all of us have a long, long way to go.

DON'T LOOK BACK

I don't mean to say that I have already achieved these things or that I have already reached perfection! But I keep working toward that day when I will finally be all that Christ Jesus saved me for and wants me to be. No, dear brothers and sisters, I am still not all I should be, but I am focusing all my energies on this one thing: Forgetting the past and looking forward to what lies ahead, I strain to reach the end of the race and receive the prize for which God, through Christ Jesus, is calling us up to heaven. (Philippians 3:12-14, NLT)

The end of a year is a time of reflecting and remembering what God has done. But there comes a point where I say, *That was then, this is NOW.* And I put the past behind me.

Paul says he is forgetting the past, the things that are behind. The word *forget* doesn't mean to fail to remember. What it means is that Paul will no longer be *influenced or affected* by what happened before. To forget, then, means that we break the power of the past by living for the future.

Now that's wonderful when we think of sin. Because when we sin and we come to God and repent of it and He forgives us, we can trust in God's promise, "For I will forgive their iniquity, and their sin I will remember no more" (Jeremiah 31:34). God isn't suggesting that He will experience a lapse in His memory concerning your sins. What He's saying is that our sins will no longer affect our standing with Him or influence His attitude towards us. So if you have sinned, if you have failed this last year, you can put it behind you. You can forget the things that are behind.

Remember, to be His disciple, Jesus said we must take up the cross daily and follow Him (Luke 9:23). Let's not be satisfied with what has happened in the past. Forget about it, and move forward.

PRESS ON

I press toward the goal for the prize of the upward call of God in Christ Jesus.
(Philippians 3:14)

You remember how God fed the Israelites with manna. Every morning they would wake up, step out of their tents, and there would be the manna just waiting for them. But this "bread from heaven" had one limiting characteristic: It wouldn't keep overnight. God didn't want His people to live off yesterday's manna. The Lord wanted them to be dependent on Him on a regular basis and gather it fresh each day.

In the same way you can't live off the experiences of last year or twenty years ago. God wants to do something fresh and new in your life today and tomorrow. No, you can't live off experiences, but you can learn from them.

Saul of Tarsus went out of his way to hunt down Christians. But he came to realize that he was not serving God, but the devil. Then he was transformed, and went on to become the apostle Paul. He could say, "Now I press on, now I reach forward." I wish this would be true in the lives of more believers. What a difference it would make in this world around us if we had that kind of ambition, that kind of drive to serve God as we used to serve ourselves.

In this new year, let's recommit ourselves to the study of the Word of God, to prayer, and to winning at least one person to Christ in the next twelve months.

As Christians, we have unprecedented opportunities for our lives to make a difference this year. There is so much to do. So much growth that needs to take place in our lives, and so much more to accomplish. It's time to step into the future. To step into what God is doing today.

KEEP GROWING

Do your best to present yourself to God as one approved, a workman who does not need to be ashamed and who correctly handles the word of truth. (2 Timothy 2:15, NIV)

Every believer, whether new or old, faces obstacles in life. I hate to pop anyone's balloon out there, but the truth is, these difficulties never go away. You will never reach some spiritual plateau where you no longer need to grow in the Lord. In fact, the moment you relax your grip or try to put your Christian experience into cruise control or rest on your laurels, that will be the beginning of your downfall.

The Christian life is one of constant growth, learning, and transformation. While the conversion process is instantaneous, becoming more like Jesus takes a lifetime. I don't have anything better in which to invest my life than that. Do you?

You hear some people say, "Oh, I tried the whole Christianity thing. It didn't work for me." But my question is, did they do their part? There are many things the Bible tells us we should do as a result of truly being converted.

For example, did they begin to study and memorize Scripture? The Bible tells us that we should hide God's word in our hearts (see Deuteronomy 11:18; Psalm 119:11; Colossians 3:16). Did they make time to be a regular part of a body of believers by becoming actively and consistently involved in a church? Did they turn from all known sin? Did they get baptized? Did they develop a prayer life? Did they attempt to keep the commandments of God? The Bible says, "He who says he abides in Him ought himself also to walk just as He walked" (1 John 2:6).

New Christian or old, the way we face obstacles is to keep moving forward and to keep on growing.

BLINDED BY SIN

*"When anyone hears the word of the kingdom, and does not understand it, then
the wicked one comes and snatches away what was sown in his heart.
This is he who received seed by the wayside." (Matthew 13:19)*

The book of Acts describes the transformational moment when
Saul of Tarsus met Jesus Christ on the Damascus road. The Lord
told him, "I will deliver you from the Jewish people, as well as from the
Gentiles, to whom I now send you, *to open their eyes*, in order to *turn them
from darkness to light, and from the power of Satan to God*, that they may
receive forgiveness of sins and an inheritance among those who are sanctified by faith in Me" (Acts 26:17-18, italics added).

Before spiritual changes can take place in a person's life, his or her eyes
must be opened. Why? Because people may hear the gospel message, but
simply don't believe. That is because sin blinds us. In fact, the Bible tells
us, "But even if our gospel is veiled, it is veiled to those who are perishing,
whose minds the god of this age has blinded, who do not believe, lest the
light of the gospel of the glory of Christ, who is the image of God, should
shine on them" (2 Corinthians 4:3-4).

There is nothing we can do to open spiritually blind eyes. We can share
the gospel with someone again and again, but it just doesn't penetrate.
Then one day, all of the sudden, it sinks in. That is why, when we pray for
unbelievers, we need to ask God to open their eyes and help them to see their
need for Him.

Don't give up on unbelievers in your life. Their resistance to the gospel
doesn't mean they will never believe. They are simply blinded to their true
spiritual state. So keep praying.

SHALLOW ROOTS

"But he who received the seed on stony places, this is he who hears the word and immediately receives it with joy; yet he has no root in himself, but endures only for a while. For when tribulation or persecution arises because of the word, immediately he stumbles." (Matthew 13:20-21)

Jesus spoke of people who hear the Word of God, but it never quite takes root. These people appear to be converted, and even motivated. They seem to be living on an emotional high, and even try to bring others to Christ. Yet they are a picture of soil embedded with rocks. The good seed of God's Word breaks ground and shoots up, but no fruit ever appears. No real change ever results. Theirs was not a true encounter with God.

Why did they fall away? It's possible they built their faith on the wrong foundation. Maybe they responded to the gospel because a friend of theirs did. But conversion is not a group effort; you have to make your own commitment to Jesus. Another possibility may be that unbelief set in, causing them to begin doubting God at their first emotional low. Or they gave up at the first sign of persecution for the gospel's sake.

If you are a true follower of Jesus, there will be hardships, times of trial, and seasons when you don't feel God is near you. And there will be times when people give you a hard time for no other reason than the fact that you say you are a Christian. So don't build your life on a friend's example or approval. Don't even build it on a church. Build it on Christ.

SEEDS AND WEEDS

"Now he who received seed among the thorns is he who hears the word, and the cares of this world and the deceitfulness of riches choke the word, and he becomes unfruitful." (Matthew 13:22)

When Jesus spoke of the seed that is sown among thorns, He was talking about ground that is embedded with weeds. There were over 2,000 types of weeds in ancient Israel, weeds that would hinder the growth of a seed. The little seedlings would be in a constant battle with these life-sapping weeds.

The trouble with a weed is that it doesn't have an immediate effect; its impact on the plant is more gradual. This is in contrast to seed sown on rocky soil, which shoots up and then falls away. A seed sown among thorns is harder to identify. A person may say, "I am a Christian," and perhaps you see some changes in his or her life. It will seem like this person is solid.

A few weeks or months go by, and slowly but surely, something happens. As Jesus said, "The cares of this world and the deceitfulness of riches choke the word, and he becomes unfruitful" (Matthew 13:22). It doesn't happen overnight. This person doesn't abandon his or her faith instantaneously. It's something that takes place over a period of time.

Gradually, material things become more important to them than spiritual things. After awhile, movies become more important than church. Parties become more important than prayer. Things on earth become more important than treasures in heaven. And slowly but surely, the weeds choke them out. These people were never truly converted; it just looked like they were. And after awhile, they just bail out.

So how can we tell who the true converts are? By time. Time will tell—time and the visible results in their lives called spiritual fruit.

GOOD GROUND

"But he who received seed on the good ground is he who hears the word and understands it, who indeed bears fruit and produces: some a hundredfold, some sixty, some thirty." (Matthew 13:23)

Believers who produce spiritual fruit aren't like the seeds sown on the wayside that Jesus spoke of in the Parable of the Sower. These symbolize people who never seem to grasp the Word of God. Nor are they like the seed sown on rocky soil, representing those who are rootless, allowing emotions to overpower obedience. Nor are they like the seed sown among thorns, signifying those who hear God's Word and plan to keep it, but gradually let worldly pursuits choke it out.

True believers hear God's Word and keep it. They respond decisively and promptly to what God shows them. They hear the message, internalize it, and make visible changes in their lives.

Outward changes don't save us, but if we really are saved, there will be changes. Works don't save us, but if we really are saved, there will be works. And if there are no changes in our lives outwardly, then there have been no real changes inwardly.

Have there been changes in your life? By "changes," I don't mean having a number of Bibles in your house in various colors to coordinate with different outfits. Nor do I mean having a bumper sticker with a Christian slogan on your car or a collection of church bulletins. What I do mean are changes to the extent that someone could look at your life and recognize you as a Christian.

If people were to look at your life today, what would they see? Would they see evidence of Jesus Christ living inside of you? Or would they see the same old you? The choice is up to you.

GOD'S HEROES

*Remember, dear brothers and sisters, that few of you were wise in the world's
eyes, or powerful, or wealthy when God called you. Instead, God deliberately
chose things the world considers foolish in order to shame those who think they
are wise. And he chose those who are powerless to shame those
who are powerful. (1 Corinthians 1:26-27, NLT)*

In many ways, we have lost the meaning of the word "hero." We throw
it around so casually. If you can put a ball through a hoop, you're a
sports hero. If you can play eight chords on a guitar, you're a rock 'n' roll
hero. If you can pretend to be something you're not, you're a Hollywood
hero. We have a strange concept as to who our heroes really are.

I remember watching a well-known journalist interview an actor about
his recent movie, which featured a politically troubled region of the world.
When the journalist asked the celebrity what he thought should be done
about the political situation there, the actor responded, "Who cares what I
think?" and went on to point out that he was just an actor. All too often, we
mistakenly think actors really are the people they portray. We think they
are heroes when, in fact, they're just people like you and me.

A hero is someone who does something sacrificial, something courageous. There are heroes today, of course. We saw many of them in action on
9/11 and in the days that followed. But often, today's heroes are operating
behind the scenes, and we never know about them.

As we look at heroes of the faith on whom God put His hand, both in
Scripture and in contemporary history, one thing stands out. It seems that
God has always gone out of His way to find individuals who did not necessarily look like heroes. And that is precisely the point. God isn't looking for
a strong man or woman per se. Rather, He's looking for someone who will
walk in His strength.

UNDER THE SPIRIT'S CONTROL

Don't act thoughtlessly, but understand what the Lord wants you to do. Don't be drunk with wine, because that will ruin your life. Instead, be filled with the Holy Spirit. (Ephesians 5:17-18, NLT)

When we hear the term "filled with the Spirit," it can sometimes frighten us. We might have seen bizarre things take place in the name of the Holy Spirit. So we think, *If that's being filled with the Holy Spirit, then I don't know if I want it.*

To be filled with the Holy Spirit doesn't necessarily involve an emotional experience. It can, but it doesn't have to. The word "filled" as used in the Bible— and specifically in Ephesians 5:18—is a word that has many shades of meaning. Not one of them, however, describes an emotional experience. One translation of the word "filled" is the idea of wind filling the sail of a ship. The wind carries that vessel along. So to be filled with the Spirit means that God fills your sails, so to speak, and guides you through life. You are led through life by the Holy Spirit.

But the idea of being filled with the Spirit also carries the meaning of being permeated. In the original language, the word was also used to describe salt permeating meat to flavor and preserve it. God wants His Holy Spirit to permeate the lives of His children in what they say, think, and do. In other words, being filled with the Spirit is not limited to one, isolated instance.

To be filled with the Spirit means that He infuses every aspect of our lives. He saturates our prayer life, our worship life, and our business life, too. He influences the way we treat others. To be filled with the Spirit is walking thought by thought, decision by decision, and act by act, under the Spirit's control.

THE DAY OF SMALL THINGS

"Who despises the day of small things?" (Zechariah 4:10, NIV)

Faithfulness. That's one consistent quality we can see in the lives of men and women God used in the pages of Scripture. We read in 2 Timothy 2:2, "And the things that you have heard from me among many witnesses, commit these to *faithful* men who will be able to teach others also" (italics added). And Jesus said, "He who is faithful in what is least is faithful also in much; and he who is unjust in what is least is unjust also in much" (Luke 16:10).

Right now, you may be at a place in life where nothing seems to be happening. You might be thinking, *Lord, come on! Use me. Call on me. I'll turn this world upside down for You.* But the Lord may be saying, "My son, My daughter, you're not ready yet. I have to prepare you first." Be faithful to do what He has set before you today to the best of your ability.

That's what Stephen did. Acts 6 tells us that his job was to serve tables. Notice the church leaders didn't say, "Stephen, go out and do miracles and then go preach the gospel to the Sanhedrin. While you're preaching, a guy named Saul of Tarsus will hear you. He ultimately will be converted, and will become the greatest preacher in the history of the church." Instead, Stephen waited on tables. And as the Lord found him faithful in the little things, He gave him more responsibility.

You can never be too small for God to use; only too big. We need to be faithful in what God has set before us. Because if we're not faithful in the little things, then we won't be faithful in greater things either.

THE PERSON GOD USES

Work hard and cheerfully at whatever you do, as though you were working for the Lord rather than for people. (Colossians 3:23, NLT)

When I was eighteen and a new believer, I quickly came to understand where the phrase "starving artist" came from. All I knew how to do was draw cartoons, so I was doing that as well as some freelance graphics on the side. I was trying to make ends meet, but most of all, I longed to be used by God. So I would hang around Calvary Chapel of Costa Mesa, waiting for an opportunity just to do something.

One day one of the pastors said to me, "Greg, I need you to do something for the church."

I said, "What is it?" Preach the gospel to the ends of the Earth? Pray for the sick? I'm ready. Here am I, send me!

"We need you to buy a doorknob."

"A doorknob?"

"Yes," he said. "We need you to go to Sears and buy a new doorknob for the church door."

It was a little job, but I was excited for the opportunity. I was on a mission from God to buy a doorknob. I went to Sears. There must have been 300 kinds of doorknobs in every size, shape, and finish. I finally bought one and took it back to the church. I was so excited. (It turned out to be the wrong size...but I tried!)

Are you excited for any opportunity to serve the Lord, even if it's a little one? The issue really isn't "big jobs" or "little jobs." It's that you are doing it for the Lord. Is that fact alone enough for you? Is it enough that God would want to guide you and use you? If so, then you're the kind of person He is looking for right now.

AN OUTLET FOR YOUR INLET

"Give, and it will be given to you. A good measure, pressed down, shaken together and running over, will be poured into your lap. For with the measure you use, it will be measured to you." (Luke 6:38, NIV)

Many believers who have known the Lord for years face spiritual stagnation. They say, "I've been a Christian for so long. I know the Bible so well. I go to church every week. What's wrong with me?"

I can tell you what's wrong. They need an outlet for their inlet. If you don't have an outlet for what you are taking in, then you will stagnate. The truth of God's Word was not designed to be hoarded, but to be shared. And the more you give out, the more God gives to you.

Proverbs 11:25 says, "The generous soul will be made rich, and he who waters will also be watered himself." The Bible is saying that if you want a full soul and a rich life, then give freely of what you have...be it time, talent, or treasure.

It's a radical thought, and it flies in the face of what we hear today—especially in our touchy-feely, narcissistic culture in which we're all trying to help our wounded inner child and build our self-esteem.

Jesus was saying, "Want to find life? Then lose it. Deny yourself." This means we stop focusing on ourselves and start thinking about other people and their needs. Then we will find what we've been looking for all along—not by searching for it, but as the byproduct of a life that is properly aligned with God.

Thursday

A LIFE THAT MATTERS

But as for me, I trust in You, O LORD; I say, "You are my God."
My times are in Your hand. (Psalm 31:14-15)

I have to admit that I'm sometimes a little amused when I read obituaries in the newspaper or hear what's said at some peoples' funerals. Whoever the deceased was, he or she was the greatest person who ever lived. There was never a person more compassionate, more loving, or more caring. This is because when someone dies, we want to say the best about him or her.

But what if we told the truth at funerals? What if someone stood up and said, "This guy was a jerk, right? He squandered his life. How many people did he rip off—including those of us right here in this room? Let's face it, he was selfish. He didn't care about others. All he cared about was himself. And quite frankly, I'm kind of glad he's gone, aren't you?"

Of course we would never say that. Instead, we might even stretch the truth about how wonderful a person was.

If someone were to sum up your life, what would they say you lived for? What will they remember you for? That will be your legacy. Wouldn't you like it to be honestly said of you, "This person loved God. She cared about the things of God. He really cared about other people. This person really lived for the Lord."

The ultimate waste is to throw your life away, to squander it. Yet so many people do. One day, you will breathe your last breath. One day, you will make your last statement. One day, you will eat your last meal. What will you be remembered for?

Live a life that matters. Live a life that makes a difference. Live a life for Him, and you will never regret it.

WHEN OPPORTUNITY KNOCKS

But in your hearts set apart Christ as Lord. Always be prepared to give an answer to everyone who asks you to give the reason for the hope that you have. But do this with gentleness and respect. (1 Peter 3:15, NIV)

To recognize opportunity is the difference between success and failure. When opportunity knocks, we have to get up and answer the door. And we never know when it will knock.

If we as Christians are going to obey the Lord's command to go into all the world and preach the gospel, then we must know what we believe and how to present it. Sadly, many Christians are unable to do that. They have little to no understanding of why or what they believe. The Bible warns that "we should no longer be children, tossed to and fro and carried about with every wind of doctrine, by the trickery of men, in the cunning craftiness of deceitful plotting" (Ephesians 4:14). When we don't know what we believe, we are vulnerable. And because of this spiritual deficiency, we are ineffective witnesses for the Lord.

In Acts 7, we read about a man who was prepared for a significant moment in his life—which turned out to be a defining moment for the young church of Jesus Christ. When Stephen was hauled before the Sanhedrin, he was ready for the opportunity God dropped in his lap. He seized the moment and made a difference.

You can do the same…because you never know when those golden opportunities will come your way. As they would say in the 19th century, "Trust in God and keep your powder dry." Be ready for that opportunity, because you never know when the Lord will drop it in your lap.

COURAGE TO STAND

If you are reproached for the name of Christ, blessed are you, for the Spirit of glory and of God rests upon you. On their part He is blasphemed, but on your part He is glorified. (1 Peter 4:14)

Throughout history, God has given special grace and courage to millions of Christians who were persecuted for the faith or who lost their lives. They were unwilling to renounce the Lord, unwilling to deny the One who had so radically changed their lives.

We may hear the stories of these Christians and say, "What a tragedy." But I don't think that's a tragedy, because everyone has to die. These believers not only lived well, but they died well. They died for the greatest cause on the face of the earth: the cause of Jesus Christ.

Sometimes we might think, *I don't know if I could handle it if my life were actually threatened for the sake of the gospel.* But if God allowed you to be put into such a situation, then I am confident He would give you the grace and strength you would need—in that moment—to face it.

Jesus told His followers, "Now when they bring you to the synagogues and magistrates and authorities, do not worry about how or what you should answer, or what you should say. For the Holy Spirit will teach you in that very hour what you ought to say" (Luke 12:11-12).

This doesn't mean you shouldn't be prepared for such a day. You simply shouldn't worry about it, knowing that God won't give you more than you can handle. He will give you just the right words for just the right situation. And not only will God give you the right words, He will also give you the power to stand up for your faith—even it means harassment or hardship or persecution.

A MATTER OF LIGHT AND DARKNESS

> *"Their judgment is based on this fact: The light from heaven came into the world, but they loved the darkness more than the light, for their actions were evil."* (John 3:19, NLT)

I have always been amazed at how upset and completely irrational some people can become when the subject of Jesus Christ comes up. You can be talking about anything, even politics, and they will be relatively nice. Even considerate. But just mention Jesus Christ, and you'll see veins pop out of the foreheads of otherwise rational and courteous people.

We wonder, *What's with this*? It is a matter of light and darkness. It's a different dynamic altogether when you talk about the things of God. There is something about the name of Jesus that arrests a person's attention. Why else would people use it for effect when they take the Lord's name in vain? There is power in that name. Even the unbeliever, in a warped sense, recognizes that.

Jesus said, "For everyone practicing evil hates the light and does not come to the light, lest his deeds should be exposed" (John 3:20). They hate the light for fear that it will expose their darkness.

The same is true of the Bible. When I travel, I will occasionally wind up in the middle seat—which I try very hard not to get. I am usually seated between two big guys who spill over their seats a little. As we are talking, I will sometimes reach into my briefcase and take out my Bible. They look at it. They see the gold pages and the ribbons. And at that point, I might as well have pulled out a live skunk. It represents truth to them, and deep down inside, they know it is the truth.

There is power in the name of Jesus and in the Word of God.

FALLING INTO HEAVEN

Then he knelt down and cried out with a loud voice, 'Lord, do not charge them with this sin.' And when he had said this, he fell asleep. (Acts 7:60)

It's a funny thing how we find sleep more and more appealing as we get older. When I was a kid, I hated to go to sleep. I still remember kindergarten, with the lukewarm milk in little cartons and having to lie down and take naps in the middle of the day. Sleep is usually the last thing kids want to do, but as we start getting older, the idea of sleep becomes more attractive.

Interestingly, the Bible describes death for a believer as sleep. You close your eyes to the only life you've ever known—life on earth—and in the next instant, you open your eyes and find yourself in the very presence of the Lord. Scripture teaches that there is no delay at all between life here on earth and life in heaven.

Stephen's statement in today's Bible passage indicates that he expected to enter the Lord's presence as soon as he died.

Again, in 2 Corinthians 5:8, we're told that a believer will enter immediately into the presence of God following death: "We are confident, yes, well pleased rather to be absent from the body and to be present with the Lord."

John Bunyan said, "Death is but a passage out of a prison into a palace." You see, when death strikes a Christian down, he or she falls into heaven.

HOW GOD SPEAKS

"My sheep hear My voice, and I know them, and they follow Me." (John 10:27)

Does God still speak to people today? Is He interested in what happens to us as individuals? Does He really have a master plan for our lives?

God truly is interested in us as individuals. He *does* have a master plan for our lives, and He *does* want to speak to us. Jesus described Himself as our Good Shepherd. And as His sheep, we can hear His voice.

So how can we know when it is God speaking? First, we need to remember that God primarily speaks to us through His Word, and He will never lead us in a way that contradicts that Word. We don't have to go any further than the Bible to know the will of God for our lives.

God also speaks through circumstances that can include failure or even hardship. We don't enjoy it when God speaks to us through tragedy and hardship, but as C. S. Lewis said, "God whispers to us in our pleasures, speaks in our conscience, but shouts in our pain: it is His megaphone to rouse a deaf world."

Often I have found that if something is the will of God, then it will be confirmed. There are times when I feel the Lord has been speaking to me through circumstances, such as an opportunity that has opened up. But I never make decisions by looking at circumstances alone.

Lastly, God speaks to us through His peace. Colossians 3:15 tells us, "Let the peace of God rule in your hearts...." God is the author of peace, not of confusion.

Maybe we hear the voice of God more often than we think. The question is, are we really listening?

THE GOOD SHEPHERD

"I am the good shepherd; and I know My sheep, and am known by My own."
(John 10:14)

Jesus, the Good Shepherd, is a familiar and comforting picture of God's feelings for us and His outlook toward us. It is a picture echoed throughout the pages of Scripture. Isaiah 40:11 tells us, "He will feed His flock like a shepherd; He will gather the lambs with His arm, and carry them in His bosom, and gently lead those who are with young."

Jesus himself told the story of a shepherd who left his flock of ninety-nine and went after one stray sheep to illustrate His attitude toward the person who strays from the flock. How easily He could write off the one who strays. But He doesn't. Instead, He goes out and looks for that sheep. When He finds it, He brings it back with great joy.

The Shepherd knows His sheep. He knows us by name. He knows our personalities, our strengths and weaknesses, our secret dreams, and what frightens us the most.

Not only does God know our natures, but He knows our needs. Don't forget that this God we serve and follow knows also what it's like to be human. He knew what it was like to face the limitations of humanity. He knew what it was like to feel the pressure of temptation and to experience loneliness, sorrow, and joy. As Hebrews 4:15 says, "For we do not have a High Priest who cannot sympathize with our weaknesses, but was in all points tempted as we are, yet without sin."

Our Good Shepherd cares about us. He knows sheep—and people—inside out. And He knows what you are going through today...down to the smallest detail.

LIKE SHEEP

All we like sheep have gone astray; we have turned, every one, to his own way.
(Isaiah 53:6)

Jesus said, "My sheep hear My voice..." (John 10:27). Of all the animals Jesus could have compared us to, He chose sheep. He didn't say, "My dolphins hear My voice," or "My chimpanzees hear My voice." He said, "My sheep hear My voice."

You may be wondering, *but aren't sheep really stupid animals?* Yes, they are. They are so dense, in fact, that if one sheep walks off a cliff and falls to its death, others will follow.

Unfortunately, there are many characteristics that we humans share with sheep. One of them is that we have a tendency to go astray, to follow the crowd—especially when we are young.

But the problem is that like sheep, we can do what everyone else does and end up doing the wrong thing. Proverbs 14:12 says, "There is a way that seems right to a man, but its end is the way of death." How we need people today to stand up for what is right and not just follow the crowd.

Daniel 3 tells the story of three Hebrew teenagers—Shadrach, Meshach, and Abed-Nego—who held positions of influence in the kingdom of Babylon. However, because they refused to bow down to the image of King Nebuchadnezzar, they were thrown into a fiery furnace. But God honored their courage and commitment to Him by preserving their lives. How we need people like them today.

Let's not be like sheep that follow the crowd to their own destruction. Let's stay on the narrow way that leads to life. If we do, we will look back and thank God. We will look back and realize that we missed nothing, but instead gained eternal life.

OUR SOURCE OF STRENGTH

I can do all things through Christ who strengthens me. (Philippians 4:13)

Sheep are timid, fearful creatures. Because of their very makeup, it's almost impossible for them to lie down unless they are free from all fear. An entire flock can go stampeding off into nowhere because a rabbit jumped out of a bush.

Yet how like sheep we are! We can be afraid of so many things. Afraid of losing our health. Afraid of losing our wealth. Afraid of losing our loved ones. In fact, sometimes it seems we can be afraid of life itself.

Certainly there are a lot of frightening things out there in the world today. Violent crime is at epidemic levels. We wonder, *Will I get on a plane and have it blown up by terrorists? Will I keep my job? Will I be robbed walking down the street? Will I contract a terminal disease?*

Jesus Christ, the Good Shepherd, will protect you, and stands as your representative before the throne of God. Jesus Christ, who paid the price for your salvation, stands as your righteousness, giving you access into the presence of God. As the Scripture says, Jesus is the One "in whom we have boldness and access with confidence through faith in Him" (Ephesians 3:12).

As believers, we can have boldness and authority, not because of who we are, but because of whose we are. Jesus is our strength. He is the one who gives us boldness. That's one more reason why we never want to stray from His side! Instead, we want to stay as close to Him as possible.

HEARING HIS VOICE

> *"To him the doorkeeper opens, and the sheep hear his voice; and he calls his own sheep by name and leads them out." (John 10:3)*

As you get to know your Shepherd, you will come to realize that when He calls you, it is always worth obeying. When He says something, it is for your benefit. If He says, "Go this way," it's because He has green pastures and still waters for you. If He says, "Stop! Don't do that," it's because He's trying to protect you from potential danger, possibly something that is even life-threatening.

The fact that God speaks to us is clear throughout the pages of Scripture. To some, like Moses, God spoke audibly. To others, like the prophet Elijah, He spoke quietly on at least one occasion.

Often we look for the big events, the earthshaking circumstances in which God speaks. And many times He is speaking to us, but it is in a still, small voice. We should try turning off the television, the radio, and the telephone and just listen. With all the noise in our world, with all the information that bombards us, we can hear all those voices but miss the most important voice of all. Maybe one reason we don't hear Him is because we never stop and listen. We should heed the words of Psalm 46:10, which says, "Be still, and know that I am God."

Once we have heard the voice of God, we need to follow. Jesus said, "The sheep follow him, for they know his voice" (John 10:4). The word "follow" means to deliberately decide to comply with instruction. It is a deliberate choice for sheep to follow the shepherd. We need to deliberately decide to follow our Shepherd, to do what He tells us to do.

When God Almighty speaks to you in that still, small voice, will you listen? Will you follow Him?

THE EXAMPLE OF ANDREW

He first found his own brother Simon, and said to him, "We have found the Messiah".... And he brought him to Jesus. (John 1:41, 42)

In the first chapter of John's Gospel, we see John the Baptist pointing to Jesus and directing his disciples to follow Him. Andrew and John heard him and followed Jesus. Then Andrew went to tell his brother Simon and brought him to Jesus.

The thing about Andrew is that once he was convinced, he was convinced. He saw for himself. He believed. And he immediately went out to tell his brother Simon. How we need more Andrews today! If we had more Andrews, we would have more Simon Peters. One person bringing another person to Jesus—it's so simple. It's so effective. And it is so neglected.

Mark 2 gives an account of four men who brought their paralyzed friend to Christ. As Jesus was teaching inside a house overflowing with people, these four persistent men climbed up to the roof and lowered their friend inside. Jesus was so impressed with their demonstration of faith that He forgave the man of his sins and healed him (see Mark 2:3-5).

When a person comes to Christ, it's often because of contacts he or she has had with a number of believers...perhaps going back years. As Paul said, "I planted, Apollos watered, but God gave the increase" (1 Corinthians 3:6). We all have a part.

Andrew was brand-new in the faith, and often the newest converts are the most zealous evangelists. That's probably because they are so aware of the fact that they have just been saved from a miserable lifestyle. That was Andrew. We may find ourselves becoming stronger witnesses for Jesus if we keep reminding ourselves time and again of what God has done for us.

JUST THROW THE NET

And he brought them out and said, "Sirs, what must I do to be saved?"
(Acts 16:30)

Many of us are afraid to ask someone if they would like to give their life to Jesus Christ for one simple reason: We're afraid the answer will be no. And it just may be. But there are those wonderful times when someone will surprise you and say, "Tell me more." Or maybe even, "I want to give my life to Jesus Christ."

Many years ago, I had the opportunity to be reunited with my father, Oscar Laurie, the man who adopted me. My mother had divorced him when I was a young boy, and that was the last time I had seen him. Years later, when I had an opportunity to preach on the East Coast, he invited our family to stay at his house for the weekend.

After dinner one night, his wife said, "Greg, tell me about how you came to put your faith in Jesus Christ." As I shared my testimony and what Christ had done for me, my dad sat there listening with his hands folded. I thought, *He's not buying this at all.* But later that night, he asked me to go walking with him the next morning.

As we walked out into the cold morning air, he said, "I was listening to what you said last night. I want to know what I need to do to give my life to Jesus Christ." He made a commitment to Christ that day, and he faithfully served the Lord for the remaining fifteen years of his life.

Sometimes, when you share your faith, you don't think you're getting through. But you never know. That is why we need to simply "throw out the net." We need to give people the opportunity.

HE KNOWS THE REAL YOU

Now when Jesus looked at him, He said, "You are Simon the son of Jonah. You shall be called Cephas" (which is translated, A Stone). (John 1:42)

John's Gospel tells us that when Andrew brought his brother Simon to Jesus, He looked at Simon. I find it interesting that the word *looked* used here could be translated "He saw right through him."

Have you ever had someone look at you that way? Mothers seem to have this special ability. But Jesus didn't have this ability in only a figurative way. He literally could look into a person's soul, see what was going on, and know everything about him or her.

So Jesus looked at Simon and said, "Your name is Simon. But I'm giving you a new name. It's Peter." I wonder what Andrew and John were thinking when Jesus said this. They knew Simon. And if there was one thing Simon was not, it was a rock. The name "Simon" means "listener or hearer." So Jesus was saying, "You are no longer going to be a listener or a hearer. You will become a rock." Jesus had looked right through him and not only saw Simon for what he was, but *saw him for what he could be.*

In the same way, Jesus knows the real *you*—not the "you" that you've created for yourself, the persona or mask that you hide behind. Jesus knows what you think about late at night…what you dream about…what troubles you…what you hope for and wish for. And He knows what needs to happen in your life to make you the person He wants you to be.

That's the key, isn't it? He not only knows you, He knows how to complete you. The best thing any of us could ever do is to commit our lives into His hands.

POWER WITH A PURPOSE

"But you will receive power when the Holy Spirit comes upon you. And you will be my witnesses, telling people about me everywhere—in Jerusalem, throughout Judea, in Samaria, and to the ends of the earth." (Acts 1:8, NLT)

What comes to mind when you hear the word *dynamite*? I automatically think of something explosive. And when something is described as *dynamic*, I know it is something unusual or special, something that stands out.

Jesus told the disciples they would receive power when the Holy Spirit came upon them. The word that Jesus used for power is from the Greek word *dunamis*, the same word from which we get our words *dynamite* and *dynamic*.

Have you ever seen a fire hose on the loose? It can knock people and things over. It can be very destructive. But if you get hold of it and aim it in the right direction, you can do a lot of good.

Power is exciting if it is used for something productive. In the same way, God has given us the power of the Holy Spirit for a purpose. God's power is practical. He didn't give us the Holy Spirit so that we would behave strangely. He gave us the Holy Spirit to be His witnesses and to effectively share our faith. It is power with a purpose.

When the Holy Spirit came upon those first-century believers on the Day of Pentecost, the Bible says that about 3,000 people made commitments to Jesus Christ (see Acts 2:41). Peter made an important statement about the Holy Spirit back then: the power they had received was not only available to them, but would be available to future generations of believers as well (see Acts 2:39).

This means that the same power is available to us to change our world.

SOWING AND REAPING

For he who sows to his flesh will of the flesh reap corruption, but he who sows to the Spirit will of the Spirit reap everlasting life. (Galatians 6:8)

A successful building contractor called in one of his employees, a skilled carpenter, and told him that he was putting him in charge of the next house the company was building. He instructed the carpenter to order all of the materials and oversee the entire process from the ground up.

The carpenter excitedly accepted his assignment. It was his first opportunity to actually oversee an entire building project. He studied the blueprints and checked every measurement.

Then he thought, "If I'm really in charge, why can't I cut a few corners, use less expensive materials, and put the extra money in my pocket? Who would know the difference? After we paint the place, no one would be able to tell."

The carpenter set about with his scheme. He used second-grade lumber and ordered inexpensive concrete for the foundation. He put in cheap wiring. He cut every corner he possibly could, but reported the use of higher-quality building materials.

When the home was completed, he asked his boss to come and see it. His boss looked it over and said, "This is incredible. You did a fantastic job. You have been such a good and faithful worker and have been so honest all of these years that I am showing my gratitude by giving you this house."

We will reap what we sow. Just as we can't plant weeds and reap flowers, we can't sin and reap righteousness. There are reactions to our actions. Think about it: every day, we are either sowing to the Spirit or we are sowing to the flesh.

What kind of seeds will you sow today?

WHAT'S ON YOUR MIND?

"So commit yourselves completely to these words of mine. Tie them to your hands as a reminder, and wear them on your forehead. Teach them to your children. Talk about them when you are at home and when you are away on a journey, when you are lying down and when you are getting up again."
(Deuteronomy 11:18-19, NLT)

People sometimes ask me to sign their Bibles, which is not something I like to do, because I didn't write it! But when someone insists, I usually write this inscription in his or her Bible: "Sin will keep you from this book, and this book will keep you from sin."

I have found that sin will always keep you away from the Bible, because the devil wants to keep you out of God's Word. He doesn't care if you read magazines, watch television, or read the latest novel on the bestseller list. But the minute you pick up the Bible and crack it open, you'd better believe that he will try to distract you with everything he has. He doesn't want you to read it.

On the other hand, if you follow what the Bible teaches, it will keep you from sin. That is why we need to know the Word of God and study it. While it's a great idea to carry a Bible in your briefcase, pocket, or purse, the best place to carry it is in your heart. Know it well. Fill the memory banks God has given you with Scripture, because the devil will attack you in the realm of your mind. The best defense is a mind that is filled with God's Word.

A Genuine Conversion

Then all who heard were amazed, and said, "Is this not he who destroyed those who called on this name in Jerusalem, and has come here for that purpose, so that he might bring them bound to the chief priests?" (Acts 9:21)

The mere mention of the name Saul of Tarsus would send chills down the backbones of the believers of his day. His conversion was such a shocking, headline event that it's mentioned three times in Scripture.

British agnostic Lord George Lyttelton certainly couldn't imagine such a transformation, and set out to prove that Paul was really never converted. He felt that if he could disprove the conversion of Paul, then he could essentially undermine the entire Christian faith. So he went to work on his treatise, entitled *Observations on the Conversion and Apostleship of St. Paul.*

But a funny thing happened. He ended up meeting the same God that Paul had met. He had set out to disprove Paul's conversion, but ultimately became converted himself after honestly looking at this amazing story. Lyttelton concluded, "Paul's conversion and apostleship alone duly considered are a demonstration sufficient to prove Christianity is a divine revelation."

In Saul, we see a man formerly controlled by hate who became controlled by love. In fact, this notorious persecutor of Christians wrote one of the most beautiful passages on love anywhere in literature, and one that certainly stands out in the pages of Scripture: 1 Corinthians 13.

After his encounter with Jesus, Paul blazed a trail that left behind many churches and converts. He preached to philosophers, Pharisees, rulers, soldiers, sorcerers, sailors, slaves, and probably to Caesar himself.

Paul wasn't some superhuman who was above temptation or incapable of falling. But he was a man who dared to follow Jesus Christ wholeheartedly as both Savior and Lord. And history has shown us the amazing results of that loyalty.

MISGUIDED LOYALTIES

As for Saul, he made havoc of the church, entering every house, and dragging off men and women, committing them to prison. (Acts 8:3)

We know from reading about Saul, or Paul, that he was raised in a strict Jewish home. This meant that he would have learned the Scriptures from youth. His family sprang from the best soil, the tribe of Benjamin, where Israel's first king, Saul, came from. No doubt young Saul was named after him.

Saul decided to become a Pharisee, a religious order characterized by strict discipline. His entire life essentially would be governed not only by Scripture, but by the various laws given by the rabbis. It was a radical commitment to make.

We also know that Saul was schooled by the famous Gamaliel, known as the teachers' teacher and famed for his wisdom and understanding. Gamaliel personally took an interest in young Saul and taught him the things of God. The young man had a ravenous hunger for knowledge. He wanted to be as devout as possible.

So how was it that a man who was so religious ultimately became nothing more than a common murderer? It's because religion can become a blinding, destructive force. Religious people conspired to put Jesus to death. And religious people had dragged young Stephen into the streets and stoned him to death.

When I say "religion," I'm not talking about faith in Christ. There is a big difference between man–made religion and true faith in God's Son. I think religion is probably keeping more people from Christ than everything else put together, because it gives such a false sense of security. But they will be in for a big shock when they find out that religion will not satisfy the requirements of a holy God.

Saul came face to face with that truth, and experienced a complete transformation in his life. The same thing can happen to your friends and family members who have put their trust in religion instead of salvation in Jesus Christ.

IMPROBABLE CHRISTIANS

And when Saul had come to Jerusalem, he tried to join the disciples; but they were all afraid of him, and did not believe that he was a disciple. (Acts 9:26)

Right now, you might be able to think of an individual you can't even visualize as a Christian. *Him, a believer? No way! Her, a Christ-follower? Not a chance!* Maybe it's one of those people who goes out of his or her way to criticize or embarrass you. Sometimes it may even seem like this person lives to make your life miserable, and to give you a hard time for your faith.

When I first became a believer, people didn't think it was real. I can't blame them! Even I never imagined myself becoming a Christian. I wasn't the religious type. And I certainly didn't envision myself as a preacher. But God had a different idea.

Amplify that a thousand times and you'll have an idea of how unexpected the conversion of Saul of Tarsus was. Saul not only went out of his way to criticize Christians, but he hunted them down like animals and arrested them. He presided over the death of the first martyr of the early church, a bold and courageous young man named Stephen.

Saul's conversion was so stunning and unexpected that many in the early church didn't believe it at first. Instead of greeting the news with joy, believers of that day responded with skepticism and suspicion. But the news was even better than anyone had imagined: This powerful man who had dedicated his life to the destruction of Christianity turned completely around and dedicated his life to taking the message of Christ into all the world. He served the Lord with as much energy, if not more, than he had served the devil.

Don't ever write off a man or woman, or say to yourself, "He or she would be the last person in the world to accept Christ." God's grace and the gospel message can penetrate the thickest walls. It can germinate, grow, and flower in places you would never imagine. Just sow the seeds and leave the results to Him.

WORTH QUOTING

For the word of God is alive and powerful. It is sharper than the sharpest two-edged sword, cutting between soul and spirit, between joint and marrow. It exposes our innermost thoughts and desires. (Hebrews 4:12)

I have always felt that when I preach, especially at Harvest Crusades, I should generously quote Scripture, because I believe there is authority in the Bible. There isn't authority in the words of Greg Laurie, unless Greg Laurie is quoting the Bible. My authority comes from God's Word. So I quote it.

People may not like what I'm saying. It may really bother them. But I have heard story after story of people who made a decision for Christ a week, even a month, after a crusade's conclusion. I have even heard a few stories of those who were converted in the parking lot following a crusade. A seed was planted. Then it germinated and eventually became fruitful... even though it was a little later than we thought it would. God's Word will not return without accomplishing its purpose, so don't be afraid to quote it.

As young Stephen was about to lose his life, the devil could have whispered in his ear, "Look at you. You gave up your life for nothing." But a little seed had been planted. And unknown to Saul of Tarsus, it was about to bear fruit.

Here were two young men, both standing up for their convictions. One was very religious. One was genuinely spiritual. Stephen was humble, saved by the grace of God. Saul was self-righteous, proud of his works and deeds. Stephen was defending the gospel, while Saul was persecuting it. But Saul ultimately carried out Stephen's task. He ended up taking his place and carrying the torch that Stephen once did.

WHO SINNED?

And His disciples asked Him, saying, "Rabbi, who sinned, this man or his parents, that he was born blind?" (John 9:2)

Sometimes the question comes up of whether our physical suffering on Earth is the result of sin. *Who sinned?* That's the question the disciples asked Jesus in John 9. Was it the blind man or his parents? Jesus responded by clearly pointing out there was no specific correlation here. In other words, the blind man wasn't being punished for his own sin or the sin of his parents.

But notice this. Jesus did not say that suffering is just a random event that has nothing to do with sin. In a broad sense, all sickness, disabilities, and the limitations that come with the physical body are a result of sin. God's original plan was that our physical bodies would never get sick, wear out, or die. God's original purpose was for this body to live forever. But because of the sin of Adam, because he disobeyed God in the Garden of Eden, sin came into human life and spread to all of humanity.

But let me add this. You *can* experience physical hardship as a result of your own sin. If you are an alcoholic, that will affect you physically. If you're a drug addict, that will affect you physically. In a sense those physical problems could be directly linked to sin. So yes, you can bring problems into your life as a result of breaking the commandments of God.

There is a reason that He gave us these guidelines in His Word. It was for our own good. God had a plan and a purpose for each rule to protect us in life that we might live life to its fullest. Every day, we have the ability to choose between right and wrong. Choose life!

BELIEVE AND SEE

And He said to him, "Go, wash in the pool of Siloam" (which is translated, Sent). So he went and washed, and came back seeing. (John 9:7)

We have all heard people say, "Seeing is believing. Show me and I will believe." But the Bible essentially teaches us that *believing is seeing*. When we say, "Show me and I will believe," God says, "Believe, and I will show you."

In John 9, we read that Jesus opened the eyes of the blind man in more ways than one. The man received his physical sight and, for the first time in his life, he was able to see. But he had his spiritual eyes opened as well. He was able to understand who God was, what right and wrong were, and what the purpose of life was.

Jesus also used a very unusual method to heal him. The Bible tells us that He spit in the dirt, made clay with the saliva, and placed it on the man's eyes. Then He told him to go wash in the pool of Siloam. Notice that Jesus didn't say, "Go wash in the pool of Siloam and you will receive your sight." That's important, because He offered this man no promise whatsoever, nor did he say that something wonderful would happen if he went. He just told him to go and do it.

Yet something activated this blind man's heart and mind and caused him to want to obey the words of Jesus as quickly as possible. And as we follow his example, we, too, can have our spiritual eyes opened.

Those who know God have come to realize that His words and commands can be trusted and immediately followed. If God tells us to do something, it's for our own good. If God says it, it's for a reason. Obey Him. Great blessings await those who wait on the Lord.

THE COST OF BELIEVING

*They answered and said to him, "You were completely born in sins,
and are you teaching us?" And they cast him out. (John 9:34)*

When Jesus healed the blind man, did everybody in town begin to rejoice because of what God had done? No, not everyone rejoiced. In fact, the man got in trouble with the religious authorities.

This man knew so little about Jesus. When he was questioned, all he could say was, "A man named Jesus did this for me" (see John 9:11). He didn't even know if he would ever meet Jesus again.

He also knew he was in big trouble. You see, in those times your entire life was wrapped around the synagogue. If they threw you out of the synagogue, you would be ostracized. You would probably lose your job. You would lose your friends. You might even lose your family. So you didn't want to offend these people. You wanted to stay in good with them. This man knew he was in jeopardy of these things, yet he made the choice to boldly speak out about what Jesus had done for him. He could not deny what had happened.

Never doubt it, following Jesus will cost you. But it will cost you even more to not follow Jesus! So whatever you give up to follow the Lord, it's worth it. Whatever sacrifices you make, it's worth it to follow Jesus. A million times over.

There's no getting around it. Either you're going to have harmony with God and friction with people, or you're going to have harmony with people and friction with God. The choice is yours. I think I would rather be in harmony with God. Wouldn't you?

IN SPITE OF SICKNESS

"And God will wipe away every tear from their eyes; there shall be no more death, nor sorrow, nor crying. There shall be no more pain, for the former things have passed away." (Revelation 21:4)

God can work in spite of sickness. He still answers prayer and heals people today, and He still does miracles. In sickness and in hardships, He can work in a person's life. Even if a person still has the sickness or problem, God can work in spite of it and give them a special strength. And no matter what happens to our physical bodies here on Earth, we have the promise of heaven and ultimate healing in heaven. At that time, God says He will wipe away all our tears. There will be no more death, sorrows, crying, or pain (see Revelation 21:4).

What a glorious promise! There is more—so much more!—beyond this life on Earth. Whatever our limitations, whatever our problems, God promises us that we will one day receive a new body that will not have the shortcomings we experience today.

And God can also use sickness to bring a person to Himself, can't He? I know of many people who have come to the Lord in the hospital or when facing death. Suddenly they reevaluate their lives. They wonder, *What am I living for? What's really important in my life? What's going to happen to me when I die?* And they begin to think about eternity.

As the psalmist says, "Before I was afflicted, I went astray, but now I keep Your word" (Psalm 119:67). God can work in spite of sickness, and He can work through sickness. Nothing is impossible for Him.

ONE THING I KNOW

He answered and said, "Whether He is a sinner or not I do not know. One thing I know: that though I was blind, now I see." (John 9:25)

Sometimes the most aggressive witnesses for Jesus are brand-new converts. You'd think it would be the people who have known the Lord for a long time, who have walked with Christ for years. With all that accumulated Bible knowledge, with all of that time around God's people, attending church and growing spiritually, you would think they'd be out there setting the world on fire for Jesus. But more often than not, those who are youngest in their faith have the most zeal.

The blind man Jesus healed hadn't even figured it out yet. But he was already beginning to talk to others. At first he simply referred to Jesus as "a man called Jesus" (John 9:11). As his understanding grew, he referred to Jesus as a prophet (John 9:17). Then he said, "If this Man were not from God, He could do nothing" (John 9:33). You can see how his faith was growing.

There is something spiritually invigorating and strengthening about making a stand for Jesus Christ. Have you ever noticed that? When you start telling someone else, you might not know much. But you do know this much: once you were blind, but now you see. You can say, "Once I was trapped in sin, but now I am forgiven. Once I was empty, now my life is full. Once I was going to hell, now I am going to heaven."

I have found that when I share my faith, it grows stronger. Why is that? Because the Holy Spirit will inspire your thoughts and He will speak through you. Faith is a lot like a muscle. The more you use it, the stronger you grow. The less you use it, the weaker you become. It's important that we step out of our comfort zone and use our faith.

THE MAN IN SATAN'S GRIP

> *When the enemy comes in like a flood, the Spirit of the Lord*
> *will lift up a standard against him. (Isaiah 59:19)*

In Mark 5, the Bible tells us of a man who was possessed by demons, had superhuman strength, and was able to break chains with his bare hands. This dangerous and frightening man lived among the tombs and on the mountains.

But underneath this horrendous exterior was a tortured soul. It's a picture of Satan's ultimate goal. This is really what the devil wants to do. He wants to destroy your life. Although it's true that God loves you and has a wonderful plan for your life, it's also true that Satan hates you and has a horrible plan for your life. The devil knows his judgment is certain. He knows that Jesus is indeed coming again. For that reason, he's pulling out all the stops, redoubling his efforts.

The good news is that although the devil may be feverishly at work 24/7, God isn't sleeping either!

This story had a very happy ending. Jesus came into this poor, tormented man's life and made him into an altogether different kind of a person. Jesus cast out the legion of demons, which went into a herd of pigs...and over a cliff into the sea. It was a dramatic transformation for this man.

Jesus can transform your life, too. Let Him lift up a standard against the enemy in your life, today.

SATAN, SOCIETY, OR SAVIOR?

"Therefore if the Son makes you free, you shall be free indeed." (John 8:36)

There were three forces at work in the life of the demon-possessed man in Mark 5. First there was Satan. Just like a roaring lion, Satan had already come into that man, intending to destroy him (see 1 Peter 5:8).

Next, there was society. What had society done for him? They had chained him up, but he broke the chains. What else could they do? Society couldn't solve the problem, because the problem was in the man's heart. No one could help this man. His situation was hopeless.

But then the Savior came into his life. What did Jesus do for him? He came to the spooky little graveyard where the man lived. Jesus saw his hurting, agonized soul and offered hope. What society could not do to release the man from Satan and sin, Jesus did with one simple command: "He said to him, 'Come out of the man, unclean spirit!'" (Mark 5:8). The demons came out of the man, and his life was changed forever.

Isn't it interesting that with all of our wonderful achievements today, society still can't deal with problems caused by Satan and sin? We can't overcome Satan in our own power. We don't know what to do. Society doesn't have the answers. We, too, need a Savior to help us.

No matter what you may be facing today or dealing with in your life, no matter how high the walls and obstacles may seem before you, Jesus has the power to step into your life today and make a difference.

HE IS GREATER

He who is in you is greater than he who is in the world. (1 John 4:4)

The devil can gain a foothold on your life in many ways. One way is through drugs. Sadly, we are seeing a real revival of drug use today. Another way you can open the door to demonic power is through dabbling in occult activities that are so fashionable in many circles. You may think of some of these activities as innocent fun, but even if they only crack the door to demonic activity just a little bit, it can invite disaster. It doesn't take much.

Now, can demons tempt Christians? Absolutely. Can demons harass us? Without question. Even the great apostle Paul spoke of a demon power that would come and buffet him (see 2 Corinthians 12:7). But God won't let you face more than you can handle. He always will put His hedge of protection around you.

When Jesus comes into your heart, it isn't a timeshare plan where He occupies the heart part of the time and the devil part of the time. No, Jesus takes control and He is there to stay.

But if you are not a Christian, if Christ is not living in your heart, you are open game for the devil. Maybe you're not a drug addict or an occultist. But I will tell you this…you're still a sinner. Every one has sinned and broken God's commandments (see Romans 3:23).

Reach out to Jesus now. He is greater than the devil. He will forgive you, transform you, and start you on a life path beyond what you have ever dreamed. Solomon had it right when he declared, "The path of the righteous is like the first gleam of dawn, shining ever brighter till the full light of day" (Proverbs 4:18, NIV).

FINDING THE LOST SHEEP

"Rejoice with me, for I have found my sheep which was lost!" (Luke 15:6)

The devil was trying to stop Jesus and the disciples from reaching a poor tortured soul, a demon-possessed man who was living among tombstones (Mark 4:3-5:20). Jesus said to the disciples, "Let us cross over to the other side." So they boarded their little boat and began to make their way across the Sea of Galilee. Suddenly a storm arose and the waves beat the boat so that even these seasoned sailors thought they were going to drown.

But Jesus would not be stopped. He explained why in the Gospel of Luke, saying:

"What man of you, having a hundred sheep, if he loses one of them, does not leave the ninety-nine in the wilderness, and go after the one which is lost until he finds it? And when he has found it, he lays it on his shoulders, rejoicing. And when he comes home, he calls together his friends and neighbors, saying to them, 'Rejoice with me, for I have found my sheep which was lost!'"
(Luke 15:4-6)

The devil is always on duty. Ever watchful, he doesn't rest day or night. He wants to destroy you and make your life miserable. This tormented man on the other side of the lake was the lost sheep Jesus was after, and he wasn't going to let high water stop Him from His intended goal.

Satan tried to stop Jesus, but he failed. He always will.

WHY PRAYER IS ESSENTIAL

> *Peter was therefore kept in prison, but constant prayer was*
> *offered to God for him by the church. (Acts 12:5)*

Have you ever been in a situation where there seemed to be no way out? Everything is going along just fine when, all of a sudden, a storm cloud overshadows you and begins to rain (pour) on your parade. Insurmountable obstacles seem to be growing worse by the minute, and you find yourself wondering what to do.

In Acts 12, we find the story of how God took a tragic, even hopeless, situation and turned it around. It was accomplished by the power of prayer, the kind of prayer that storms the throne of God and gets an answer.

Both James and Peter were in prison. Tragically, James was put to death. But Peter was still incarcerated, awaiting his fate. Though all doors were closed, one remained open: the door of prayer. The church recognized that "We use God's mighty weapons, not mere worldly weapons, to knock down the Devil's strongholds" (2 Corinthians 10:4, NLT).

Prayer was and is the church's secret weapon. Although the devil struck a blow against the church, the church gained victory through prayer as Peter was miraculously released.

Sadly, we don't pray often enough. Yet it is essential that Christians learn more about effective prayer, because all of us will certainly face difficulties, hardships, and problems. So we need to discover what God can do through the power of prayer.

Prayer for the Christian should be second nature, like breathing. We should automatically pray, lifting our needs and requests before the Lord. Jesus said that we should always pray and not lose heart (see Luke 18:1).

Prayer is something we should never avoid and never grow tired of. Prayer should be woven through our day like a bright gold thread woven through a piece of fabric. The more we pray, the more we will see the kingdom of God break through the darkness of seemingly "impossible" situations.

Thursday

JUST ASK

You want something but don't get it. You kill and covet, but you cannot have what you want. You quarrel and fight. You do not have, because you do not ask God. (James 4:2, NLT)

It is my firm conviction that some Christians today don't have God's provision, healing, or blessing in their lives *simply because they haven't asked for it.*

I'm not saying God will give us everything we ask for. But I am saying that many of us are going through life missing out on many of the things God has for us. The Bible says, "You do not have, because you do not ask God."

Some Christians pray only as a last resort, when everything else fails, after they've called all their friends and all their relatives. When no one can help them, they say, "What else can I do? All I can do now is pray." But prayer should not be a last resort. It should be the first thing we do.

As the old hymn says, "Satan trembles when he sees the weakest saints upon their knees." The devil doesn't want you to pray. He will do everything he can to keep you from it, because he is afraid of the power that can be exercised through prayer. He whispers, "Don't pray. Try this. Try that. You aren't worthy to pray. God won't hear you." He will do anything to keep you from approaching the throne of God.

Prayer is a privilege given to the child of God. God will hear the prayer of an unbeliever who calls out to Him for forgiveness, but only a person who has put his or her faith in Christ can have a prayer life. So pray with fervor. Pray with energy. Pray continually. Don't give up, because you never know what God will do.

MAKE EVERY DAY COUNT

So teach us to number our days, that we may gain a heart of wisdom.
(Psalm 90:12)

It's hard to explain when someone's life has been cut short, dying at a relatively young age. We expected that person to live a much longer life. But who is to say that it wasn't his or her appointed time to go? Who is to say that it wasn't the exact length of life that God had preordained for that man or woman from the very beginning?

That is why we want to make every day count. To paraphrase the words of Moses in Psalm 90:12, "Lord, help us to realize our lives can end on any day, so please show me how to use each day wisely."

We don't know when our day will come. When God calls you home, you're going home! You can live on vitamin C, zinc, and Echinacea. You can drink green tea, eat tofu, and avoid all the toxins you can, but when your number is up, your number is up.

On the other hand, you will be around until God is done with you. You won't go before your time. You may or may not be the healthiest person, but you will live to the time that God has appointed for you…and worrying about it won't extend your life for one moment.

At the same time, however, we are not to take foolish risks and "put the Lord to the test."

We can be assured that we are here until God is done with us. As the apostle Paul said, "For to me, to live is Christ, and to die is gain" (Philippians. 1:21). So let's make the most of the lives God has given us.

Missionary Jim Elliot once wrote: "Wherever you are, be all there. Live to the hilt every situation you believe to be the will of God."

A GUIDE FOR PRAYER

*Once Jesus was in a certain place praying. As he finished, one of his disciples
came to him and said, "Lord, teach us to pray, just as John taught his disciples."
(Luke 11:1, NLT)*

For prayer to be powerful and effective, there has to be at least a
few moments of recognizing the One to whom we are speaking.
"What? Isn't all prayer offered to God?" some might ask.

Not necessarily. I think it's entirely possible to pray and never think of
God at all! We can rush into God's presence and rattle off our grocery list
as though we are talking to Santa Claus, without even taking a moment
to contemplate whom it is we are addressing. Often in prayer, there is little
thought of God Himself. Instead, our mind is taken up with what we need.

Jesus gave us a model prayer that we call the Lord's Prayer. In reality,
the Bible doesn't call it that. It could be more accurately called the Disciple's
Prayer, because one day, the disciples came to Jesus and said, "Lord, teach
us to pray, just as John taught his disciples." Notice they didn't say, "Lord,
teach us a prayer." Rather, they said, "Teach us to pray...."

Some people will attach a mystical significance to the reciting of this
prayer. They view it as sort of the big-gun prayer to pull out when all else
fails. But this isn't a prayer that Jesus gave as much as it was a *model* for
praying. No, there's nothing wrong with praying the Lord's Prayer. If you
choose to pray it as it is written, that's fine, as long as it's coming from your
heart. But more importantly, it is a prayer that gives us a guide to all prayers
that we would offer to God.

Check it out! Let every sentence of this prayer be a launching point
to lead you into deeper conversation with the God who loves you.

WHEN NOT TO PRAY

> *Now this is the confidence that we have in Him, that if we ask anything according to His will, He hears us. (1 John 5:14)*

In a broad sense, we should pray about everything. But there are certain things we don't need to pray about. For example, if someone were to say, "Greg, I'm praying about robbing a bank. Would you pray with me?" I will pray for that person, but I won't pray that God will bless their efforts. Why? Because the Bible says, "You shall not steal" (Exodus 20:15). We don't need to pray about that.

Yet there are certain things God tells us we can pray for. He tells us we can pray for wisdom: "If any of you lacks wisdom, let him ask of God, who gives to all liberally and without reproach, and it will be given to him" (James 1:5).

We can pray for His provision. Philippians 4:19 says, "And my God shall supply all your need according to His riches in glory by Christ Jesus."

We can pray for protection. Psalm 91:5-7 says, "You shall not be afraid of the terror by night, nor of the arrow that flies by day, nor of the pestilence that walks in darkness, nor of the destruction that lays waste at noonday. A thousand may fall at your side, and ten thousand at your right hand; but it shall not come near you."

The key to effective prayer is getting our will in alignment with God's will, as the verse at the top of today's devotional explains.

Nothing lies outside the reach of prayer except that which lies outside of the will of God.

AWAY WITH JESUS?

"He who is not with Me is against Me." (Luke 11:23)

After Jesus cast the demons out of the man who lived among the tombs, they went into a herd of pigs and ran over a cliff. When the people saw that, instead of rejoicing that their neighbor was saved, "they began to plead with Him to depart from their region" (Mark 5:17).

That really sums up the reaction of all humankind to Jesus Christ. You're either saying, "Jesus, I want to be close to You," or you're saying, "Jesus, go away. I don't want You in my life."

You might protest, "Now wait a second. I admit that I haven't yet made a commitment to Christ. I'm simply saying I haven't decided yet." But if you don't say yes to Jesus, you are essentially telling Him to go away. Jesus said, "He who is not with Me is against Me" (Luke 11:23). Either you have faith and trust in Christ or you have unbelief. There is no other option.

Have you said, "Away with Him?" You say, "What do you mean, away with Him? I have never said, 'Jesus, go away.'" Maybe you have, indirectly. Maybe you resisted God's work in your heart. Maybe you don't want to give up some things in your life that you know are wrong. Or maybe you're just too busy—you have time for everything but Jesus.

It really boils down to this: what have you done with Jesus? What are you going to say right now? "Away with Jesus"? Or are you going to ask Him to become a part—the very center—of your life? He offers you His forgiveness. Take it. The choice is yours. Don't put it off.

NUCLEAR GIANTS AND ETHICAL INFANTS

Woe to those who call evil good, and good evil; who put darkness for light, and light for darkness; who put bitter for sweet, and sweet for bitter! (Isaiah 5:20)

In 1948, General Omar Bradley made a statement with a prophetic ring to it: "We have grasped the mystery of the atom and rejected the Sermon on the Mount.... Ours is a world of nuclear giants and ethical infants."

What an accurate description of our times right now. Today, with all our technology, we have simply discovered new ways to kill one another and to eradicate what God has done. Despite our sophisticated technologies and amazing abilities, we have made no progress in solving our basic human problems. That's because the world is upside down.

While the early church turned their world upside down, it seems today that the world is turning the church upside down. The early church consisted of a relatively small group of Christians. Their numbers weren't large like ours today. They didn't have the technology like we have today to get the Word out. Yet they made a dramatic difference wherever they went.

Today, even with so many naming the name of Christ, our impact on the world seems to be smaller than ever. And that's my point. Christians are allowing secular attitudes to find their way into the church and into their lives. It seems like our culture is affecting us more than we are affecting our culture.

The world needs to see a genuine man or woman of God living the Christian life. They need to see the real thing. In short, they need to see you. God can use you. Maybe you're not a preacher, but you can proclaim the gospel message through your life and through your words. You can turn *your* world upside down.

NOT OF THIS WORLD

"Jesus said, 'My kingdom is not of this world. If it were, my servants would fight to prevent my arrest by the Jews. But now my kingdom is from another place.'" (John 18:36, NIV)

So often the world misconstrues what Christians say. It draws erroneous conclusions because it never takes the time to really listen carefully to the gospel message.

The early Christians were insulted and criticized for what they were doing—and even accused of treason. It was suggested they were actually advocating the overthrow of Caesar—which really wasn't the case. It was a complete misunderstanding of what the objectives of these Christians really were. Anyone who would have given them even a brief hearing would have realized that these followers of Jesus weren't seeking to establish an Earthly kingdom—and they certainly weren't plotting to overthrow Caesar or Rome.

Yet it's worth noting that the first-century Christians made no attempts to conquer paganism by reacting blow by blow. Instead, they outthought, outprayed, and outlived the unbelievers. Their weapons were positive, not negative. They prayed, preached, and proclaimed the message of the gospel.

As a result, these Christians dramatically impacted their world. In the end, they prevailed. In retrospect, where is Rome today? It's no longer a world power. Do we remember the names of more than a few of the great emperors of Rome? For the most part, no.

There have been numerous attempts throughout history to destroy the Christian faith. But those efforts will always fail for one simple reason: Christianity is Christ. He *will* prevail in the end and establish His kingdom. And because we are with Him, we will win in the end, too.

COMPELLED TO PREACH

Now while Paul waited for them at Athens, his spirit was provoked within him
when he saw that the city was given over to idols. (Acts 17:16)

Do you ever feel righteous indignation as you look at our confused society today? Righteous indignation is the result of seeing something that disturbs you deep in your soul.

Maybe you see something on television that is wicked and perverse. Maybe you see someone misrepresenting God, or a situation in which you realize that people are turning to false gods. It grieves you, and stirs something deep within you.

The Book of Acts tells us that when Paul arrived in Athens, he was grieved to see the absolute absence of the living God, and in His place, every conceivable substitute. Acts 17:16 says that Paul's spirit "was provoked within him." Another way to translate this is, "His spirit was exasperated," or "He was irritated or aroused to anger," or my favorite, "He was hot and mad."

This doesn't mean that Paul simply lost his cool; this was righteous indignation.

Does it grieve you inside as you see generation after generation going down the same path that leads to destruction, buying into the same lies the generation before them bought into? Does that concern you?

Here's what it comes down to. We can take as many classes as we want on how to share our faith. We can memorize verses. We can prepare ourselves. But unless we have a God-given burden for unbelievers, it won't matter.

Paul said, "Woe is me if I do not preach the gospel!" (1 Corinthians 9:16). But if some Christians were honest, they would say, "Woe is me if I have to preach the gospel." We need to ask God to change our hearts.

ONE AT A TIME

When they heard Paul speak of the resurrection of a person who had been dead, some laughed, but others said, "We want to hear more about this later."
(Acts 17:32, NLT)

The apostle Paul was probably the greatest communicator the church ever produced. As a brilliant orator and a great student of Scripture, history, and culture, he knew how to make his case. That is clear when you read anything that the Holy Spirit inspired him to write. Yet even Paul's preaching of the gospel was rejected by some.

It serves as a reminder that even if you are the greatest witness, even if you live a truly godly life, even if you are an effective communicator, even if you usually have the answer to every hard question people come up with, not everyone will be convinced.

After all, Jesus Christ was the perfect example. He never slipped up, not even once. He was God in human form. He was absolutely flawless and perfect. Yet in spite of that, Judas Iscariot sold Him out for thirty pieces of silver.

This refutes the timeworn argument of those who say the reason they are not a Christian is because there are so many hypocrites in the church. Jesus was never a hypocrite. But Judas sold Him out anyway.

Even if you are a godly person, you're won't convince everyone. No preacher or apologist for Christianity has even come close to that.

So what do we do? We need to start with the world around us. We should seek to live godly lives and share the Good News with those we come in contact with. But we also need to remember that the process won't always be easy. Even so, just as it was in Paul's day, God is in the business of changing lives, one person at a time.

MOVED TO ACTION

For out of much affliction and anguish of heart I wrote to you, with many tears,
not that you should be grieved, but that you might know the love which
I have so abundantly for you. (2 Corinthians 2:4)

Even before *Titanic* arrived on the big screen in 1997, people have been fascinated by its story. Clearly, many mistakes were made that led to its sinking. Although it was called the unsinkable ship, it sank— and relatively easily, at that.

We know that 1,500 people perished in an icy grave. We know there weren't enough lifeboats on board. We know that many of them went out half-full, some with only four or five people when they had the capacity to carry at least sixty.

But one of the greatest tragedies about the Titanic is the fact that while there was room in the lifeboats, no one went back to save anyone else. They had rowed out a distance from the sinking vessel because they were afraid of its suction. Survivors said they could hear the screams of the people as the Titanic finally disappeared below the surface.

Here were people in lifeboats that had room for more! They could have rowed back and pulled others in. Yet they did nothing about it. They waited for about an hour, and then they went back. By then, they were only able to save a handful of people. They waited until it was too late.

Right now, there is a lost world around us. People are going down, and we have room in our lifeboat. Do we care enough to go and pull them on board? Do we care enough to do something for them? Or will we say, "They should have gotten into the boat when there was time"?

Do you have a concern in your heart for lost people? That is where it starts.

LIFE DURING LIFE

"I have come that they may have life, and that they may
have it more abundantly." (John 10:10)

An interest in life on Mars seems to run in cycles. At this writing, our nation has a new exploration robot prowling around and digging little holes in the dirt near the Martian north pole.

A few years ago, I was even interviewed for an article about life on other planets. I said, "I don't see anything in the Bible that would indicate there is life on other planets, but if there is, God created it." They closed the article with another of my statements: "Maybe we shouldn't be so worried about life on other planets and ask ourselves the question, 'Is there life on Earth, and are we living it the way God wants us to?'"

We often wonder if there is life after death. But is there life *during* life? That is a question we should all consider.

When I was seventeen, that was my question. I wasn't so concerned with what happened beyond the grave at that age, because I thought I would live a long, long time. My primary concern at that time was, "What's life all about? What's the purpose of life?" I knew in my heart there had to be more than what I'd experienced to that point. I was desperately searching for some kind of meaning in life. I just had to know.

Thankfully, I didn't have to look very far, because there was a group of very outspoken Christians on my high school campus. They practiced what they preached, and I was intrigued by them. So I began to watch them. I saw that they were experiencing a dimension of life that I had never known. Not long after that, I gave my life to Jesus and discovered the truth of Jesus' great statement from John 10:10: "I have come that they may have life, and that they may have it more abundantly." That's what I had been searching for, life during life.

Ask the Lord to point you toward someone today who may be searching for that very thing.

CHOOSE LIFE

"I call heaven and earth as witnesses today against you, that I have set before
you life and death, blessing and cursing; therefore choose life, that both
you and your descendants may live." (Deuteronomy 30:19)

God has provided us with a radical contrast regarding the choice that we can make in life. Jesus has essentially told us, "Here is your choice: you can either follow the thief who wants to kill and destroy you, or you can follow Me, because I want to give you life. So here is your choice in life: you can have fullness or emptiness. You can choose life or death. As a result, you can face eternity in heaven or in hell."

Yet it's amazing to me how many people today are consciously choosing death. Not only do they choose a lifestyle that can lead to a premature death on Earth, but they also choose a lifestyle that can certainly lead to an eternal death.

People are choosing death, choosing to throw their lives away. And as society watches its so-called heroes destroying their lives, many people simply follow. It's the blind leading the blind.

That is the devil's plan for you. So if you want to do what everyone else is doing, then here is his plan—get ready for it: it is death. It is misery. It is emptiness. And it will result in a life of regret when you look back one day.

Contrast that option with the promise Jesus made when He said, "A thief is only there to steal and kill and destroy. I came so they can have real and eternal life, more and better life than they ever dreamed of" (John 10:10, The Message).

Check that out....and choose life.

PEACE IN THE KINGDOM

For the kingdom of God is not eating and drinking, but righteousness and peace and joy in the Holy Spirit. (Romans 14:17)

Jesus calls us His sheep, and we know that the Shepherd's primary objective for His sheep is that they flourish. He wants His sheep to be well-fed, well-cared for, content, and satisfied. It is the joy of the Shepherd to lead His sheep to green pastures and still waters.

Jesus also has given His sheep a great promise. He said, "My sheep hear My voice, and I know them, and they follow Me. And I give them eternal life, and they shall never perish; neither shall anyone snatch them out of My hand" (John 10:27-28). There is great security in knowing that the Lord is our Shepherd, and that we are under His protection.

Did you know that God loves to bless you? Delights to pour His grace out upon you? Truly enjoys working in your life? He wants to bless you more than you want to be blessed! He wants to answer your prayers more than you want them answered. He wants to speak to you even more than you want to be spoken to. And He wants to use you even more than you want to be used. He loves you. Jesus said, "Do not fear, little flock, for it is your Father's good pleasure to give you the kingdom" (Luke 12:32). It is His joy, His pleasure, to give you the kingdom.

And what is that kingdom? The Bible says the kingdom of God is "righteousness and peace and joy in the Holy Spirit" (Romans 14:17). He wants His righteousness, peace, and joy to permeate every level of your life.

THE KEY TO CONTENTMENT

Now godliness with contentment is great gain. (1 Timothy 6:6)

As you begin to know God's love and purpose for you, you can live a life that overflows with purpose, peace, and joy. This is life as He intends you to live it, and this is exactly what David meant when he said, "The Lord is my shepherd; I shall not want" (Psalm 23:1).

Have you been able to say that? Have you been able to say, "Lord, if You want to give me more, fine. If You don't want to, fine. I shall not want, because I have found my contentment in You."

The apostle Paul found that contentment. He said he was content, regardless of his circumstances (see Philippians 4:11-12). But how many of us have thought, *I would be content if I just had a little more money...if I could just land that promotion... if I could get married....* But somehow, we never quite reach that place of contentment. We're always looking for something just a little beyond what we have.

There are certain things that only God can give. And when you are in a relationship with Him in which you say, "The Lord is my Shepherd," you can say with David, "I shall not want."

Our contentment doesn't come from what we have. It comes from Whom we know. Hebrews 13:5 tells us, "Let your conduct be without covetousness; be content with such things as you have. For He Himself has said, 'I will never leave you nor forsake you.'"

So when you get down to it, everything you need in life is found in a relationship with God.

A TUNE-UP FOR YOUR LIFE

"For a good tree does not bear bad fruit, nor does a bad tree bear good fruit."
(Luke 6:43)

People can talk all day about their love and deep sense of devotion for God, but the proof is in the pudding, so to speak. If you are a real Christian, if you have really asked Christ into your life, there *will* be evidence.

So here are a few tune-up questions we should ask ourselves as believers:

Do I obey the Word of God? We can't obey it if we don't know what it says. So first, we need to read it. Are we keeping His commandments?

Do I reject this world system that is hostile to God? When a person becomes a Christian, he or she sees this world for what it is, because his or her priorities have changed.

Do I eagerly await Christ's return? If we truly are followers of Christ, we will look forward to the day when He will come again.

Do I see a decreasing pattern of sin in my life? That's not to say true Christians don't sin, because they do. We all do. But there is a difference between continuing in sin and trying to sin less and less.

Do I love other Christians? Jesus said, "By this all will know that you are My disciples, if you have love for one another" (John 13:35). If we are children of God, then we will love His people, and love to be around them.

You might be thinking, *After that little list, I don't think I measure up.* Welcome to the club! I don't measure up in every way, either. There's always room for improvement. That is why it's good to periodically step back and ask for the Lord's perspective on our lives, to see whether we're in the place where He wants us to be, doing what He wants us to do.

Solomon said it like this: "The wisdom of the prudent is to give thought to their ways, but the folly of fools is deception" (Proverbs 14:8, NIV).

DEATH TURNED TO VICTORY

Jesus said to her, "I am the resurrection and the life. He who believes in Me, though he may die, he shall live." (John 11:25)

The older we become, the more this question will gnaw away at us: Is there life after death? Sometimes we ask that question earlier in life, when someone close to us dies without warning, and we come face-to-face with the uncomfortable fact of death. This shouldn't come as a revelation to you, but we are all going to die.

Some Christians will say, "I'm going to go to heaven, so when I die, don't weep for me." But death is hard for everyone, and there's nothing wrong with feeling sorrow over the loss of someone you care about. Christians experience that sorrow, too. It's a natural part of the grieving process. As the Bible says, there is "a time to weep, and a time to laugh" (Ecclesiastes 3:4).

Death even brought tears to the eyes of Jesus when His friend Lazarus died (see John 11:35). But, of course, we know there is life beyond the grave for Christians. We know that life is not limited to this time on Earth, and that our stay on this planet is temporary. Of course we will feel sorrow and loss for a Christian who has died. But as believers, we know we will see that person again in heaven. That is God's great gift to us. His Son Jesus personally intervened and turned death into victory.

The writer of the book of Hebrews put it like this: "Because God's children are human beings—made of flesh and blood—Jesus also became flesh and blood by being born in human form. For only as a human being could he die, and only by dying could he break the power of the Devil, who had the power of death. Only in this way could he deliver those who have lived all their lives as slaves to the fear of dying" (Hebrews 2:14-15, NLT).

TEMPORARY UNKNOWNS

For now we see in a mirror, dimly, but then face to face. Now I know in part, but then I shall know just as I also am known. (1 Corinthians 13:12)

Will we know one another in heaven? I can't give a definite answer to that question, because the Bible doesn't specifically address this, although it does say we will know as we are known (see 1 Corinthians 13:12).

For the time being, I don't have a complete knowledge of life beyond this life. The fact of the matter is, there's so much about the person of God, His ways, and His dwelling place that I don't know. But one day in a new body, I will see Him face-to-face, and all of my questions will be answered.

The apostle Paul had a remarkable experience in which he died and then was revived (see Acts 14:19-20). This wasn't a near-death experience; Paul literally died. But he didn't write a book about it or go on the talk-show circuit. He basically said, "I was caught up in the third heaven and heard things that I can't even describe to you, but it was paradise" (see 2 Corinthians 12:2). That's all he would say.

It does appear, however, that we will recognize one another in heaven. After all, when Moses and Elijah met with Jesus on the Mount of Transfiguration, the disciples recognized them immediately. So you might ask, "How will I know you if I'm looking for you?" Well, look for the guy with the full head of brand-new hair. That will be me.

Yes, someday very soon we will be with the Lord. And though we don't know a great deal about heaven now, we can be sure its reality will exceed our wildest dreams. We will see the Lord and we will see one another. And all of the mysteries will be solved.

TRUST HIS PLAN

Now Jesus loved Martha and her sister and Lazarus. (John 11:5)

When Mary and Martha informed Jesus that Lazarus was sick, they expected to see their brother recover as soon as He received their message. But to their surprise and disappointment, nothing happened. And instead of coming right away, Jesus intentionally waited for two more days. By the time He arrived in Bethany, Lazarus had been dead four days.

Like Mary and Martha, maybe you had a need that you brought before the Lord, only to receive an answer you didn't want. You may have concluded that God doesn't love you. But God had a different plan than you did. Isaiah tells us, " 'My thoughts are not your thoughts, nor are your ways My ways,' says the Lord. 'For as the heavens are higher than the Earth, so are My ways higher than your ways, and My thoughts than your thoughts'" (55:8-9).

Martha and Mary's message said, "Lord, behold, he whom You love is sick" (John 11:3). Their word for "love" can be translated, "brotherly love," which speaks of love that a friend has for a friend.

Jesus said, "For God so loved the world that He gave His only begotten Son..." (John 3:16). This word "love" speaks of a sacrificial, agonizing love, which loves a person in spite of anything. And this is how Jesus loved Lazarus, Mary, and Martha.

Mary and Martha only thought of friendship, while Jesus thought of sacrificial love. They thought of their temporal comfort, while Jesus thought of their eternal benefit. They wanted a healing, while Jesus wanted a resurrection. Jesus wanted to do above and beyond what they could ask or imagine. He loved them with a deeper love. And He loves us with a deeper love as well.

WHEN GOD CRIED

Therefore, when Jesus saw her weeping, and the Jews who came with her weeping, He groaned in the spirit and was troubled. (John 11:33)

At the tomb of Lazarus, Jesus surveyed the scene. Mary, Martha, and the others were all weeping and mourning. And Jesus wept. Tears rolled down His cheeks.

Jesus wept tears of sympathy for Mary and Martha and for all of the sorrow caused by sin and death through all the long centuries of human existence. The Bible says that He was "a Man of sorrows and acquainted with grief" (Isaiah 53:3). When you have lost someone you love, He knows and understands the pain and hurt deep inside your soul. Maybe other people will never completely understand, but Jesus has wept with you.

His tears were also tears of sorrow for Lazarus. Those tears were for one who had known the bliss of heaven and now would have to return to a wicked earth, where he would have to die all over again.

Jesus also wept tears for the unbelief of the people: "Therefore, when Jesus saw her weeping, and the Jews who came with her weeping, He groaned in the spirit and was troubled" (John 11:33). Jesus was troubled. And He was angry.

The ravages of sin in the world He had created stirred deep emotion in His heart. His wonderful original plan, His perfect creation, had been deeply marred by sin. Death was a part of the curse, and it angered Jesus to see the devastating effect sin had on humanity.

Some may wonder, *Well, why doesn't He do something about it?* He has. He went to the cross of Calvary and died for our sins so that death doesn't have to be the end. There is life beyond the grave for the Christian. There is something beyond… something we can look forward to.

And it's all because He laid down His life to rescue us.

Do You Believe?

> *Jesus said to her, "Did I not say to you that if you would believe*
> *you would see the glory of God?" (John 11:40)*

People always knew where they stood with Martha. That's what I like about her. After Lazarus died, she said to Jesus, "Lord, if You had been here, my brother would not have died." That was classic Martha, calling it as she saw it. She was disappointed, but she was honest.

So what did Jesus say? "I am the resurrection and the life. He who believes in Me, though he may die, he shall live. And whoever lives and believes in Me shall never die. Do you believe this?" (John 11:25-26).

After He had also spoken to Mary, Jesus commanded Lazarus to come out of the tomb. The same voice that spoke creation into existence spoke beyond the veil that separated eternity from life on Earth. Only Jesus could call to the other side of eternity and be heard.

You would think this would be the miracle that would convert everyone. John tells us, "Then many of the Jews who had come to Mary, and had seen the things Jesus did, believed in Him. But some of them went away to the Pharisees and told them the things Jesus did" (verses 45-46).

Ultimately they decided to put Jesus to death. It just goes to show that miracles—signs and wonders—won't necessarily convert a person. What will bring people to faith in Christ is the message of the gospel, the recognition that we are all sinners and have sinned against a holy God. But God loves us so much He sent His own Son to die on the cross in our place, and to take all the sin of the world upon Himself.

Salvation is the greatest miracle of all.

NEW KNOWLEDGE FOR THE SKEPTIC

And Thomas answered and said to Him, "My Lord and my God!" (John 20:28)

Thomas, one of Jesus' disciples, has earned the nickname "Doubting Thomas," but I think that's a bit unfair. I have always thought of Thomas as more of a skeptic than a doubter. After all, Thomas didn't ask for a special revelation from Jesus. He simply asked for the same proof the other disciples had (see John 20:25). Thomas was the kind of guy who wanted to know for himself. He was his own man, and wouldn't let others do his thinking for him.

What did Jesus do with such a man? He made a special resurrection appearance for him. He condescended to Thomas and his desire to know for himself. What amazes me about this is that Jesus came to Thomas on his level. He didn't rebuke him. He didn't humiliate him. He could see that deep down in Thomas's heart, he really wanted to know God. Jesus came to him and said, "Reach your finger here, and look at My hands; and reach your hand here, and put it into My side. Do not be unbelieving, but believing" (John 20:27).

I like Thomas, because by nature I, too, am a skeptical person. I have never been one to believe something just because someone says it's true.

You might be someone who is a bit skeptical, a bit unsure of your faith. You may have a lot of questions. Deep down inside, you want to know God. You want to know for yourself. The risen Lord has something for you. He can turn your skepticism into belief.

Just come to Him with your questions and with your doubts. (He knows them anyway!) And when He has revealed Himself to you in a fresh way, you, too, will be able to say, "My Lord and my God!"

NEW COMFORT FOR THE GRIEVING

Jesus said to her, "Mary!" She turned and said to Him,
"Rabboni!" (which is to say, Teacher). (John 20:16)

Mary Magdalene was one of the most devoted followers that Jesus ever had. The book of Luke tells us that she and others ministered to Him out of "their substance," which simply means that she financially supported Him. She traveled with Him, wanted to be near Him and hear Him, and had the courage to stand at the foot of the cross after most of the disciples had run for their lives. Imagine how her heart broke at His crucifixion.

She was the last one at the cross, and early Sunday morning, she was the first at the tomb. She wasn't there to see a risen Lord, but to anoint His dead body. But she was in for a great surprise, because Jesus came to her in the midst of her sorrow.

And Jesus comes in the same way to the grieving person today. Maybe you feel desperate in your own grief. Maybe it's over a death. Maybe it's the breakup of a marriage or child who has gone astray spiritually. But you are broken and grieving.

The good news is that things can change. Circumstances in your life may look absolutely bleak today, but that husband or wife may return. That prodigal child may come back to God. And as a believer, you will again see that Christian loved one who has died. No matter what your circumstances, Jesus will be there with you. Maybe He will resolve your problems immediately. Or maybe your problems will continue. But you will never, never be alone.

That is the message of the resurrected Lord to us. He knows what we are going through. He understands. And He cares.

RIGHT WITH GOD

Since his days are determined, the number of his months is with You;
You have appointed his limits, so that he cannot pass. (Job 14:5)

The Bible says our days are numbered, which means there is a day coming (we don't know when) when we are out of here. We can worry about that, or we can simply trust that God knows when that day will be. It doesn't mean we take up bungee jumping off of bridges or swimming with sharks, putting our lives at unnecessary risk. But it does mean we recognize the fact that our lives belong to God. We are in His hands.

This is a very comforting thought, because it means that until God is finished with us, nothing will happen to us. That's great to know. But it also means when our number is up, it is up. When that day comes, there is nothing we can do to turn the clock back.

So what are we to do? As Christians, to live is Christ and to die is gain, as the apostle Paul says (see Philippians 1:21). So we should praise God for each new day, thank Him for the opportunities He provides, for the blessings He gives us, and for our family and friends. Then we should be available and willing to serve Him in whatever plans He has for us.

God values you. He loves you. But if death came for you today, would you be ready? If not, you would face a certain judgment. That is the last thing God wants to happen to you. That is why He sent Jesus to die on the cross and shed His blood for every sin you have ever committed.

Only the person who says, "To live is Christ" can then say, "To die is gain." That is a person whose soul is right with God.

A New Start for the Distant

Therefore, if anyone is in Christ, he is a new creation; old things have passed away; behold, all things have become new. (2 Corinthians 5:17)

I t all started to fall apart for Peter in the upper room. Jesus warned the disciples that one of them would actually betray Him and the others would desert Him.

Peter couldn't believe that Jesus would make such a statement! He boldly protested, "Even if all are made to stumble because of You, I will never be made to stumble" (Matthew 26:33). Then Jesus told Peter that not only would he deny Him, but he would deny Him *three* times. Peter couldn't conceive of that. He thought that was absolutely impossible. But Jesus knew Peter better than Peter knew Peter.

It wasn't too much later that Peter fell asleep in the Garden of Gethsemane when he should have been praying with Jesus. Then after Jesus' arrest, he followed at a distance and denied the Lord not once, not twice, but three times.

Immediately after that third denial, the eyes of Peter and the eyes of Jesus met. Peter was devastated, and he went out and wept bitterly (see Luke 22). Imagine how heartbroken he must have felt over his cowardice and failure. Then, a few days later, he heard that wonderful message that the Lord had risen. Not only that, but Jesus said to the women at the tomb, "But go, tell His disciples—and Peter—that He is going before you into Galilee; there you will see Him, as He said to you" (Mark 16:7). *Tell the disciples—and Peter....*Jesus singled him out. Why? Because He knew Peter needed encouragement.

Maybe you need encouragement today. Maybe you've gone astray, or drifted from your faith. If you would like to come back to Christ again, you can. In spite of your failures, the risen Lord can give you a new start today.

NEW LIFE FOR US ALL

Blessed be the God and Father of our Lord Jesus Christ, who according to His abundant mercy has begotten us again to a living hope through the resurrection of Jesus Christ from the dead. (1 Peter 1:3)

A couple from Chicago was planning a vacation to a warmer climate, but the wife couldn't join her husband until the next day, because she was on a business trip. Her husband scribbled down her e-mail address on a little scrap of paper, but upon his arrival, he discovered that he had lost it. He wanted to send off a quick e-mail to let her know he had arrived safely. So trying his best to remember her e-mail address, he composed a brief message and sent it off.

Unfortunately, his e-mail didn't reach his wife. Instead, it went to a grieving widow who had just lost her husband, a preacher, the day before. She had gone to her computer and was checking her e-mail when she let out a loud shriek and fainted on the spot. Her family came rushing in to see what was on the screen: "Dearest wife, I just checked in. Everything is prepared for your arrival tomorrow. P. S.: It sure is hot down here!"

The good news is that because of the death and resurrection of Jesus Christ, we don't have to be afraid of that real place that's "hot down there." In fact, we don't even have to fear death. Because Christ died and rose again from the dead, we know that for us as believers, there is life beyond the grave.

If that were all the resurrection did for us, it would be worth the price of the ticket. Of course, we didn't buy the ticket. Christ did. But if all that Christianity offered was the hope of life beyond the grave, it still would be worth it to be a Christian.

But there is a whole lot more that the resurrection has for us. Our risen Lord will give us a new heart and put a new spirit within us (see Ezekiel 36:26). He will give us new knowledge, new comfort, new peace, and a new life in Him.

THE RIGHT KIND OF FEAR

The fear of the Lord is the beginning of wisdom; a good understanding have all those who do His commandments. His praise endures forever. (Psalm 111:10)

Even the most committed believer has those moments when fear or worry can kick in. Anxiety can overtake us. Maybe we're concerned about our future, or perhaps discouraged about some of our failures.

But far too often, we are afraid of the wrong things in life, and we are not afraid of the right things—or the right One. Many people don't fear God, giving Him the awe and the reverence that is His due. Yet the Bible tells us that the fear of the Lord is the very beginning of wisdom.

To fear God doesn't mean that we must cower in terror before Him. Rather, the fear of God has been properly defined as a wholesome dread of displeasing Him. So if I have sinned, my fear should not be based on the anticipation of what God will do to me, but on what I have done to displease Him. That is what it is to fear the Lord. It is to love the Lord so much that you don't want to sin against Him.

David wrote, "The fear of the Lord is clean, enduring forever" (Psalm 19:9). It is *good* for us to fear Him. The remarkable thing is that when you fear God, you fear nothing else. On the other hand, if you don't fear God, then you fear everything else.

In another psalm, David stated, "The Lord is the strength of my life; of whom shall I be afraid?" (Psalm 27:1). Only the person who can say, "The Lord is the strength of my life" can then say, "Of whom shall I be afraid?"

Maybe you feel that your life has been a failure, or maybe you find yourself discouraged, depressed, or afraid of something. If you're gripped by fear and worry today, then let the Lord be the strength of your life.

STANDING BY

Be of good courage, and He shall strengthen your heart,
all you who hope in the Lord. (Psalm 31:24)

Paul had gone to Jerusalem to preach the gospel, and the next thing he knew, he was locked up in a cold, damp, dark prison cell. I'm sure that on his first night there, he was a discouraged man.

Why do I say that? Because of the Lord's words to him that night: "Be of good cheer, Paul; for as you have testified for Me in Jerusalem, so you must also bear witness at Rome" (Acts 23:11). The phrase "be of good cheer" could also be translated, "be of good courage." In Scripture, whenever an angel of the Lord would appear and say, "Fear not," it was usually because someone was afraid at that given moment. So I conclude that when the Lord himself told Paul, "Be of good courage," he needed a special word of encouragement at that particular moment.

Acts 23:11 includes this important detail: "But the following night the Lord stood by him and said, 'Be of good cheer....'" The Lord stood by him. Sometimes, it may seem as though the Lord is the only one standing by us. But if everyone else had abandoned Paul, Jesus was company enough. If all others despised him, the smile of Jesus was approval enough. Though his circumstances were less than ideal, I am sure Paul knew that it was better to be in jail with the Lord than anywhere else without Him.

Jesus is there in your prison as well. For some, it might be a literal prison cell. For others, it might be the prison of a hospital room or the prison of mourning. Whatever or wherever that prison is in your life, Jesus is standing by you. And He is saying, "Be of good courage."

IT'S NOT OVER YET

Being confident of this very thing, that He who has begun a good work in you will complete it until the day of Jesus Christ. (Philippians 1:6)

Are you discouraged today? Afraid of an uncertain future? The Bible tells the story of a time when Jesus' disciples were not only discouraged, but they were afraid for their very lives.

Jesus had told them to get into a boat and go over to the other side of the Sea of Galilee, and they obeyed. But when they were a considerable distance from land, a fierce storm arose that terrified them. Jesus, who had been on a mountain praying, went to meet the disciples, walking on the water. Thinking He was a ghost, the disciples cried out in fear. So Jesus immediately told them, "Be of good cheer! It is I; do not be afraid" (Matthew 14:27).

There are two simple reasons the disciples didn't have to be afraid: First, Jesus would help them weather the storm. And second, He had told them to go to the other side, which meant that they *would* reach the other side.

Jesus knows where you are at this very moment. He knows what you are experiencing. He is telling you to be courageous, because He is with you and there is a brighter tomorrow for you. Even if you have failed, even if you have made a mistake, it isn't over. You can still learn from that mistake and get out of the situation in which you find yourself.

God has a future for each of us. Jeremiah 29:11, one of my all-time favorite verses, says, "For I know the thoughts that I think toward you, says the Lord, thoughts of peace and not of evil, to give you a future and a hope." God will complete the work He has begun in your life.

WORTH WAITING FOR!

He has made everything beautiful in its time. Also He has put eternity in their hearts, except that no one can find out the work that God does from beginning to end. (Ecclesiastes 3:11)

Jairus was a well-known, powerful, wealthy individual who was the head of the local synagogue. When his twelve-year-old daughter, his only child, was in great need, he sought out Jesus to heal her.

We don't know whether Jairus was a believer in Jesus. As the head of the synagogue, he would certainly have been a religious man. He'd probably heard about Jesus. Maybe he had already put his faith in Him. The Scripture doesn't say. Nevertheless, Jairus believed that Jesus could save his daughter's life. So he went and found the Lord and begged Him to heal his daughter. He placed his complete trust in Jesus.

But as they were on the way to his house, the news came that his daughter had died. The reason they hadn't arrived at his daughter's side more quickly was because a woman in need of healing came along and touched Jesus, and He stopped and demanded to know who it was that touched Him.

Jairus, however, didn't complain. He had committed himself and his situation to Jesus, believing that God knew what He was doing. His faith was dramatic, especially because at this particular time in Jesus' ministry, He had not raised anyone from the dead. Granted, He had healed people. But there had been no resurrections.

Jairus had to wait, and sometimes we have to wait. A lot of us grow impatient with God, and in our impatience, we may foolishly take things into our own hands and make them far worse. Know this: God's delays are not necessarily His denials. We need to wait on the Lord. He's worth waiting for! God's timing is just as important as His will. He doesn't ask for us to understand, He just asks us to trust.

CORRECTIVE SUFFERING

Before I was afflicted I went astray, but now I keep Your word. (Psalm 119:67)

In the much-loved Psalm 23, David wrote: "Your rod and Your staff, they comfort me." The rod and the staff were shepherd's tools. The staff was a long, crooked instrument the shepherd would use when a sheep was going astray. But the rod was simply a club, which was used when the staff wasn't working anymore.

We may think that a club is extremely cruel to use on a poor sheep. But better to get whacked with a club than to be eaten by a wolf. Sheep are incredibly dumb. They will actually line up to die. If one sheep goes over a cliff, the other sheep will say, "Get in line. We're all going to die today. Let's go. Single file." The shepherd sometimes has to use extra corrective measures on a wayward sheep that could lead others astray.

I have seen the Lord use the rod of suffering or sickness to get someone's attention. He will say, "You really shouldn't do that," and then convicts them by His Spirit. But they might ignore Him. So He tells them, "Don't do that. I don't want you to do that." If they continue to ignore Him, BAM! God will use His rod: "I told you…don't do that." I have met a lot of people in hospitals who have come to Christ. Unfortunately, a lot of them don't stay with Christ. But others continue to walk with the Lord.

Maybe God has recently whacked you with His rod to get your attention. Maybe He has given you a wake-up call in the form of suffering or sickness, and you've been wondering why.

Don't ever doubt it: It is because He loves you.

THE SUM OF OUR LIVES

For with You is the fountain of life; in Your light we see light. (Psalm 36:9)

Someone has calculated that the average American spends up to fifteen years of his or her life in front of the television. *Fifteen years.* I'm not saying we should throw our TVs into a dumpster. But I am saying that we can sure waste a lot of time in front of it.

I sure have.

I'm a channel surfer. My wife likes to watch cooking shows and…well, I don't. Therefore, I try to gain possession of the remote so I can start madly clicking through the channels. I like to watch about eight things at once. Yet I've been amazed at how I will sit down and say, "I'm going to watch TV for five minutes," but when I look at my watch, an hour-and-a-half has gone by. I've wasted all that time and feel half brain-dead as a result.

We can squander time watching television, but we can squander time doing other things as well. So let's not throw our lives away. Let's wisely use the precious moments God gives to us each day, each month, and each year, and let's use them for Him. We will stand before Him on that final day. We should be able to sum up our lives like the apostle Paul and say, "For to me, to live is Christ, and to die is gain" (Philippians 1:21).

Some people might say, "To me, to live is sports," or "To me, to live is music." Everyone lives for something. What do you live for? Another way to look at that question might be, what are you investing in? What occupies your time, your attention, your thoughts, and your loyalties?

Life is way too short to leave such questions unexamined!

REAL WORSHIP

"Worthy is the Lamb who was slain to receive power and riches and wisdom, and strength and honor and glory and blessing!" (Revelation 5:12)

A number of words in the Bible are translated "worship." The one used the most often means "to bow down and do homage." Another biblical word for worship means "to kiss toward." Put the two words together, and you will have a good idea of what real worship is. We worship God because He is worthy. In doing so, we bow down and pay homage to Him. That speaks of reverence and respect for God. But we also "kiss toward" Him, which speaks of tenderness and intimacy.

We ought to be learning all we can about worship, because it will be one of the primary activities of heaven. And Jesus made it clear that there is a right and a wrong way to worship. There is true and false worship.

The Pharisees, who considered themselves the worship experts of their day, missed the target by a mile. Jesus said of them, " 'These people draw near to Me with their mouth, and honor Me with their lips, but their heart is far from Me. And in vain they worship Me, teaching as doctrines the commandments of men'" (Matthew 15:8-9).

Some people are too flippant and casual with God. They seem to think of Him as their celestial Big Buddy and approach Him that way in prayer: "Hey, Lord, how are You doing?" Others recognize God as holy and all-powerful and may even tremble before Him, but they don't realize that God wants to be known in an intimate and personal way.

We are to revere and honor God. But we're also to embrace Him in closeness. We are to engage our hearts, with no hypocrisy. And that's where true worship begins.

TIME DOES TELL

"For what will it profit a man if he gains the whole world, and loses his own soul? Or what will a man give in exchange for his soul?" (Mark 8:36-37)

A while ago, I ran into a guy that I once hung out with in school. I hadn't seen him in about twenty-five years. He had called to say that he was coming to hear me speak, so we arranged to meet beforehand.

As we talked, he told me he had been married twice and was presently divorced. Then he said, "I basically drank my marriages away." He went on to explain that he had fallen prey to alcoholism, and had never gotten free of it. It had ruined his life.

I told him, "You know, in the Bible, God says, 'You will seek Me and find Me....'"

"You can quote your book, and I'll quote mine," he said. "I'm in fellowship, too. ...I'm in a 12-step program."

We used to hang out and party together, but although I left that lifestyle at age seventeen, he never did. As I look at the course his life has taken and the course my life has taken, it's clear who really gave up the most.

There might be times as a Christian when you look at unbelievers and think, *I don't know. Maybe they're having the good time and I'm not.* It might look like they are having fun today, but there is a price for sin. You will reap what you sow.

If you live for Christ, if you determine to do things God's way, you won't regret it. Because you won't find happiness or fulfillment through sex, drugs, or drinking. You won't find it through relationships, success, possessions, or accomplishments. You *will* find happiness and fulfillment by walking in your Creator's true purpose for your life: a living, dynamic relationship with God through Jesus Christ.

OPEN ACCESS

Having predestined us to adoption as sons by Jesus Christ to Himself, according to the good pleasure of His will, to the praise of the glory of His grace, by which He made us accepted in the Beloved. (Ephesians 1:5-6)

Within the first few verses of Jude's short New Testament letter, he uses an important word twice: "beloved." In verse 1, he writes, "To those who are called, sanctified by God the Father, and preserved in Jesus Christ...." The word "sanctified" could better be translated "beloved." Jude begins verse 3 with the same word. Here we have a foundational truth, which Jude brings front and center: We are beloved of God.

How often we hear about what we are supposed to do for God. Yet the emphasis of the Bible is not so much on what we are supposed to do for God, but rather on what God has done for us. If we can get hold of that in our minds and hearts, it will change our outlook and actions. The more we understand of what God has done for us, the more we will want to do for Him.

This is no small truth. In fact, it's fundamental to our spiritual lives. The devil would love to keep you from praying at all by reminding us how "unworthy" we are—telling us in effect that we have a lot of nerve to even think we could approach a holy God. He whispers, *Do you think that God would hear your prayers after what you've done?* But the real question to ask is this: "Is Jesus Christ worthy to come into the presence of the Father whenever He wants?" Of course He is.

The fact is that we are "accepted in the Beloved." Because Christ has open access to the presence of the Father at any time, we have the same access as we come to God the Father through our relationship with Jesus. It's not on the basis of what we have done for God, it is solely on the basis of what Christ has done for us.

And that's the best news I've ever heard.

AN ITCH FOR NOVELTY

For the time will come when they will not endure sound doctrine, but according to their own desires, because they have itching ears, they will heap up for themselves teachers; and they will turn their ears away from the truth, and be turned aside to fables. (2 Timothy 4:3-4)

In these two verses from his letter to his young disciple Timothy, Paul describes conditions during the last days before the return of Jesus Christ. The phrase "itching ears" in verse 4 could be translated, "an itch for novelty." Isn't that an apt description of people in the church today? I am amazed at the crazy things that people who profess to be Christians will buy into. It seems as though every few years some new doctrinal fad or teaching comes along that everyone gets worked up about.

People get caught up in nonsense, and it is an itch for novelty. After awhile, they tire of it and run off to some new thing. It's because they have never learned to love the Word of God.

The Bible tells us that in the last days, there will be false teachers, there will be a false gospel, and there will be false miracles. Only those Christians who are conversant with the Word of God and are biblically literate will be able to identify them.

Jesus said we are to go "and make disciples of all the nations" (Matthew 28:19). The church is a place where the Bible should be taught and where God's people should learn the teachings and the requirements of the Word of God. It should be a place where we worship, pray, and use the gifts God has given to us.

Novelty isn't what we need, it is *consistency*. A steady day-by-day walk with Jesus and a daily commitment to mine the treasures of His Word will not only bring us the maximum amount of joy in life, it will also protect us from false teaching and false messiahs.

THE REAL JESUS

He said to them, "But who do you say that I am?" Simon Peter answered and said, "You are the Christ, the Son of the living God." (Matthew 16:15-16)

Without question, Jesus Christ is the most fascinating person ever to walk the face of the Earth. He is undeniably the most extraordinary, influential individual in human history. More books, music, and dramas have been written about Jesus Christ than any other figure in our past...from Day One. In fact, His arrival and death were so significant that we actually divide human time and mark off human history by them.

But who is the real Jesus? Is He merely some distant figure in stained glass who can't be touched or known? Was He a radical revolutionary who had come to change His world? Or was He some kind of guru or one of many "sons of god" who had come as an example to follow? Peter knew the answer: Jesus is the Son of the living God.

If your desire is to see who the real Jesus is, then the place to look is in the Bible. Jesus said, "In the volume of the book it is written of Me..." (Hebrews 10:7). You don't have to look any further than this. You don't have to look for a prophet or a guru or someone with a special revelation. You can find everything you need to know about Jesus in the pages of Scripture. The Holy Spirit will illuminate these truths for you. You can begin to know Him, and He will begin to work in your life.

TO SEE JESUS

Now there were certain Greeks among those who came up to worship at the feast. Then they came to Philip, who was from Bethsaida of Galilee, and asked him, saying, "Sir, we wish to see Jesus." (John 12:20-21)

I remember visiting a mental hospital years ago with a fellow pastor. We were visiting the patients and sharing the gospel. Back then, I wore very long hair and had a full beard. My pastor friend began talking with one patient and said, "Have you ever personally met Jesus Christ?"

"No," the man replied, "But I've always wanted to." Then he turned to me, shook my hand, and said, "Jesus, it's good to meet you! I've heard so much about you."

"I'm not Jesus!" I told him. "My name is Greg."

Imagine what it would be like to actually reach out and shake hands with the real Jesus, to actually touch Him. The opening verses of today's devotional tell us about some individuals from Greece who wanted an opportunity to do just that.

Instead of simply granting them an audience, however, Jesus used their request to illustrate a point: "The hour has come that the Son of Man should be glorified. Most assuredly, I say to you, unless a grain of wheat falls into the ground and dies, it remains alone; but if it dies, it produces much grain..." (verse 23-24).

Jesus was essentially saying, "Do you really want to see Me? Do you want to see God? You *will* see Me through My death. Soon, I will die on a cross for you and pay the price for your sins. Through My death, you can have life. You can see God, and you can know God."

A DIFFERENT KIND OF KINGDOM

Then Jesus, when He had found a young donkey, sat on it; as it is written: "Fear not, daughter of Zion; behold, your King is coming, sitting on a donkey's colt."
(John 12:14-15)

The Bible tells us that when Passover took place, Jerusalem—being the spiritual capital of Judaism—teemed with visitors. People were everywhere. Not only that, but word traveled like wildfire that Jesus was there. Everyone was talking about it.

You see, Jesus was getting ready to make a very significant move. This was the moment He had been waiting for. The hour had come for Him to begin His road to Calvary. He was about to fulfill Scripture's prophecies.

The next day a great multitude that had come to the feast, when they heard that Jesus was coming to Jerusalem, took branches of palm trees and went out to meet Him, and cried out: "Hosanna! 'Blessed is He who comes in the name of the Lord!' The King of Israel!" Then Jesus, when He had found a young donkey, sat on it; as it is written: "Fear not, daughter of Zion; behold, your King is coming, sitting on a donkey's colt."
(John 12:12-15)

Luke's gospel tells us they thought the kingdom of God would appear immediately. They thought Jesus Christ would come in and say, "I am now the King of Israel," and then overthrow the Romans who had kept them in bondage. *Hosanna! Finally, we're going to be free from this tyranny!*

But there was a different significance. For the Jews, Jesus was saying, "I am your Messiah." And for Rome, He was saying, "I am your King. But My kingdom is not of this world."

Jesus' entry into Jerusalem that day was not to take the crown, but to wear a crown of thorns—for all of us.

GOD'S TRADE-IN DEAL

"He who loves his life will lose it, and he who hates his life in this world will keep it for eternal life." (John 12:25)

Most of us are suspicious of the trade-in deal. Maybe you've tried to buy a car and trade in something else. The salesman says, "Trade that in, and I'll give you a deal." Then you tell your friends, "I got this great deal for my trade-in." The real question, however, is what they charged you for the new one you bought.

In spite of what they might tell you on the TV used car ads, you can't get something for nothing.

God Almighty, however, says to us, "I will give you eternal life. I will forgive all of your sins." So we say, "What's the catch? Surely there's something I need to do." It's hard for us to accept that God could simply forgive us.

God says, "No, you have broken all the laws. There is no way you could earn My grace or forgiveness. I offer it to you for free. I give you everything. Now you give Me your life. I don't care what shape it's in. I'm in the restoration business. You watch what I can do." So you bring your life to Him.

Jesus said, "Whoever loses his life for My sake will find it" (Matthew 16:25). You will be a new creation, because in Him, all things have become new (see 2 Corinthians 5:17).

"Do you want to find life?" Jesus says to us. "You won't find it by looking within yourself. You won't even find it by looking for life. You will find it by looking to Me. And as you trade your life in, I will give you life. The very thing you want, you'll find by coming to Me."

This is God's trade-in deal.

A LIGHT IN THE DARK

"If the world hates you, you know that it hated Me before it hated you."
(John 15:18)

Jesus became very popular during His earthly ministry. He spoke in a way that people could understand. Reaching out to hurting people and down-and-outers, He became known as a friend of sinners. All that really irritated the religious authorities. Clearly, He was a threat to their legalistic system of works. For that reason, He became public enemy number one. Jesus Christ, the Son of God, was a wanted man.

In the same way, there are people today who hate Jesus Christ and everything He stands for. They despise His teachings. And if you follow Jesus Christ and His teachings and stand up for what you believe, then they will hate you, too. In fact, Jesus said we should remember that if the world hates us, it hated Him first. He chose us out of the world, and therefore the world hates us. We can expect to be persecuted (see John 15:18-20).

We are representatives of Christ. And if you think people hate Christians in general, then try being a pastor! Because I'm a representative of God, some people will take all their anger out on me. "Why does God do this?" they demand. "Why doesn't God do that?" Actually, I accept the fact that I'm a representative of God. I'm not ashamed of it. But some people will hate us for it.

It isn't easy being rejected or scorned by others, is it? Most of us like to be liked. We have no desire to offend people unnecessarily, and we try to live our life in a kind and gracious way. But because we are representatives of Christ—simply for that reason—we *will* bother and even anger people. Why? Because they know we stand for biblical values and biblical truth. It's like being a light in a dark place.

The Bible offers no consolation for Christians who are hated for being jerks or hard to get along with. But if you are hated simply because you love and follow Jesus, you have real cause to celebrate. (See Matthew 5:10-12.)

A STRONG COMMUNITY

*"For where two or three are gathered together in My name,
I am there in the midst of them." (Matthew 18:20)*

We live in a time in which our society is becoming more and more disjointed and divided. Rather than celebrating what we have in common, it seems nowadays we emphasize the things that separate us. In fact, I don't know of a time, at least in my brief life, when our culture has been more divided (perhaps with the exception of the tumultuous 1960s).

Families are falling apart like never before, and the result is that people are looking for a place where they can belong, a community where they can feel safe, a family they can belong to...a place where they can genuinely love and be loved in return.

And that is exactly what the church is!

I know the church isn't perfect, made up as it is of imperfect people. But foibles and all, it is the only organization that Jesus Christ Himself ever established. And after two thousand years, it's still going strong.

Any attempt that has ever been undertaken to eradicate the church that Jesus established and maintains has met with failure, because Jesus said of His church, "I will build My church, and the gates of Hades shall not prevail against it" (Matthew 16:18). He is with His church, and it is still going strong!

Step out and invite that neighbor or coworker you're so sure wouldn't be interested to church with you. Hard as it may be for you to imagine, they may be just waiting for an invitation.

CALLED OUT AND CALLED TOGETHER

Now all who believed were together, and had all things in common. (Acts 2:44)

There is nothing in this world quite like Christian fellowship. We know that the early church worshipped, prayed, and studied the Scriptures together. They also ate together, gave their tithes and offerings together, shared the gospel together, helped one another, and stuck together. In short, they loved one another.

The word that describes this phenomenon is the Greek word *koinonia*, which is usually translated "fellowship." But it is also translated into the words "communion," "distribution," "contribution," or "partnership." This means there is something wonderful and supernatural that people in the church experience. It's a bond we share that those outside that fellowship can't begin to understand.

God has a unique purpose and place for the church in the world today. Paul tells us that we Christians are "the called of Jesus Christ" (see Romans 1:6). God's people are called out of a world system that is hostile to the teachings of Scripture. As Jesus said, "You are not of the world, but I chose you out of the world, therefore the world hates you" (John 15:19).

This doesn't mean we are to isolate ourselves from the world, because Jesus said, "Let your light so shine before men, that they may see your good works and glorify your Father in heaven" (see Matthew 5:16).

We are to be salt and light in this culture. But at the same time, we are called out of the culture and warned not to love it. Called out...and called together. In the world...but not of the world. The apostle Paul called the church "a mystery," and there is nowhere better to be in this world than right in the middle of it.

A PLACE FOR YOU

But now God has set the members, each one of them,
in the body just as He pleased. (1 Corinthians 12:18)

The Bible likens the church to a family and to a physical body. We are called as Christians to be functioning, participating, contributing members of the body of Christ. We need to be a part of a body where there is accountability, friendship, and *koinonia*. We need to be a part of a body where we come to receive and to learn, but we also need a place where we can contribute and serve the Lord with the gifts He has given us.

In comparing the church to a body, the apostle Paul wrote, "But now indeed there are many members, yet one body. And the eye cannot say to the hand, 'I have no need of you'; nor again the head to the feet, 'I have no need of you' " (1 Corinthians 12:20-21).

I do many things with my hands, but I don't really think about how I'm going to use them. My hands just sort of do what they do. Underneath the skin everything is working together so I can use my hands. Each part of my body is dependent on another part of my body.

In the same way, the church as a body is interdependent. We cannot live and flourish apart from other believers. God wants us to engage. He wants us to be a part of what He is doing. Attending church is not a spectator sport. We are here to be a functioning part of His church.

Everyone has a job to do. Everyone has a need to serve. And yes, there is a place for you. Are you doing your part?

THE LOVING CHURCH

> *My little children, let us not love in word or in tongue,*
> *but in deed and in truth. (1 John 3:18)*

The Bible tells us again and again that we should love one another. Love is like the glue that holds us all together. The apostle John wrote, "Beloved, let us love one another, for love is of God; and everyone who loves is born of God and knows God" (1 John 4:7).

The Bible's definitive chapter on love, 1 Corinthians 13, is the most comprehensive description of love in all of Scripture. In these classic verses, Paul shines love through a prism, so to speak. We see many of its colors and hues, so we can more easily understand love and apply it in a practical way. Each ray gives a different facet of God's *agape* love.

The Bible doesn't focus so much on what love is, but on what love does and doesn't do. The love of God that we are to demonstrate toward one another is not merely feeling or emotion. Nor is it abstract or passive. It is active. It engages. It works. It moves. God's love doesn't merely feel patient; it is patient. God's love doesn't simply have kind feelings; it *does* kind things. Love is fully love only when it is active. As the apostle Paul said to the Romans: "Don't just pretend that you love others: really love them" (Romans 12:9, TLB).

At the same time, the Bible tells us the goal of the Christian is to be conformed to the image of Christ (see Philippians 3:10). This is what God wants you to strive for and aim toward—so that the love He speaks of will work its way into every aspect of your life.

LOVE IS PATIENT AND KIND

Love suffers long and is kind. (1 Corinthians 13:4)

Can you imagine the world we would live in if people operated by the principle that says, "Don't look out for your own needs and interests, but for the needs of others"? Yet we live in a culture that tells us to forget about others and to look out for number one.

One thing we should bear in mind is that God's love is patient. And as part of the body of Christ, our love should be patient as well.

Another way to translate the phrase, "Love suffers long" from 1 Corinthians 13 is "Love is long-tempered." This common New Testament term is used almost exclusively in speaking of being patient with *people*, rather than being patient with circumstances or events. Love's patience is the ability to be inconvenienced again and again.

The last words of Stephen, the first martyr of the church, were those of patient forgiveness: "Lord, do not charge them with this sin" (Acts 7:60). As he was dying, he prayed for his murderers rather than for himself. This is the same kind of love Jesus spoke of that turns the other cheek. It's the kind of love that has as its primary concern not its own welfare, but the welfare of others.

And love is kind. Just as patience will take anything from others, kindness will give anything to others. To be kind means to be useful, serving, and gracious. It is active goodwill. Love not only feels generous; it *is* generous. Love not only desires the welfare of others; love works *for* it.

If, however, you wait for this emotion to come and settle over you like the morning dew, you may be waiting a long, long time. Remember, love is active. Love is kind. So just *be* kind, even if you don't feel kind. Step out with kind, loving actions, and your feelings will follow along behind.

WHEN TO RUN

Run from anything that stimulates youthful lusts. Instead, pursue righteous living, faithfulness, love, and peace. Enjoy the companionship of those who call on the Lord with pure hearts. (2 Timothy 2:22, NLT)

Some years ago, there was a story in the news about a man who had a tree fall on his leg. With no one around to come to his rescue, he took out a pocketknife and proceeded to amputate his leg. Then he made his way up the road until someone picked him up and raced him to help. Amazingly, this man who had a severed leg still had enough presence of mind to tell the driver of the vehicle not to go too fast. He said, "I didn't come this far to die on the road. Take it easy."

I remember reading that story and thinking, "He did *what*? How could this guy cut off his leg? I would have laid under the tree and just waited for help." But the doctors who treated him later said that if he hadn't taken such a drastic measure, he would have died. The action had saved his life.

Sometimes we must take radical, drastic steps to remove ourselves from whatever it is that is hurting us spiritually. That may mean immediate change. It may mean physically getting up and saying, "I'm out of here."

You might be at a party, watching a movie, in a particular relationship, or in a place where you have no business being. Wherever it is, you realize you shouldn't be there. God is convicting you. He is saying, "What are you doing here?" Don't be foolish. Just get up and go. That's not always possible, but many times it is.

Is there a relationship or a situation in which you don't belong? Has God been speaking to you about it? You'll be glad you took the time to listen.

LETTING GOD CHOOSE

Now glory be to God! By his mighty power at work within us, he is able to accomplish infinitely more than we would ever dare to ask or hope. (Ephesians 3:20, NLT)

When my oldest son was a little boy, I would take him to the toy store. We would look around, and I would tell him to pick out something for himself. He would look at the Star Wars figures, and I would look at the X-wing fighter with the remote control, thinking that I would like to get it for him. The truth was that I wanted to play with it, too. He would pick out his little figure. Then I would say, "I was thinking of getting you something better than that." He always went along with my idea!

After a while, he started learning something about Dad, which was that Dad liked to get presents for his kids. He came to realize that it was better to say, "I don't know what to get, Dad. You choose it for me." He figured out that my choices were often better than what he would choose for himself.

Have you ever said to the Lord, "Here is the way I think You ought to work. But not my will, but Yours, be done"? Some might say, "I'm not saying that to God. If I say that, He might make me do something I don't want to do." I think that a person who believes that has a warped concept of God, a misconception that His will is always going to be something undesirable.

God may be saying "no" to something you have asked Him for, because He wants to give you something far better than what you could ask or think. Don't be afraid to let your Father choose for you.

LEARNING TO YIELD

> *For our present troubles are quite small and won't last very long. Yet they*
> *produce for us an immeasurably great glory that will last forever!*
> *(2 Corinthians 4:17, NLT)*

I read a story—perhaps apocryphal—about a radio exchange that took place some time ago between a U.S. Navy ship and Canadian authorities off the coast of Newfoundland. The Canadians warned the Americans, "Please divert your course 15 degrees to the south to avoid a collision."

The Americans responded, "Recommend you divert your course 15 degrees to the north to avoid a collision."

The Canadians said, "Negative. You will have to divert your course 15 degrees to the south to avoid a collision."

The Americans: "This is the captain of a U.S. Navy Ship. I say again, divert your course."

"No. I say again, you divert your course."

"This is the aircraft carrier USS Lincoln, the second largest ship in the United States Atlantic fleet. We are accompanied by three destroyers, three cruisers, and numerous support vessels. I demand that you change your course 15 degrees north. I say again, that is 15 degrees north or counter-measures will be undertaken to assure the safety of our ship."

After brief moment of silence, the Canadians responded: "This is a lighthouse. It's your call."

Sometimes we don't like what God wants us to do, and we want Him to change course when, in reality, it is you and I who ought to change course.

We need to understand that God's plans are better than ours. Having said that, it doesn't mean that they are always the easiest or even the most appealing at the moment. There are times in our lives when we might not like the plan of God—not at all! Even so, God's plans are always better for us in the long run.

HALF-HEARTED COMMITMENT

"Look how far you have fallen from your first love! Turn back to me again and work as you did at first...." (Revelation 2:5, NLT)

At first glance, you might think that Abraham and his nephew Lot were both spiritual men. But a closer examination reveals that this was not the case.

You see, Abraham lived for God. Lot, on the other hand, lived for himself. Abraham walked in the Spirit. Lot walked in the flesh. Abraham lived by faith. Lot lived by sight. And most significantly, Abraham walked with God, and Lot walked with Abraham.

Unfortunately, because of Lot's half-hearted commitment to the Lord, he was becoming a spiritual drain on Abraham. Their relationship was gradually pulling Abraham down. That is why, earlier in Genesis, God said to Abraham, "Leave your country, your relatives, and your father's house, and go to the land that I will show you" (Genesis 12:1, NLT).

But Abraham was reluctant to part ways with Lot. When a famine came, Abraham actually went down to Egypt. It was a definite step backward. But Abraham eventually came to his senses and realized he was in a backslidden state. He decided to return to God and to the place where He had called him.

Sadly for Abraham, he reaped in the years ahead the results of that wrong choice. It was in Egypt that a woman named Hagar became Sarah's servant. Abraham ended up having a child with Hagar. The child's name was Ishmael, and conflicts between his descendents and the descendents of Isaac continue to this very day.

Are there any ungodly influences in your life that have been wearing you down lately? Has a certain relationship or pursuit become a spiritual drain in your life? Have you been compromising? Then make a change. It isn't too late.

AGAINST ALL ODDS

And Jehoshaphat feared, and set himself to seek the Lord, and proclaimed a fast throughout all Judah. So Judah gathered together to ask help from the Lord; and from all the cities of Judah they came to seek the Lord.
(2 Chronicles 20:3-4)

Jehoshaphat, King of Judah, faced a terrifying dilemma. His enemies greatly outnumbered him. To make matters worse, his enemies had joined forces with Judah's other enemies and were coming to destroy him.

One day, someone came to King Jehoshaphat and warned him that a gigantic army was headed his way, bent on his destruction. It was hopeless. There was no way that he could meet this mighty army with what he had. It looked for all the world like doomsday for the little nation of Judah.

What did Jehoshaphat do? The Bible says that he "set himself to seek the Lord." He prayed, "O our God, will You not judge them? For we have no power against this great multitude that is coming against us; nor do we know what to do, but our eyes are upon You" (2 Chronicles 20:12).

The Lord told Jehoshaphat, "Do not be afraid nor dismayed because of this great multitude, for the battle is not yours, but God's…. Position yourselves, stand still and see the salvation of the **Lord**, who is with you" (2 Chronicles 20:15, 17).

Jehoshaphat and his army went out to meet their enemies, but they put the worship team out in front of the soldiers! The Bible says that when they began to sing and praise the Lord, the enemy started fighting among themselves and destroyed each other.

Maybe you are facing what seems like an impossible situation right now. You may not be able to see a way out. But God can. Call on Him. Then stand still and see what He will do.

HEART TROUBLE

"Let not your heart be troubled; you believe in God, believe also in Me."
(John 14:1)

Have you ever felt troubled in your heart—agitated, stressed–out, or uncertain about tomorrow?

There is a lot to be afraid of these days, isn't there? Maybe something has happened to you recently that has turned your world upside down. Maybe you've found yourself wondering whether God really is aware of the problems you're facing right now.

That is exactly how the disciples of Jesus felt. They were downhearted and discouraged. When they were all gathered in the Upper Room for the Passover feast, Jesus told them that one of them was going to betray Him. Then He identified Judas Iscariot as the betrayer. Not only that, but Jesus also said Simon Peter would deny Him—not once, not twice, but three times. Peter! Could it really be? The whole world turned upside down for these men. And then, worst of all, Jesus began talking about leaving them, about being crucified. Can you blame them for wondering, *What in the world is going on here?*

Maybe you feel that way. Maybe there is uncertainty in your future. As you survey your fears and concerns today, take a few minutes to consider what Jesus said to His disciples and to us in that tense Upper Room: "Let not your heart be troubled; you believe in God, believe also in Me" (John 14:1). This verse could also be translated, "Let not your heart be agitated, or disturbed, or thrown into confusion...."

In other words, "Don't let these things throw you! Put your full trust and faith in Me!" It was good advice for some deeply troubled believers two thousand years ago and I can tell you right now with complete confidence... it's the best counsel anyone will give you all day today.

THE BIG PICTURE

And we know that all things work together for good to those who love God, to those who are the called according to His purpose. (Romans 8:28)

There are times in our lives as Christians when God will do things or fail to do things that we want Him to do, and it won't make a bit of sense to us. And because we don't see the big picture, we may falsely conclude that God has abandoned us. But we need to trust Him during these times, remembering that Jesus Christ is the author and finisher of our faith. In other words, what God starts, He completes.

It seems as I get older, I get distracted and forget things all the time. But what if God forgot about us? What a frightening thought. Imagine being in the midst of a fiery trial as God is watching and waiting for that moment to take us out of it. Then the phone rings, and He's gone for a decade! Thankfully, God never forgets about us. He is in full control. He knows exactly what He is doing. He will complete what He has begun.

Sometimes in the middle of that process, we may think the Lord is missing it. But He isn't. We're the ones who are missing it. From our limited human viewpoint, we think of the temporal, but God lives in the eternal. We are thinking of today, but God is planning for tomorrow...in fact, He's already been there. We are thinking of comfort, but God is thinking of character. We are thinking of an easy time, but God is thinking of how to make us better people.

So let's trust Him. Whatever our circumstances or hardships, let's believe His promise to His children.... All things *are* working together.

Tuesday

OUR GREAT HOPE

"In My Father's house are many mansions; if it were not so, I would have told you. I go to prepare a place for you." (John 14:2)

We don't have to be stressed-out or troubled in our hearts, because as Christians, our destination is eternal life in heaven. No matter what happens, no one can rob us of that great hope. Maybe you've lost your job or your car won't start. Maybe you have all kinds of problems in your life right now. But you are still going to heaven.

The apostle Paul encouraged the church with these words: "Therefore we do not lose heart. Even though our outward man is perishing, yet the inward man is being renewed day by day. For our light affliction, which is but for a moment, is working for us a far more exceeding and eternal weight of glory" (2 Corinthians 4:16-17).

The troubles we see now will soon be over, and the joys that are yet to come will last forever. Jesus promises there is a real place called heaven, and you have His word on it. You have the word of God Himself on that...the surest word in all the universe.

Now when Jesus said, "In My Father's house are many mansions," I don't believe He was speaking of a celestial Beverly Hills with beautiful, palatial mansions for those who live really godly lives on Earth. I don't believe there will be actual houses on streets when we get to heaven.

But Jesus has promised us that we will be together with Him in heaven, for eternity, in the place He has prepared for us. And He will keep His word.

WATCHING AND WAITING

For the Lord Himself will descend from heaven with a shout, with the voice of an archangel, and with the trumpet of God. The dead in Christ will rise first. Then we who are alive and remain shall be caught up together with them in the clouds to meet the Lord in the air. And thus we shall always be with the Lord.
(1 Thessalonians 4:16-17)

The Bible says that God has loved us so that in the ages to come, He might show us the exceeding riches of His grace and kindness toward us in Christ Jesus (see Ephesians 2:4-7). In other words, God is saying, "I can hardly wait until you get home so I can show you how much I love you."

So we don't need to be stressed out. Jesus is coming again. And someday, in the not-too-distant future, He will set foot back on planet Earth and say, "I have returned."

As a student of Bible prophecy for many years, I can say that I know of no prophecy in Scripture that needs to be fulfilled before the Lord returns. In my understanding of what the Bible teaches, Jesus Christ could come back for His people today. And it will happen in a moment, in the twinkling of an eye.

He might return today for those who are watching. Are you ready for that moment?

Thursday

A VISION OF HEAVEN

"And God will wipe away every tear from their eyes; there shall be no more death, nor sorrow, nor crying. There shall be no more pain, for the former things have passed away." (Revelation 21:4)

Have you ever tried to explain something to someone and couldn't quite find the words? Have you ever tried to describe something complex to a child? For God to describe heaven to us in a way we could understand would be like trying to describe the beauty of Hawaii to a three-month-old child. We're not able to comprehend, in our finite human understanding, all the infinite glories of heaven.

In fact, the apostle Paul, who had the unique experience of dying and actually going to heaven, said that he heard things so astounding that they couldn't be told (see 2 Corinthians 12:2-4). Paul was essentially saying that he couldn't put his experience into words.

Heaven is beyond our comprehension. While there aren't many verses in the Bible that tell us about it, Scripture does tell us a few things. It says that in heaven there will be no night. There will be no fear. There will be no suffering or death. All of the pain and disabilities that we face in this life will be gone in heaven.

But the glory of heaven is even more than having new bodies—and even more than the absence of darkness and sorrow and pain and death. The fact that Jesus Christ will be there is better than all the beauty and all the answers to all our questions.

"Your eyes will see the king in his beauty and view a land that stretches afar" (Isaiah 33:17, NIV).

IN SEARCH OF BIBLICAL LITERACY

"My people are destroyed for lack of knowledge...." (Hosea 4:6)

Whenever I'm invited to speak somewhere, I can discern the biblical IQ of the group I'm addressing in the first few minutes of my message. I observe the way they track, the way they listen, what interests them, and what doesn't interest them. I note how they will come alive when an illustration is rolled out. But as soon as I get back to the biblical text, they go into a daze, as if to say, *Wake me when the next illustration or joke is coming.*

This is because they have never learned to love the Bible. They have never developed a hunger for it. We love worship at our church—and no one walking in the door way on a Sunday morning could believe otherwise. We love having various artists coming in and sharing their music with us. But the main event is the teaching and the preaching of the Word of God.

Yet tragically, so many people in the church today are biblically illiterate. They don't have a biblical worldview. I can't tell you how many times I've gone to a church as a guest speaker and said, "Turn in your Bibles to..." and no one has a Bible! When I will refer to certain biblical passages or a biblical story, they will look at me with blank expressions. That is not a good sign.

I believe the cry of Hosea 4:6 rings true for many in the church today: "My people are destroyed for lack of knowledge."

It doesn't have to be that way. No matter what the level of Bible teaching might be in your church, you can study the Word of God for yourself. Find a Bible translation that you can understand, plug into a daily Bible reading program, ask the Holy Spirit to open your understanding...and launch into the greatest of all journeys!

DESTRUCTION BY DECEPTION

For certain men have crept in unnoticed, who long ago were marked out for this condemnation, ungodly men, who turn the grace of our God into lewdness and deny the only Lord God and our Lord Jesus Christ. (Jude 4)

Is it possible to preach and not be a true believer, or to even do miracles and not necessarily be saved? Absolutely.

Jesus said, "Not everyone who says to Me, 'Lord, Lord,' shall enter the kingdom of heaven, but he who does the will of My Father in heaven. Many will say to Me in that day, 'Lord, Lord, have we not prophesied in Your name, cast out demons in Your name, and done many wonders in Your name?' " (Matthew 7:21-22).

Notice that Jesus said, "*Many* will come in that day." This reminds us there will be an abundance of false miracles in the last days. Many will say they have been producing signs and wonders and casting out demons. But Jesus will say, "I never knew you; depart from Me, you who practice lawlessness!" (Matthew 7:23). The worst thing imaginable is to spread wickedness under the veneer of true faith. Tragically, this does happen in the church today.

I wish that we could spot these people more easily. But Jude pointed out that they come in unnoticed (see Jude 4). That's the whole idea. Satan is a deceiver, and that is why, on more than one occasion, the Bible compares him to a snake. Having been an avid collector of snakes as a kid, I know how easily they can get out of the tightest little spots and escape. In the same way, Satan sneaks into the church unnoticed.

False teachers come into the church secretly. And their numbers grow by preying on unsuspecting believers. Beware of false teachers. And be careful of those who say they have a message you won't hear anywhere else. Be like the believers from Berea, in Paul's day, of whom it was said: "Now these were more noble-minded than those in Thessalonica, for they received the word with great eagerness, examining the Scriptures daily to see whether these things were so" (Acts 17:11, NASB).

CONTEND FOR THE FAITH

> *Beloved, while I was very diligent to write to you concerning our common
> salvation, I found it necessary to write to you exhorting you to contend
> earnestly for the faith which was once for all delivered to the saints. (Jude 3)*

Without question, the gospel is under attack today. And I believe
that most Americans, not to mention the rest of the world, have
not really heard the gospel message. The fact is that when a lot of people are
supposedly "preaching the gospel," they really aren't doing any such thing.

That is why Jude 3 says that we need to contend for the faith. We want
to make sure that we know what the essential gospel is, because there are
certain elements that must be in place for the gospel to be the gospel.

I often hear people oversimplify or overcomplicate the Good News of
Jesus Christ. Either they load it down with a bunch of rules and regulations
that have nothing to do with the essential gospel, or they strip it of its essential meaning by offering forgiveness without mentioning repentance—or by
telling people about a wonderful place called heaven without mentioning a
very real place called hell. We need to find that balance and do it properly.

What would you think of a surgeon who just opened you up and started
randomly cutting away? It would be frightening for him or her to say,
"Hmmm…I'm really not sure where to start!" It's the same with the gospel
message. We want to make sure that what we declare is the real deal, the
genuine article, because sharing the message of Jesus Christ has
ramifications that stretch through time right into eternity.

So let's contend for the faith. Let's declare it. Let's defend it.
And let's live it.

Tuesday

CONTENDING WITH CARE

Instead, speaking the truth in love, we will in all things grow up into him who is the Head, that is, Christ. (Ephesians 4:15, NIV)

I remember walking down Kalakaua Avenue in Waikiki and seeing a man holding a big sign with red flames and the words, "The wages of sin is death." He was yelling out to people, "God hates you! God is going to judge you! God is going to get you!" I watched as people passed by, intentionally turning away from him.

Finally, I walked up to him and said, "Excuse me, I have a question. I just wanted to say that while it's true that the wages of sin is death, as your placard says so boldly, it is also true that the rest of that verse says the gift of God is eternal life through Jesus Christ our Lord. Why don't you put that on the other side of your placard, and you could flip it around periodically? You could give them the whole message."

The man then told me that I was going to hell. He was intent on delivering a certain degree of truth in a contentious way.

When we read in Jude 3 that we are to contend for the faith, it doesn't mean that we're to *assault* with the truth. It doesn't mean we are to bludgeon people with it. The word "contend" in this verse actually speaks of delivering the truth, but doing so in a loving manner. The Bible tells us to speak the truth in love, which means professing God's truth in a loving way.

It is important to know your theology and to know what the Bible teaches. But it is also so very important to just love people. If we can find the balance of lovingly presenting truth, it will be a powerful combination.

BUILDING AND DEFENDING

But from then on, only half my men worked while the other half stood guard
with spears, shields, bows, and coats of mail. The officers stationed themselves
behind the people of Judah who were building the wall. The common laborers
carried on their work with one hand supporting their load and one hand
holding a weapon. (Nehemiah 4:16-17, NLT)

W hen God called Nehemiah, the cupbearer of King Artaxerxes,
to rebuild the walls of Jerusalem, Nehemiah was living in the
lap of luxury. He was in a position of power and prestige.

But Nehemiah was stirred in his heart, because he knew that while he
lived in comfort, his fellow Jews were basically living in ruin. The once-
high walls of Jerusalem lay in rubble, burned-out and charred. God told
Nehemiah to use his position of influence for Him. Nehemiah prayed
and then went to the king and asked for permission to rebuild the walls.
Permission was granted, and Nehemiah returned to Jerusalem and set
about the task of getting the people to rebuild the wall.

At first, they weren't all that interested, but eventually Nehemiah rallied
the troops. Everyone began to work together. And as soon as the Israelites
began to rebuild the walls of Jerusalem, there was opposition.

It is a reminder to us that whenever God's people say, "Let's rise up and
build," the devil and his cohorts are going to say, "Let's rise up and oppose."
One of the greatest challenges when we go into a community to hold a
Harvest Crusade is not booking the venue or printing the materials or doing
the other things that are so visible. The hardest thing is getting the churches
to wake up to the need of getting the gospel out in their own community.

That is what Nehemiah had to do, and that is what we need to do. On
one hand, we are to be building ourselves up in the faith. And on the other
hand, we are to be contending for the faith. We build and defend, and it all
goes together.

MISUNDERSTOOD GRACE

What shall we say then? Shall we continue in sin that grace may abound?
Certainly not! How shall we who died to sin live any longer in it?
(Romans 6:1-2)

I am shocked at what some people today will do and still claim to be Christians. They will blatantly do what the Bible tells them they should never do.

The idea that you can do whatever you want as a Christian and still be forgiven isn't unique to our day, however. Paul had to refute that fallacy, as we see in the above verse.

It is a false teaching that says that you can go out and blatantly disobey God, reassuring yourself that "God's grace will cover it all." It is a perversion of the teaching of the grace of God.

The Bible says that the grace of God is given to us so that we might say no to ungodliness and worldly passions and live self-controlled, upright, and godly lives in this present age as we wait for the return of Christ.

It doesn't say that the grace of God was given to us so that we can do whatever we want and break His commandments with abandon. Grace and law work closely together. The law tells me that I am a sinner. Grace tells me how to deal with my sin.

While it's true that the Christian is no longer under the constraint or the extreme limitations of the law, it doesn't mean that he or she should disregard it altogether. It means we should obey it because we want to, not because we have to.

What you believe determines how you will behave.

THE IMPORTANCE OF DOCTRINE

Take heed to yourself and to the doctrine. Continue in them, for in doing this
you will save both yourself and those who hear you. (1 Timothy 4:16)

Theology and doctrine are not trivial matters. Yet there are people today who set aside biblical teaching and say, "I just want to experience God. I don't want to argue over doctrine. I just want to love Jesus." That is a nice sentiment, but it is also a very dangerous one. It means they might end up loving the wrong Jesus. They might end up believing the wrong doctrine.

That is why the Bible exhorts us again and again to have our lives and doctrine in order. One of the reasons so many people are falling prey to false teachings today is that they do not have a grip on good Bible teaching.

I once heard a statistic that 80 percent of people who are pulled into various cult groups were once part of a church. That isn't necessarily saying they were believers, but it is saying that these people had some church involvement at some point in their lives. If that statistic is correct, then it is alarming. It shows there are people who could have spent time in church, maybe a lot of time, but because they didn't have their doctrine in order, they were led down the wrong road.

If you have your doctrine in order, if you know what the Bible teaches, then you will be able to refute false teaching and defend your faith. It's what Jude means by exhorting Christians to "contend earnestly for the faith which was once for all delivered to the saints" (Jude 3).

THE RESULT OF REBELLION

And I remind you of the angels who did not stay within the limits of authority God gave them but left the place where they belonged. God has kept them securely chained in prisons of darkness, waiting for the great day of judgment. (Jude 6, NLT)

Sometimes the question arises as to how a God of love could create someone as wicked as Lucifer. The answer is that God did not create Lucifer as we know him today. In fact, that being was once a high-ranking angel and, according to Ezekiel 28, was the model of perfection, full of wisdom and beauty.

So what happened? What was his specific sin? Very simply, it began when his heart was lifted up with pride because of his incredible beauty. He was not satisfied with worshiping God. He instead wanted to be worshiped. So Lucifer, once a high-ranking, beautiful angel of God, lost his exalted position in heaven. Lucifer became Satan when he fell to the earth. Lucifer means "star of the morning," which he once was. Satan means accuser, which he now is. And when Satan fell, he took one-third of the angels with him, who are now in rebellion against God.

It's staggering to think that angels turned against God. After all, apart from humanity, who has greater privilege than angels? Certainly they have been given the unspeakable privilege to have access to the very throne of God and worship before Him. Yet the Bible tells us there was a major angelic rebellion.

Here is the warning for us today: Even the angels are facing judgment because they rebelled against God, reminding us of the danger of thinking we can use the grace of God as a license for sin. The Bible cautions us that just because we know what is right and have been taught in the truth, does not mean that we are incapable of rebelling against God. The angels rebelled and faced God's judgment. And if we rebel, we will face His judgment as well.

If on the other hand we cling to our faith in our redemption through the blood of Jesus Christ our Lord, we will one day enter into an eternity of worship and fellowship with our great Creator…the very privilege Lucifer has lost forever.

A TIME-TESTED WARNING

And don't forget Sodom and Gomorrah and their neighboring towns, which
were filled with immorality and every kind of sexual perversion.
Those cities were destroyed by fire and serve as a warning
of the eternal fire of God's judgment. (Jude 7, NLT)

It may seem like a bit of a stretch to use Sodom and Gomorrah as an example and warning to us in the church today, but that is exactly what Jude did. One of the most obvious reasons we are to remember this biblical account of sin and judgment is that it is prophetic of the condition of the last days.

I cannot think of a time in my years of following the Lord when I have seen greater immorality among those who claim to be followers of Jesus Christ. I cannot personally think of a time when I have seen more open and blatant sin taking place on the part of those who profess to be Christians.

When we hear the names Sodom and Gomorrah, we immediately think of immorality. But there were other things at the root of these sins. Ezekiel 16:49 offers God's assessment: "Look, this was the iniquity of your sister Sodom: She and her daughter had pride, fullness of food, and abundance of idleness; neither did she strengthen the hand of the poor and needy." These people were proud, they had more food than they needed, and they had too much time on their hands. What an accurate description of our nation today.

The pride of those who lived in Sodom and Gomorrah was a nationalistic pride. They felt strong and indestructible—precisely the way many of us feel today within the borders of the United States.

The problem is that we have forgotten God. We have done our level best to push Him out of our schools, out of our courtrooms, and out of our culture, and we are now reaping the results of those actions…a shocking moral breakdown in our society.

Let's walk in the conscious, moment-by-moment fellowship of Jesus Christ today, remembering that our true security lies in Him.

Tuesday

OUR BACK-UP PLAN

*Keep yourselves in the love of God, looking for the mercy of our
Lord Jesus Christ unto eternal life. (Jude 21)*

When police officers are in trouble, what do they do? They call
for backup. That is what believers need to do as well. When we
are being hassled or tempted, we need to call for backup. We are to stand
strong in the Lord and in the power of His might.

James 4:7 says, "Therefore submit to God. Resist the devil and he will
flee from you." Notice it doesn't say that we are to submit to God and carry
on extended conversations with the devil. We want to keep our distance
from the enemy, being careful never to yield to his suggestions.

Disobedient and persistent waywardness provides the enemy a foothold
from which he can attack and influence the Christian. So flee temptation
and don't leave a forwarding address. Keep your distance from the things
that could drag you down.

We must learn from the example of the Israelites who, in spite of their
privileges and exposure to miracles, did not keep themselves in the love of
God. As a result, they faced judgment.

We must learn from the example of the fallen angels who, even though
they once worshiped God in heaven, rebelled against Him and became
demons in hell.

We must learn from the example of the people living in Sodom and
Gomorrah who, in spite of the fact that they were exposed to the preaching
and ministry of Abraham, Lot, and even Melchizedek, they rebelled against
God.

These all failed to keep themselves in the love of God. So let's make sure
we are taking every step to succeed.

LETTING THE HOLY SPIRIT WORK

> *"And when He has come, He will convict the world of sin,*
> *and of righteousness, and of judgment." (John 16:8)*

Why has the Spirit come into this world? What does God's Holy Spirit want to do in the life of the unbeliever? The Holy Spirit is very involved in the actual work of conversion. You see, before we were Christians, it was the Holy Spirit who convicted us of our sin (see John 16:8). Another way to translate the word "convict" in John 16:8 is "convince."

Notice this verse doesn't say He will convict the unbeliever of a specific sin. Rather, He wants to convince him or her of sin in general, the root cause of all sins.

Now we can try to produce in someone a sense of guilt and wrongdoing. In an effort to "help" the conversion process along, we want to make them feel really bad or guilty about something. (Mothers seem to have an unusual ability in this area.) But only the Holy Spirit can effectively produce a guilt that will bring a person to their senses.

Sometimes we get in the way of someone's conversion. We get impatient, or we try to assist the Spirit. We can be telling someone about the Lord, maybe a friend or a coworker or a family member, and as they become interested and start asking questions, we start trying to convert that person in our own strength. We try to complete the transaction while the Spirit is still working.

The best thing we can do after we have shared the Word of God with someone is to simply pray that it takes root. We should just do our part and leave it in the hands of God. We don't need to force the issue. He will do the convincing. Let God's Spirit do His work.

SIMPLE THINGS

Because the foolishness of God is wiser than men, and the weakness
of God is stronger than men. (1 Corinthians 1:25)

Have you ever wished you could do a miracle for friends or family members who weren't believers? You think, "If this happened—right before their eyes—then they would believe." We think we need something dramatic or earthshaking. But so many times, God works in simple ways to reach people.

For example, I read about a hardened atheist who had a young daughter. He didn't want her to believe in God. So one day, he wrote down the words "God is nowhere" on a piece of paper and told his little girl to read them aloud. She picked up the piece of paper. She was just learning to read, so she sounded out her words and said, "God is...let's see, N-O W-H-E-R-E. Oh, I understand, Daddy. God is now here." The atheist was so touched by that simple little event that he became a believer in Jesus Christ.

I'm reminded of a couple that attended one of our Harvest Crusades events in Southern California. As they were walking down the street, they spotted a crumpled but colorful piece of paper on the ground. When they picked it up and smoothed it out, they discovered a Harvest Crusade flyer. They read it, and then prayed and received Christ. They also went to the crusade and walked forward at the invitation. What a simple thing God used: a crumpled little flyer that contained a gospel message.

So often, we think we need something dramatic to reach nonbelievers—or maybe some brilliant, flawless argument. And so often, God does His work in unexpected ways, using people, methods, and circumstances you could have never predicted.

Our part is to pray and to be a good witness of what Christ has done in our lives...and then just watch Him work.

OUR HELPER

> *"And I will ask the Father, and he will give you another Counselor, who will never leave you. He is the Holy Spirit, who leads into all truth."*
> *(John 14:16-17, NLT)*

In the Upper Room, on the night Jesus was betrayed, the disciples were upset and discouraged by what He had been telling them about His impending betrayal and crucifixion. So Jesus shared some words of encouragement with them. He told them about the Holy Spirit for the first time:

"If you love Me, keep My commandments. And I will pray the Father, and He will give you another Helper, that He may abide with you forever—the Spirit of truth, whom the world cannot receive, because it neither sees Him nor knows Him; but you know Him, for He dwells with you and will be in you. I will not leave you orphans; I will come to you."
(John 14:15-18)

I am certain that those words of Jesus brought comfort to their hearts. He was saying to His disciples, "I'm not going to leave you comfortless or abandon you without help. I will ask the Father, and He will send someone alongside to help you."

During the days that Jesus walked the Earth, He was always there for His people. They could reach out and touch Him. If they had a question, they could ask Him. He always had time for His own. They could get close to Him.

Then He told His disciples (and essentially all followers of Jesus to this day) that He would guide them and lead them in an entirely new way: through the Holy Spirit. As Christians, then, we know that the Holy Spirit is actively involved in our lives. He is the Helper Jesus has given us.

OUR TEACHER

"But the Helper, the Holy Spirit, whom the Father will send in My name,
He will teach you all things, and bring to your remembrance
all things that I said to you." (John 14:26)

W e may not even realize it, but the Spirit of God teaches us all the time. The Holy Spirit can unfold passages from the Bible in an incredible way through our reading and study of Scripture. Needless to say, that is why we should spend regular time in Bible study and memorization. In doing so, we are opening the door for the Spirit to illuminate God's Word for us.

I don't have startling insights or some kind of deep spiritual experience every time I open the Bible to read. But I read because I know I need to, in obedience to God. It might be that very day or the next day when a situation will arise, and suddenly the passage I committed to memory is activated by the Holy Spirit. All of a sudden, the Spirit takes that Scripture and uses it to minister to someone. It's the Holy Spirit speaking through me, and that's a wonderful experience.

When I step up to the pulpit, I depend on the Holy Spirit to speak through me. Yes, I have prepared. I have done my homework. But at the same time, I want God to speak to the people who are listening.

Sometimes, we will hear speakers and think they are the greatest preachers who have ever lived. But in reality, it is the Holy Spirit speaking through those people to us. So let's give the glory to God and not to them.

The Holy Spirit will give us the power to live the way God wants us to live. And He will continue to teach us day by day, hour by hour.

THE PURSUIT OF PLEASURE

You will show me the path of life; in Your presence is fullness of joy;
at Your right hand are pleasures forevermore. (Psalm 16:11)

The Bible tells us that one of the signs of the last days would be that people are lovers of pleasure rather lovers of God (see 2 Timothy 3:1-3). That is an accurate assessment of our culture today. Ours is a pleasure-obsessed culture.

Yet the Bible doesn't tell us that pleasure is necessarily wrong. In fact, God promises a pleasure that comes from knowing Him and walking in His presence.

The problem is when we allow pleasure to become the driving force in our lives. The Bible says, "She who lives in pleasure is dead while she lives" (1 Timothy 5:6). Peter describes those who revel in their pleasures as blots and blemishes (see 2 Peter 2:13).

Besides all of that, the pursuit of pleasure rarely brings what we are searching for! Rather, it brings emptiness. One only has to read the writings of Solomon to recognize this.

Jesus told us how to deal with this selfish pursuit: "If anyone desires to come after Me, let him deny himself, and take up his cross daily, and follow Me" (Luke 9:23). Jesus didn't say we are to love or esteem ourselves; He said we are to deny ourselves. We are to take up the cross daily and follow Him.

And that's where the irony of it all comes in. As we deny the impulses of our flesh and set our hearts to follow and obey Jesus Christ...we find the pleasure and satisfaction we'd been looking for all along.

LOVE YOU CAN COUNT ON

Having loved His own who were in the world, He loved them to the end.
(John 13:1)

We have all probably heard someone say at some time, "God loves you." And sometimes we may wonder, *Does God really love me?* Maybe you've been let down and sorely disappointed by people. Maybe someone said he loved you and then turned against you. Maybe someone said she was your closest friend, but ultimately betrayed you.

When it comes to God's love, we tend to ask ourselves whether it is for real. We wonder whether He, too, will turn away from us if we let Him down.

Jesus knew what it was like to be betrayed. As Jesus celebrated the Feast of the Passover with His disciples, the devil had already put it into the heart of Judas to betray Him. The other disciples didn't stand by Jesus, either. They forsook Him, but He did not forsake them. They denied Him, but He did not deny them. He loved His own who were in the world, and He loved them to the end.

The story is told of a little boy who was troubled one night by a thunderstorm. He cried out from his room, "Daddy! I'm scared!"

The father responded, "Son, don't worry. God loves you, and He will take care of you."

The boy replied, "I know God loves me, but right now I need someone with skin on."

Jesus is God with skin on. Jesus is God demonstrating His love for His own.

Aren't you glad that God doesn't treat you the way that you treat Him? Aren't you relieved He doesn't reciprocate that way? No matter what you do, no matter where you go, God will always love you.

TWELVE HOURS TO LIVE

Jesus knew that His hour had come.... (John 13:1)

At the first Passover in Egypt, the blood of the lambs that protected the Israelites was pointing to Jesus Christ. It was foreshadowing what He would do on the cross, when Jesus himself would become the Passover lamb, the lamb that was slain for all of humanity. His blood was shed in our place.

Jesus had been waiting for this moment. He was always in full control of everything that was happening in His life and ministry. He knew exactly what would take place next. He knew time was short and that His departure was at hand, when He would leave this world to return to the Father. But He had certain things He had to accomplish before He went to the cross, a certain chain of events that had to take place. And the night before, He knew He basically had twelve hours before He would be crucified.

What if you had only twelve hours to live? Would you make any changes in your life? Would you be prepared to meet God? The Bible says, "Prepare to meet your God" (Amos 4:12).

God told Hezekiah, "Set your house in order, for you shall die and not live" (Isaiah 38:1). Is your house in order? By that I mean, are you ready to meet the Lord? If He were to come back today and call His own to be with Him in heaven, would you be ready to go? If you died, would you be sure that you would go to heaven? If not, you ought to make some changes.

Jesus knew what was coming. He dreaded it. He even recoiled from it. But for the sake of His love for us all, He pressed on.

FATHERLY LOVE

Behold what manner of love the Father has bestowed on us,
that we should be called children of God! (1 John 3:1)

What do you think God's love is? Do you envision a permissive love that allows you to do whatever you want? That doesn't describe the love of God. You see, God loves you enough to put restrictions in your life. He loves you enough to say, "Do this. It will help you. And don't do this. It's bad for you."

Suppose a child asks his mother, "Mommy, can I play in the street?" Of course she would say, "No, you may not. I love you and don't want you to be in a place where you would be endangered. One day, you will realize that I did this not from a lack of love, but because I do love you."

It's the same with us. When God says no to us, it's not because He doesn't love us. It's just the opposite.

In the Garden of Eden, God told Adam, "'Of every tree of the garden you may freely eat; but of the tree of the knowledge of good and evil you shall not eat, for in the day that you eat of it you shall surely die'" (Genesis 2:16-17). So the devil tempted Eve: "Has God indeed said, 'You shall not eat of every tree of the garden'?" (Genesis 3:1). Essentially he was saying, "If God really loved you, then He would let you do whatever you want." The truth was that because God loved Adam and Eve, He didn't want them to fall into sin. Yet they disobeyed God and that's exactly what happened.

Those limits that you find in the pages of the Bible are there for your own good. God has put a fence around you, so to speak. But it's not to keep you confined—it's to keep you safe from the many dangers in this world—and in the invisible spiritual world that surrounds us.

CONSTANT CLEANSING

After that, He poured water into a basin and began to wash the disciples' feet, and to wipe them with the towel with which He was girded. (John 13:5)

Before the Passover meal, Jesus took off His outer robe. He got down on His hands and knees, picked up the basin, and began to wash the disciples' feet.

As Jesus made His way around the room, Peter was watching. Always one to speak his mind, he blurted out, "Lord, are You washing my feet?" (John 13:6). It's almost as though he didn't want to humble himself in this way. Perhaps he saw that it had symbolic meaning and, in spite of the fact that he had already bathed, the implication was that he was dirty again.

There are people like that today who say, "I haven't sinned. I haven't done anything wrong. I'm a good person. I don't need God's forgiveness." But everybody needs it.

Jesus told Peter, "He who is bathed needs only to wash his feet, but is completely clean..." (verse 10). In other words, once you have received Jesus Christ as your Savior and Lord, you don't need to be saved again and again. You don't have to shower over and over. Once you have received Christ into your life and have asked Him to forgive you, then you are forgiven. Christ has already come into your heart...but you do need regular cleansing.

I know that my sin is forgiven; I know my final destination is heaven, but on a daily basis I do need to say, "Lord, forgive me." Jesus taught us that we should regularly pray, "And forgive us our debts, as we forgive our debtors" (Matthew 6:12). So it's a good thing to say, "Lord, cleanse me. Forgive me." Because we need constant cleansing.

DARKNESS OR LIGHT?

Having received the piece of bread, he then went out immediately. And it was night. (John 13:30)

The ultimate betrayal is done by someone you love. And that was the case with Judas. It wasn't just that he turned against the Lord, but that he had pretended to love Him. Worse yet, Judas betrayed Jesus with a kiss. At the moment Judas appeared to be the most holy, he was at his most wicked.

Why is that? It is the hardness of sin. Judas had a series of choices. But he hardened his heart. He sealed his fate. Judas left the table of fellowship that night, and slipped out into darkness to betray his best Friend...and he never returned. He preferred to go into the night rather than to be in the light. Why? Because he loved darkness rather than light, because his deeds were evil (see John 3:19).

The Bible describes our lives without Christ as living in darkness. Walking with God and knowing God is walking in the light. The Bible warns that we as Christians do not belong to the night or to the darkness, because we are sons of light and sons of day (see 1 Thessalonians 5:5).

Have you ever noticed that the later it gets at night, the weirder the people seem to be? You read about so many crimes and bizarre things happening after midnight, in the wee hours of the morning. It seems like really strange people come out really late at night.

How much better it is to walk in the light. The Bible tells us, "But if we walk in the light as He is in the light, we have fellowship one with another, and the blood of Jesus Christ His Son cleanses us from all sin" (1 John 1:7).

God says, "Come out of your dark life. Come into My light. I will forgive you." Which way are you going? Into the darkness? Or into the light?

THE PURSUIT OF GOD

"Abide in Me, and I in you. As the branch cannot bear fruit of itself, unless it abides in the vine, neither can you, unless you abide in Me." (John 15:4)

A glance at today's headlines could lead us to conclude that we live in pretty bleak times. There is great uncertainty about the future, especially among teens and twenty-somethings. Many feel they have nothing to grasp, no one to believe in, and no one to trust except themselves.

I would like to say that there is something to grasp. There is someone to trust in, but it is not ourselves. It is the God who created us.

Why am I here? What is my purpose in life? These are questions that everyone should ask as they look to the future, especially if they are young. If we have no goals, purpose, or guiding principles, then we will waste our lives like so many others have wasted theirs. As it has been said, if we aim at nothing, we're bound to hit it.

According to the Bible, you don't find happiness, fulfillment, and joy by just looking for them here and there. These things are *by-products* of a relationship with the living God, in Christ. Let me put it this way: if you seek God and live according to His plan for your life, then you will find happiness. You will find joy. You will also find fulfillment—not through the pursuit of those things, but through the pursuit of God. So seek Him!

FILLING THE VOID

Let us hear the conclusion of the whole matter: fear God and keep His commandments, for this is man's all. (Ecclesiastes 12:13)

I f you are seeking fulfillment, purpose, or meaning from this world and from human accomplishments, I have some bad news: you will never find it. There is nothing in the world that will fill the deepest void in your life—not the ultimate car, not the greatest job, not the most beautiful girl or the most handsome guy, not the greatest education. There is nothing that can even come close.

King Solomon, one of the wealthiest men who ever lived, had everything he wanted. Yet he went on a binge, trying to satisfy his appetites with the wrong things. He went after passion. He went after possessions. He went after things of beauty and buildings and land. He drank and he partied. After all of that, here was his conclusion: "Then I looked on all the works that my hands had done and on the labor in which I had toiled; and indeed all was vanity and grasping for the wind. There was no profit under the sun" (Ecclesiastes 2:11).

Have you ever been ravenously hungry and tried to satisfy your appetite with snacking? It just doesn't work. You want a real meal. In the same way, we were created with a God-shaped hole in our lives. We have been created to love God, to know God, and to bear fruit. Everything else is secondary.

Think about it: *Everything* else in life, every other responsibility, no matter how significant, must be ordered behind the central purpose of your existence on Earth: knowing, loving, and serving your Creator. Yes, God cares about your career, your marriage, your family, and your ministry. But knowing Him, prioritizing Him, is number one. And when you do, the Bible says you will never be a loser for it!

"Your heavenly Father already knows all your needs, and he will give you all you need from day to day if you live for him and make the Kingdom of God your primary concern" (Matthew 6:32-33, NLT).

WHAT SPIRITUAL FRUIT LOOKS LIKE

"But he who received seed on the good ground is he who hears the word and understands it, who indeed bears fruit and produces: some a hundredfold, some sixty, some thirty." (Matthew 13:23)

The concept of bearing fruit is used often in Scripture. In the Gospels, Jesus told the story of a sower who went out to sow seed. The seed fell on various types of ground. Some of the ground was rocky and hard. Other ground was receptive, but weeds choked out the seed. But there was a portion of ground that was neither rocky nor weedy, and in that soil the seed took root. Jesus said that this was a picture of the different people who hear the gospel. Those who are true believers will bring forth fruit (see Luke 8:4-15).

What is bearing fruit? Essentially, it is becoming like Jesus. Spiritual fruit will show itself in our lives as a change in our character and outlook. As we spend time with Jesus and get to know Him better, His thoughts will become our thoughts. His purpose will become our purpose. We will become like Jesus.

The Bible gives an excellent description of a life characterized by the fruit of the Spirit. Galatians 5:22-23 says, "But the fruit of the Spirit is love, joy, peace, longsuffering, kindness, goodness, faithfulness, gentleness, self-control."

Is that what others see in your life? If not, then either you don't know God or you are living outside of fellowship with Him. If that is the case, then a commitment or a recommitment to Him would be in order. God isn't asking for a perfect life. But He is asking that these fruits be primary characteristics of a life that is lived for Him.

Thursday

MAKING A COMMITMENT

Then He said to them all, "If anyone desires to come after Me, let him deny himself, and take up his cross daily, and follow Me." (Luke 9:23)

Although it has been more than three decades, I still remember clearly the day I was joined in marriage to my wife Cathe. She walked down the aisle looking beautiful. I, on the other hand, resembled Jeremiah Johnson with my shoulder-length hair and big beard. I cringe when I look at the photos. But that day, I committed myself to Cathe. I said, "I take you to be my lawfully wedded wife, to have and to hold from this day forward, for better for worse, for richer for poorer, in sickness and in health, to love and to cherish, 'til death do us part." I made a public commitment to her.

And although I have already made that commitment, I make a recommitment every day to love Cathe and to be the husband that God wants me to be. I don't always do this perfectly. But I recognize that it is a continuing commitment.

I have also committed myself to Jesus Christ, and every day I honor and affirm that commitment. One practical way I do this is simply by staying in fellowship with Him. Jesus said, "If anyone desires to come after Me, let him deny himself, and take up his cross daily, and follow Me" (Luke 9:23). By obeying God, listening to and heeding the "still, small voice" of His indwelling Holy Spirit, I remain in unbroken fellowship with Him.

If you want to grow in Jesus Christ, it will take time—and lots of it. It will take a daily commitment for the rest of your life. But do you have anything better to do with the rest of your life than to follow Jesus and learn more about Him? That is the best thing you could possibly do with your life and future. Nothing is better than that.

You could say the same thing hour by hour through your day. Nothing is better, no matter what your activities or responsibilities, than walking in the sweetness and radiance of His conscious presence.

IN HARMONY WITH GOD

He who says he abides in Him ought himself also to walk just as He walked.
(1 John 2:6)

The word "walking" speaks of regularity, of moving at a certain pace. The Bible tells us in Genesis 5 about Enoch, who walked with God. But what does it mean to "walk with God"? Is it just a religious cliché?

The prophet Amos asked, "Can two walk together, unless they are agreed?" (Amos 3:3). The idea is to be walking in pace with someone, in harmony with another.

I have a problem with this when I walk with my wife. I always walk a little faster than she does. I will walk ahead. I'll stop. Then she will catch up with me. So I'll walk more slowly, but the next thing I know, I'm walking fast again.

When it comes to walking with God, some of us run ahead of Him. Some of us lag behind. We need to move in harmony with Him. We need to stay close to Him, and make a continual commitment to do so.

But what does this mean in practice? How do we do this? It means we take time for the things of God. It means when we get up in the morning, we take time to read the Bible. If we neglect the Word of God, it will show in our lives. Abiding in Jesus also means that we spend time in fellowship with God's people.

Make time for the things of God. Don't wait for time to simply materialize; deliberately carve out room in your schedule. If it means an hour less of sleep, fine. If it means skipping a meal, okay. If it means missing a television program, so be it. Do what you need to do, because these things are essential to spiritual growth, to abiding with God, and to bearing spiritual fruit.

And it is a walk—the best of all walks—that will bring indescribable richness to your daily life.

PROMISES...WITH A PREREQUISITE

*He who dwells in the secret place of the Most High shall abide
under the shadow of the Almighty. (Psalm 91:1)*

Without question, Psalm 91 is a real gem among the psalms.
Next to Psalm 23, it has probably brought more encouragement and comfort throughout the centuries than any other psalm.

But it is worth noting that the blessings promised in Psalm 91 aren't for just anyone. They are specifically given to believers—and not just to believers in general. These benefits are targeted toward believers who specifically meet the requirements found within the psalm. Psalm 91 is full of conditional promises. In other words, God promises to do certain things for us, hinging on us doing certain things that are required.

Verse 1 begins, "He who dwells in the secret place of the Most High....." The word "dwells" could be translated as "quiet and resting, enduring and remaining with consistency." It is very similar to the word "abide," which we see often in the New Testament. Jesus said, "He who abides in Me, and I in him, bears much fruit" (John 15:5). That word "abide" means, "to stay in a given place, to maintain unbroken fellowship and communion with another."

Here's what God is saying: "If you want to experience the promises of Psalm 91—My protection, My provision, and My blessing—you must dwell in the secret place of the Most High. You must remain in constant fellowship with Me."

We have a relationship with God because we have put our faith in Jesus Christ and have turned from our sin. But are we living in constant fellowship with God? Many believers are not.

God is interested in a relationship with you, not just on Sundays, but throughout the week. He wants you to dwell in the secret place of the Most High.

KEPT IN HIS WAYS

For He shall give His angels charge over you, to keep you in all your ways.
(Psalm 91:11)

The angels of God are nearer than you may think. They are all around us all the time, taking care of us and ministering to us, even when we're not aware of their presence. That's fine with them, because essentially they are God's secret agents, doing His bidding and the work He has called them to do. Many, many times they have intervened in our lives and we didn't even know they were doing so.

According Psalm 91 and other passages of Scripture, angels are actively involved in the life of the believer. Hebrews 1:14 says that they are ministering spirits, sent forth to minister to those who will inherit salvation. Hebrews 13:2 tells us not to be forgetful to entertain strangers, for in doing so, some have entertained angels without even knowing it. There are so many stories in the Bible of angels who delivered the people of God—we read about Jacob, Lot, Daniel, Peter, and Paul, among others.

But as wonderful as the promise of angelic involvement in our lives is, we must first recognize what the conditions are for this promise to be activated in our lives: "For He shall give His angels charge over you, to keep you in all your ways" (Psalm 91:11). Recognize the fact that the phrase "to keep you in all your ways" is not referring to whatever path you choose, but to *God's* ways.

There is a difference between trusting the Lord and testing Him by taking unnecessary chances with your life or even endangering your spiritual safety by doing stupid things, expecting God to bail you out. God will keep you in all your ways—but your ways must be *His* ways.

Tuesday

WHEN TROUBLE COMES

"He shall call upon Me, and I will answer him; I will be with him in trouble; I will deliver him and honor him. With long life I will satisfy him, and show him My salvation." (Psalm 91:15-16)

Are you facing an emergency today? Dial 911...Psalm 91:1, that is. This psalm of David speaks of both great adversity and the wonderful help and protection of God. The fact is, God can use difficulty and crisis in the life of the Christian. None of us wants adversity in our lives, but God can be glorified through such times. You may have faced a serious, even life-threatening illness and experienced the healing power of God. Or perhaps you're still dealing with a troublesome physical condition, and you haven't experienced that longed-for healing. Either way, we bring glory to His name right in the midst of it all.

Psalm 91 doesn't say you will never die. But it is saying that you won't die before your time. It is saying that until God is done with you, His angels will keep you in all your ways...in your ups and downs, when you're awake and asleep, in the sunshine and in the rain.

What's your part? It is to dwell in the secret place of the Most High and abide under the shadow of the Almighty. Your objective as a Christian should be to stay as close to the Lord as you possibly can, leaning on Him with quiet faith and confidence. Because this all-powerful, all-knowing God who possesses heaven and earth, has made a covenant with you, loves you, and offers to protect and provide for you, you should make it *your* objective to get closer to Him, asking, *How can I walk so closely with Him that I will be in His very shadow?*

You should periodically ask yourself whether you are meeting the criteria of this great psalm, whether you are living up to the conditions that have been set forth. If your answer is yes, then you have God's word that these promises will be activated in your life.

ONLY THE LONELY

*"And the Lord, He is the One who goes before you. He will be with you, He
will not leave you nor forsake you; do not fear nor be dismayed."*
(Deuteronomy 31:8)

Years ago, Roy Orbison recorded one of the great rock and roll
classics, entitled, "Only the Lonely." A couple of the lines from the
song were, "Only the lonely know the way I feel tonight…. Only the lonely
know the heartaches I've been through." That song resonated with a lot of
lonely people who knew what it was like to be abandoned.

Maybe you have been abandoned—perhaps it was by your parents,
your spouse, or your children. Or maybe you even feel that you have been
abandoned by God Himself. There are many people who feel estranged and
alienated from God. Even if they have everything they want in life, they may
still face loneliness.

We read in John 5 of a man at the pool of Bethesda who was in a seemingly hopeless situation. He had been abandoned. He was uncared for and
unable to help himself. He must have been desperately lonely.

In this account, we learn that Jesus changed the man's life forever. It's
a story that tells you and me how to change as well. Before Jesus brought
transformation and healing into this man's life, however, He first asked him
a rather pointed question: "Do you want to be made well?"

In the same way, is there something you want changed in your life? Do
you want to be made well? Maybe it's an addiction to a certain vice or a
lifestyle you are trapped in. Maybe it's something you have tried to shake
time and time again.

Jesus turned the course of this man's life around forever, giving him the
ability to live a life free from loneliness and the power of sin. We can live
that life, too—with Him.

GOING INTO BUSINESS

Can two walk together, unless they are agreed? (Amos 3:3)

There are a number of things included in the concept of walking with God. The Bible says that we need to walk in the Spirit (Galatians 5:16). We should walk rooted in Him (Colossians 2:6-7). We should walk humbly with Him (Micah 6:8). Walking with God means moving in harmony with Him, staying close to Him. This phrase "walking with God" speaks of a joint effort.

If you go into business with someone, it means pooling your resources. Maybe you both have small businesses, even competing businesses, and one day you go to that person and agree to work together. You draw up the contracts and pool your resources. He has his clients, you have your clients, and suddenly you broaden your base.

Walking with God is like going into business with God. This means that I take all of my resources, which obviously are quite limited, and say, "Lord, here is what I have to bring. I give myself to You."

Then God says, "Here is what I bring to the table. I bring My omniscience. I bring My unlimited power. I bring My grace. I bring all that I have."

Essentially it would be like a millionaire going into business with a homeless person. That's a pretty good deal. The homeless person will benefit because all the millionaire's resources are now at his or her disposal. But it also means that all of his or her resources (such as they are) will now be at the millionaire's disposal.

When we walk with God, He brings all He has and all He is to the table…but He also asks us for all we are and all we have. Through all of time and eternity, we are the ones who get the better end of that arrangement!

UNDER NEW MANAGEMENT

"And you will hear of wars and rumors of wars. See that you are not troubled; for all these things must come to pass, but the end is not yet. For nation will rise against nation, and kingdom against kingdom. And there will be famines, pestilences, and earthquakes in various places." (Matthew 24:6-7)

From the beginning of time, humanity has searched for peace. We have joined peace movements, marched for peace, given prizes for peace, even gone to war for peace. And when we hear that people have been arrested for disturbing the peace, we wonder where they actually found any to disturb! Some people tell us via their bumper stickers to "Visualize world peace." Then they cut us off on the freeway.

Displayed above the doors of the United Nations are the words of Isaiah 2:4: "They shall beat their swords into plowshares and their spears into pruning hooks." We are a people who want peace. But we need to know this: neither the United Nations nor politicians nor people who visualize it will bring about the long-awaited peace on Earth that humankind so desperately longs for. The peace that we long for will only happen when the Creator Himself returns, repossesses what is rightfully His, and hangs a sign over this war-weary planet that says, "Under New Management."

It would be nice to think that with all of our sophistication and technology, we could somehow bring about global peace. But according to Jesus, in the last days we "will hear of wars and rumors of wars. See that you are not troubled; for all these things must come to pass...." (Matthew 24:6). Tragically, war will be a part of the future of humanity until Christ Himself comes and establishes His kingdom.

Until that day...until the Prince of Peace returns to take charge of a troubled world, we can still find peace of heart and mind, peace that surpasses all understanding, as we rest in Him.

FRIENDS OF GOD

But God demonstrates his own love for us in this: While we were still sinners, Christ died for us. (Romans 5:8, NIV)

Two men camping in the forest were enjoying their morning coffee when, all of a sudden, they spotted a very large, hungry grizzly bear running toward them. One of the men quickly pulled on his running shoes. "Do you actually think you can outrun that grizzly bear?" his friend asked.

"I don't need to," he replied. "All I have to do is outrun you."

We've all had friends like that, haven't we? At the first threat of danger or hardship, or difficulty, they're out the back door. So what makes for true friendship? It has been said that a true friend is one who walks in when others walk out. Thankfully, there have been people in my life who have stood by me and have been honest friends. But there's one thing of which I'm confident: I have found a true and loyal friend in Jesus Christ.

Jesus Christ offers His friendship to us. But do we really expect a friendship without a response on our part? A genuine relationship, obviously, is made up of two people committing themselves to one another. I can extend friendship to you, but until you return it to me, I can't legitimately say we're really friends.

Jesus demonstrated His willingness to have a friendship with us by what He did for us. He said, "Greater love has no one than this, than to lay down one's life for his friends" (John 15:13). He forever proved just how dedicated He was to us when He did just that.

TRUE FRIENDS

*A man who has friends must himself be friendly, but there is a friend
who sticks closer than a brother. (Proverbs 18:24)*

We can't choose all of our coworkers. For that matter, we can't choose all the members of our family. But we can choose our friends. And we need to be very careful as we do so.

Knowing what an influence a close friend can have on our outlook and our lives, we need to look for godly friends. Look for friends who love God, who will speak the truth to you, who will help to build you up, and who will be godly influences on you.

Shadrach, Meshach, and Abed-Nego, those three Hebrew teenagers we read about in the book of Daniel, appeared to be great friends, supporting one another in times of trial. When everyone else turned against them and everyone else was worshiping a false god, these three stuck together as godly friends, even in the fiery furnace. We need friends like this.

So how do we find out which of our friends are true friends? Here is one way: wholeheartedly commit your life to Jesus Christ, and you will find out who your true friends are. Before I was a Christian, I thought I had a lot of friends. Then when I asked Christ to come into my life, I realized that I didn't have any real friends. They all deserted me, because they had no desire to follow the God I had chosen to follow.

Here's another way to determine who your friends are. These are the ones who will be standing by you when a hardship or crisis comes. Jesus had a lot of fair-weather friends. They were there when He was doling out bread and fish, speaking words of love and compassion, and sticking it to the Pharisees. But where were they when He was arrested and taken away? They were gone. A true friend will be loyal to the end.

Do you have such a friend? More important, are *you* such a friend?

Tuesday

FRIENDSHIP WITH JESUS

"You are My friends if you do whatever I command you." (John 15)

How do we show our love and friendship for Jesus? In John 15:14, Jesus points out three things we can do to show our friendship with God.

First, true friends of Jesus will obey Him. Quite simply, we will do what He says. If we don't, then we have no right to call ourselves His friends.

What kind of obedience are we talking about here? An *active* obedience. Some people think it's enough if they avoid what He specifically forbids. And certainly being a Christian means ceasing to do certain things. But it also means setting out to *do* certain things. It's not merely avoiding the wrong thing, but it's doing the right thing.

How do we find out what God wants us to do? By reading the Bible and becoming familiar with its content. The more we know of this Book, the more we will know of God. The more we know of this Book, the more we will know about what He requires of us—and what friendship with God really looks like.

Lastly, true friends of Jesus obey Him continually. In other words, we are constantly obedient. Not always perfect, but always trying. And if we fail, then we repent and get up and try again.

Remember, this is *Jesus* who asks for our obedience. This the One who has loved us, offered His friendship to us, and laid down His life for us. We obey Him joyfully because we love Him and know how much He loves us. When we are in love with God, obedience won't be a duty; it will be a delight. And if our Christian life has become drudgery, merely consisting of rules and regulations, then we are missing out on what friendship with God is all about.

THE PLACE OF BLESSING

Because, although they knew God, they did not glorify Him as God, nor were thankful, but became futile in their thoughts, and their foolish hearts were darkened. Professing to be wise, they became fools. (Romans 1:21-22)

Though God's love toward us is undeserved, unconditional, and even unsought, it is still possible for us to fall out of harmony with Him. To keep ourselves in the love of God, as Jude 21 urges us, means to keep ourselves in a place where God can actively show His love toward us.

Take the prodigal son, for example. He rebelled against his father, went to a distant land, and did things he shouldn't have done. Was he still his father's son? Of course he was. Was he in a place where his father could actively show his love to him? No, he was not.

Though this loving father missed his son, longed after his son, and grieved over the young man's rebellion, the prodigal was in a far country. He had removed himself from his father's love, blessing, and protection.

We, too, can do the same thing. We can still be children of God, but if we are out of fellowship with Him and His people, pursuing a path that we know violates His Word and breaks His heart, then we are not in a place where God can actively demonstrate His love toward us. So we must keep ourselves in a place where God can do that.

Keep yourself from all that is unlike God. Keep yourself from any influence that would violate His love and bring sorrow to His heart. Enjoy His richest blessings by making yourself "blessable."

GETTING TO THE ROOT

We use God's mighty weapons, not worldly weapons, to knock down the strongholds of human reasoning and to destroy false arguments.
(2 Corinthians 10:4, NLT)

So often when something is going wrong in our country, we want to protest, circulate a petition, or maybe organize a boycott. But did you know that as believers, we have something infinitely more powerful than those methods? It's called prayer, and the Bible tells us to devote ourselves to it (see Colossians 4:2).

We need to pray for our country. We need to pray for people who need to hear the gospel. And we need to share that gospel! We need to offer the good news of Jesus Christ to that woman who wants to abort her child. We need to speak forth the gospel message with that man or woman who is trapped in the homosexual lifestyle. We need to explain the way of salvation to gang members and those in our society who are hurting.

As people learn there is another kingdom, it will change the way they live in this one. Far too often, we Christians have been preoccupied with the symptoms in our society and haven't touched the root of the problem. The root is sin. The solution is the gospel.

So let's get the solution to the root. Our country needs to turn back to God. We keep thinking that a new president will solve all of our problems—or maybe some new members of congress—or some new government program. But our nation's problems won't be solved through any efforts of our own doing. We need to turn back to God.

Let's tell others about Christ and not be so preoccupied with what they're doing because of their sin. Let's try to reach people where they are really hurting.

And let's never forget that prayer isn't wishing or hoping…it is power.

THE MASTER ARSONIST

God wants you to be holy, so you should keep clear of all sexual sin.
(1 Thessalonians 4:3, NLT)

W hen wildfires swept through Southern California in the fall of 1993, I noticed a photograph in the newspaper of an entire neighborhood that had been leveled by the fires. All that was left were the foundations. In the midst of all the burned, charred, rubble stood one house that remained completely untouched, even by smoke. This gleaming white house stood in stark contrast to all of the ruin around it.

When asked why his house was left standing when all the others fell, the homeowner explained how he had taken great care to make his house flame-retardant. This included double-paned windows, thick stucco walls, sealed eaves, concrete tile, and abundant insulation. This man went the extra mile and, as a result, his house survived when the fires came.

Today, our country is being devastated by the wildfires of immorality. Satan, a master arsonist, is causing massive devastation. Sexual infidelity and immorality destroys homes and devastates families. And if we aren't careful, we could become its next victims.

The writer of Proverbs asked, "Can a man scoop fire into his lap and not be burned?" (6:27, NIV). The answer is no. Fire can burn out of control so easily.

If we as believers allow temptation to infiltrate our lives and permit our sinful natures to prevail, we will likely fall, as surely as the hungry flames of a wildfire consumes dry wood and grass. But if we take practical steps to guard ourselves and stay close to the Lord, then we don't have to fall. Let's go the extra mile to protect our families and our lives against the wildfires of immorality.

With God's help, we can make our homes "fire free" zones.

KEEP RUNNING!

Therefore we also, since we are surrounded by so great a cloud of witnesses, let us lay aside every weight, and the sin which so easily ensnares us, and let us run with endurance the race that is set before us, looking unto Jesus, the author and finisher of our faith. (Hebrews 12:1-2)

In the ancient Greek games, a judge would stand at the finish line holding, in plain sight, the laurel leaves that would be rewarded to the victor. As runners came down the final stretch, they were exhausted, perhaps in agony, and feeling as though they couldn't go another step. But suddenly there was the prize in sight, and a new burst of energy would kick in.

This is the picture behind the phrase "looking unto Jesus" in Hebrews 12:2. We have to keep our eyes on Jesus Christ. And our prize is the privilege of standing before Him and receiving the crown of righteousness that He will give us.

That is why we try to live godly lives, and why we try to reach people for Him. It isn't for brownie points. It isn't for applause. It isn't for notoriety. It's so we can hear Jesus say to us on that final day, "Well done, good and faithful servant." No, we can't earn our salvation, because He has already provided it. But we want to please the One who laid down His life for us. Ultimately, we want to be able to say, "Lord, I took the life You gave me and tried to make a difference. Here it is. I offer it to you."

"Looking unto Jesus…." That keeps you going, doesn't it? After all, you can get discouraged at times. People will let you down. They will disappoint you. They won't appreciate your hard work or notice your efforts. Not bothering to understand your real motives, they'll criticize that which they don't (or won't) understand. And that is when you need to remind yourself, *I am not running my race for this person or that person. I am running for You, Lord. And I will keep running…with my eyes fixed on You.*

LOOKING UP?

> *Keep yourselves in God's love as you wait for the mercy of our*
> *Lord Jesus Christ to bring you to eternal life. (Jude 21, NIV)*

There is a lot of disagreement in the church as a whole over what we call "eschatology," or prophetic events. Most often, it seems, the differences lie in the order of events. Some don't believe Christ could return at any time. Some believe the church will go through the Tribulation.

Here's my bottom line: There is room for honest disagreement as to the timing and order of events in the book of Revelation. But the imminent—at any moment—return of Jesus Christ is a teaching we need to hold onto. The fact that Jesus could come back at any time is a New Testament emphasis that not only fills our lives with hope, it also has a *purifying* effect. As 1 John 3:3 says, "Yes, dear friends, we are already God's children, and we can't even imagine what we will be like when Christ returns. But we do know that when he comes we will be like him, for we will see him as he really is. And all who believe this will keep themselves pure, just as Christ is pure" (NLT).

A literal translation of this verse would be, "Whoever has this hope continually set on Him is constantly purifying himself." If I live my life in a sense of expectation that Christ could come back at any time, then it will purify me.

Children who are prone to get into trouble will be on their best behavior if they know their parents might walk into the room at any moment. In the same way, if we know that Christ could come back at any moment, it should affect the way we live.

In contrast to disobedient children who dread the arrival of their parents, we should look forward with great excitement to the return of our Lord. Like John, we should be able to say, "Even so, come, Lord Jesus!" (Revelation 22:20). If you can't say this, it could be an indication that something is not right spiritually.

I enjoy life and the opportunities God sets before me. But if tonight were the night for Christ's return, I would say, "Bring it on!" Wouldn't you? That is the way to live.

WHEN CHRISTIANS STUMBLE

For what does the Scripture say? "Abraham believed God, and it was accounted to him for righteousness." (Romans 4:3)

Contrary to what some might believe, the Bible doesn't teach that if you are a Christian, you will never stumble, fail, or fall short. But it does teach that if you are a true believer and have had a lapse or a stumble, you will always get up and move forward. That is one strong way to truly determine whether someone is a real believer.

Although Abraham was a friend of God, which Scripture specifically mentions three times, it is also clear that he had his lapses of faith. Yet the Bible says that "Abraham believed God, and it was accounted to him for righteousness" (Romans 4:3). Does this mean that Abraham was declared righteous because of the good things he did? Did God justify Abraham because he lived such a holy, pure, and flawless life? Hardly. Any honest look at the life of Abraham would clearly show that he was a flawed man.

Having said that, it is also important to point out that although Abraham deviated occasionally from the straight and narrow, he always came back.

If someone says he or she is a Christian but falls away and never returns to the faith, then he or she was not a believer. As 1 John 2:19 says, "They went out from us, but they were not of us; for if they had been of us, they would have continued with us; but they went out that they might be made manifest, that none of them were of us."

True believers will be miserable in their sin and will eventually beat a quick path back to the cross of Calvary.

REMEMBER TO FORGET

Where is another God like you, who pardons the sins of the survivors among
his people? You cannot stay angry with your people forever, because you
delight in showing mercy. Once again you will have compassion on us. You will
trample our sins under your feet and throw them into the depths of the ocean!
(Micah 7:18-19, NLT)

Have you ever done anything that you're ashamed of? Have you
ever done things you wished you hadn't? If you have repented of
those sins and have turned your back on them, the Bible clearly teaches that
you are forgiven.

There is something in us that wants to keep dredging up our sins. Maybe
we feel that by doing so, we are somehow making amends for the wrong
that we've done. Maybe by punishing ourselves, we think we are somehow
appeasing God. But this is wrong—and thoroughly unscriptural.

The book of Acts tells us: "Brothers, listen! In this man Jesus there is
forgiveness for your sins. Everyone who believes in him is freed from all
guilt and declared right with God—something the Jewish law could never
do" (Acts 13:38-39, NLT).

Speaking of our sins, God said, "And I will forgive their wickedness,
and I will never again remember their sins" (Hebrews 8:12, NLT).

In the verse that opens today's devotional, the prophet speaks of God
throwing our sins into the depths of the ocean. Have you ever lost anything
in a lake or in the ocean? It's pretty much a lost cause. Once it goes down,
it goes way down. And that is what God has done with our sins: He has
thrown them into the deepest part of the ocean. Simply put, our sins are
G-O-N-E…and you and I shouldn't choose to remember what God has
chosen to forget.

No Approval Necessary

In love he predestined us to be adopted as his sons through Jesus Christ, in accordance with his pleasure and will—to the praise of his glorious grace, which he has freely given us in the One he loves. (Ephesians 1:5-6, NIV)

As a young Christian, I remember thinking that the reason God was blessing me was because of my disciplined and regular Bible study. I would get up before school every morning and study the Bible for about an hour, and then I would pray for an hour or more (I know I prayed for an hour or more because I kept checking my watch). I thought when I got to school that God would use me that day because I had "done so much for Him."

Then one morning, my alarm didn't go off. I woke up very late. I didn't have time to pray or read my Bible. That day, God allowed me the privilege of leading someone to Christ.

Some people think, just as I did as a young believer, that they must do certain things to earn God's approval. They think they have to somehow appease Him. But that is as wrong as can be. Why? *Because God's righteous demands were satisfied at the cross of Calvary.* We don't have to do things like read the Bible, pray, or go to church to find God's approval. We should do these things because we *want* to, because we love our heavenly Father and want to be near Him and learn from him. We should want to serve Him, but not to earn His approval. We already have that!

The Bible tells us that God has "made us accepted in the Beloved" (Ephesians 1:6, NKJV). This means that when we put our faith in Christ, God has put His righteousness into our account. He loves us when we do well. But He also loves us when we don't.

Just Getting Started

He has made everything beautiful in its time. (Ecclesiastes 3:11)

When I look back on my life at the things God has allowed me to do and the opportunities He has opened up, I can see the wisdom of His perfect timing.

Our tendency is to rush things. But just because something has never happened in your life today doesn't mean it won't happen tomorrow. And just because it doesn't happen tomorrow doesn't mean it won't happen a month or a year from now. Maybe one phase of your life is ending and another is beginning. Maybe everything that has happened to you up to this point in your life has been preparation for what is still ahead.

Moses didn't get going until he was eighty. Then there was Caleb, another Israelite who left Egypt in the Exodus. Along with Joshua, Caleb came back full of optimism and belief when they were sent to spy out the Promised Land. But when the Israelites believed the pessimistic report of the ten other spies, God was so displeased that He refused to allow them to enter the land.

Years later, when Joshua led a new generation of Israelites into the Promised Land, Caleb was among them. And at eighty years old, he said to Joshua, "I'm asking you to give me the hill country that the LORD promised me. You will remember that as scouts we found the Anakites living there in great, walled cities. But if the LORD is with me, I will drive them out of the land, just as the LORD said"

(Joshua 14:12, NLT). Joshua gave him his little segment of land as was promised, and Caleb drove out all of its inhabitants. Caleb believed God's promises, and God was faithful. We need to do the same.

EYES ON HIM

Since we have such a huge crowd of men of faith watching us from the grandstands, let us strip off anything that slows us down or holds us back, and especially those sins that wrap themselves so tightly around our feet and trip us up; and let us run with patience the particular race that God has set before us. Keep your eyes on Jesus, our leader and instructor. He was willing to die a shameful death on the cross because of the joy he knew would be his afterwards; and now he sits in the place of honor by the throne of God. (Hebrews 12:1-2, TLB)

Holocaust survivor Corrie ten Boom once said, "Look within and be depressed. Look without and be distressed. Look at Jesus and be at rest." Looking without, she had reason to be distressed. She lived in a concentration camp. She saw her sister and father—and many others—die at the hands of the Nazis. Looking within, she felt depressed as she saw the darkness of her own heart. But seeing the example of her godly sister Betsy, who saw the bright side of everything and was always trusting God, she concluded, "Look at Jesus and be at rest."

The Bible says that Abraham "did not waver at the promise of God through unbelief, but was strengthened in faith, giving glory to God, and being fully convinced that what He had promised He was also able to perform" (Romans 4:20-21). The word "waver" used in this verse could also be translated "stagger." It would imply that this unwavering walk of Abraham took place with his eyes fixed on the promise of God.

As we walk with God, people will let us down. People will disappoint us. Circumstances will be difficult. The enemy will hassle us. This is when we need to remember why we started to walk with God in the first place. It was because of Jesus. So keep your eyes fixed on Him. That will keep you moving forward, because the only way we will make it as Christians is by keeping our eyes on Jesus Christ.

CONDITIONS FOR PEACE

Don't worry about anything; instead, pray about everything. Tell God what you need, and thank him for all he has done. If you do this, you will experience God's peace, which is far more wonderful than the human mind can understand. His peace will guard your hearts and minds as you live in Christ Jesus. (Philippians 4:6-7, NLT)

One of the first things I remember about the day I put my faith in Christ was the sense of peace filling my heart. It was as though someone had lifted a heavy burden from me. It wasn't until later, when I read the Bible, that I learned about God's promise of peace to every believer. He has given it to us as a gift.

This peace, however, doesn't come from what or who we are, but from what God has done—how He has justified us in response to our faith. A wonderful by-product of this reality is a deep inner peace that floods our soul.

But we can't have this wonderful effect without the beginning cause. If we are fighting with God, if we are resisting His plan and purpose for our lives, then we won't experience this supernatural peace.

I think many people would like to have the beautiful results and benefits of the Christian life without having to pay the price. In other words, they would like to know they are forgiven and going to heaven when they die, but they still want to live as they please. They don't want to put their complete faith and trust in Jesus.

That sort of attitude just won't fly. We can't have the pleasing, life-transforming privileges of God's peace without first meeting God's requirements. Colossians 1:20 (NLT) says that through Jesus Christ, "God reconciled everything to himself. He made peace with everything in heaven and on earth by means of Christ's blood on the cross." The only way we will experience the peace of God that passes all human understanding is through the blood of the cross, the blood Jesus shed.

You cannot have the peace *of* God until you first have peace *with* God.

THE TRAP OF TEMPTATION

Therefore submit to God. Resist the devil and he will flee from you. (James 4:7)

Right after I became a Christian, other believers warned me, "Greg, watch out. There is a devil who will tempt you."

I said, "Right, devil." I thought of the red figure with the pitchfork and horns.

They said, "No, the devil is real. He is a real spirit power and he will tempt you."

I said, "Get out of town. He's not going to tempt me."

I was in high school at the time, and there was a certain girl in my art class who I sort of had a crush on, but I hadn't mustered up the courage to walk up and talk to her. I was sitting in class one day as a brand-new Christian, when suddenly she walked up to me and said, "Hi. What's your name?" We had been in the same class for months, and she had never even acknowledged my existence.

I told her my name. She said, "You know, you're kind of cute. My parents have a cabin up in the mountains, and I'm going up there this weekend. Why don't you just come up with me? Let's get to know each other better."

I thought, *This is it. This is what they told me about. It's temptation!* I declined her invitation and realized there had to be something to what had just happened. I thought, *I'm not an idiot. No girl has ever come up to me and said this before. This is a set-up.*

That experience made me want to follow the Lord even more, because I saw the reality of the spiritual world beginning to unfold. Remember, the devil wants to keep you from coming to Christ. And once you have come to Christ, he wants to keep you from moving forward, and to steal away your joy, your victory, and your witness.

But today's Scripture verse gives us the powerful truth: if we resist the devil in Jesus' name, he'll back off. In fact, he'll run!

EMBRACING HARDSHIP

> *And not only that, but we also glory in tribulations, knowing*
> *that tribulation produces perseverance. (Romans 5:3)*

The apostle Paul didn't merely endure his hardships. He gloried in them. He celebrated them. The meaning of the word "tribulation" that Paul used in Romans 5:3 comes from a term that describes a threshing instrument which a farmer would use to separate the grain from the husks. It's the idea of being under pressure, such as squeezing olives in a press to extract the oil, squeezing grapes for their juice, or pounding garlic to release its aroma. Through the pounding process, something comes out that wasn't visible or discernible before. In the same way, our lives can be pounded out on the threshing floor of tribulation.

Paul made a choice about his hardships. He said he gloried in tribulation because it produced something he needed. We have a choice as well. We can become bitter. Or we can become better.

Like it or not, tribulation will come into our lives. Scripture is clear on that. Jesus said, "These things I have spoken to you, that in Me you may have peace. In the world you will have tribulation; but be of good cheer, I have overcome the world" (John 16:33). The apostles encouraged the believers in Acts 14 to continue in the faith, saying that through much tribulation they must enter the kingdom of God (see Acts 14:22). And Philippians 1:29 says, "For to you it has been granted on behalf of Christ, not only to believe in Him, but also to suffer for His sake."

When hard times come, you can either get mad at God, or you can try to learn what He wants to teach you. It's a choice. Hardships will come, but how you react to them is entirely up to you.

Thursday

FINDING FORTITUDE

And not only that, but we also glory in tribulations, knowing that tribulation produces perseverance; and perseverance, character; and character, hope.
(Romans 5:3-4)

When you want to get in shape, it's actually through the process of tearing your muscles down that you build them up. The first day of your workout isn't so hard. But the next day, you're in pain. Everything hurts. The next time, you feel weak, but you work out anyway. A couple of days later, you're still weak and sore, but you're also a little stronger. You increase the weights a bit, then you do a little more. Pretty soon, you notice that you're getting stronger. It is through the breaking-down process that the building up comes.

In the same way, we need to build up our spiritual muscles. God allows us to go through difficulties. He increases the weights on us. Pretty soon, we are benching a whole lot more than we ever thought possible. We're learning more than we ever thought we would learn. We're doing more than we ever thought we would do. Iron is entering our souls, and we are developing that heroic endurance, perseverance, and strength that only comes through difficulty.

The Bible tells us, "My brethren, count it all joy when you fall into various trials, knowing that the testing of your faith produces patience. But let patience have its perfect work, that you may be perfect and complete, lacking nothing" (James 1:2-4). In the original language, the word used here for "patience" means "perseverance," "endurance," "steadfastness," or simply "staying power."

If you are going through a time of testing and trial, realize that God has a purpose in it. Most likely, He is preparing you and training you today for what He will do in your life tomorrow.

PREPARED FOR CHOICE WORK

For we are His workmanship, created in Christ Jesus for good works, which God prepared beforehand that we should walk in them. (Ephesians 2:10)

A traveler was visiting a logging area in the Pacific Northwest and was interested to see how logs were chosen that eventually would be used for furniture. As the logs came down the stream, the logger would suddenly reach out and hook one, pull it up, and then set it down. He would sometimes wait for a few minutes before grabbing another. There didn't seem to be any rhyme or reason to his choices.

After a while, the visitor said to him, "I don't understand what you're doing."

"These logs may all look alike to you," said the logger, "but I can recognize that a few of them are quite different. The ones that I let pass came from trees that grew in a valley. They were always protected from the storms. The grain is rather coarse. The logs that I pulled aside are from high up on the mountain, where they were beaten by strong winds from the time they were quite small. That toughens the trees and gives them a fine grain. We save these logs for choice work. They're too good to be used for ordinary lumber."

It was through the trying and testing that the logs were prepared for choice work. The same could be said of us as Christians.

If you were to ask Moses how he became who he was, he would remind you of his trials with Pharaoh and his times of testing in the wilderness. If you were to ask Peter, he would probably point back to his denial and how he learned many difficult yet important lessons.

Maybe you find yourself facing something similar in your life today. Maybe God is preparing you for a choice work.

FALSE PROMISES

These are grumblers, complainers, walking according to their own lusts; and they mouth great swelling words, flattering people to gain advantage. But you, beloved, remember the words which were spoken before by the apostles of our Lord Jesus Christ: how they told you that there would be mockers in the last time who would walk according to their own ungodly lusts. (Jude 16-18)

A common characteristic of false teachers is the offer of false promises. You see them promising, for example, that God will prosper those who give $10 with a hundredfold blessing—multiplying that amount and returning it to them. This is a false message, however. We should never give to get.

If I were to give an amount of money to God's work, thinking it would multiply a certain number of times and would ultimately return to me, that would be a wrong motive. God won't honor it. It is also a false promise.

All believers should give on a regular basis out of the resources and income that God has given to them. The Bible says that God loves a cheerful giver (see 2 Corinthians 9:7). We give because we have received. We give because we recognize that all that we have comes from God. We give because we want to share in the eternal reward of what God is doing by investing in the work of His kingdom. We give because God has commanded us to do so.

Jude wrote his New Testament letter to refute those who were teaching that the grace of God gives people a license to sin. And Paul wrote in Romans 3:8, "And why not say, 'Let us do evil that good may come'?—as we are slanderously reported and as some affirm that we say. Their condemnation is just."

In other words, there are those who say, "Go ahead and do wicked things, and God will bless you, because you are covered by grace." Paul was saying that this is a perversion of the teaching of the grace of God.

We don't need to be diverted and distracted by false promises. The pages of our Bible brim over with *real* promises—"exceedingly great and precious promises" (2 Peter 1:4)—that God wants us to cling to with all our hearts.

JUST BEFORE DAWN

Now in the fourth watch of the night Jesus went to them, walking on the sea.
(Matthew 14:25)

In Matthew 14, we read about the disciples being tossed by the wind and waves in their boat on the Sea of Galilee. Then Jesus came, walking on the water, at the fourth watch of the night. The fourth watch was the last part of the night, just before dawn. This means the disciples had been at sea for at least nine hours in this fierce storm. So we see that Jesus came to them at the last conceivable moment.

This reminds us that God's delays aren't necessarily His denials. Jesus knew what He was doing all along. Why did He wait so long before He intervened? Probably because it took a long time for them to exhaust their resources and completely trust in Him.

Lifeguards will tell you that often the hardest person to save is the one who is panicking. But when an individual is exhausted, when he or she has no energy left, the lifeguard can pull that person back in to safety. In the same way, sometimes God will allow us to get to the end of our rope, to the end of our resources, so we will finally cling to Him.

The disciples were exhausted and afraid. "[Jesus] said to them, 'It is I; do not be afraid.' Then they willingly received Him into the boat, and immediately the boat was at the land where they were going" (John 6:20-21). For many of us, that is what Jesus is waiting for. He is waiting for us to say, "Come on board." He will step into your storm-tossed boat and take control, if you will invite Him. He will be there for you…even in the darkest night, just before dawn.

READY AND WAITING

"And at midnight a cry was heard: 'Behold, the bridegroom is coming; go out to meet him!'" (Matthew 25:6)

Some people may believe they are going to heaven and may even be looking forward to the return of Jesus, yet still not necessarily be Christians. As they look at the world today and realize that Bible prophecies are being fulfilled, they might even believe that Christ is returning soon. But that doesn't necessarily mean they are Christians.

In the parable of the ten bridesmaids, Jesus told the story of bridesmaids who were attending a wedding (see Matthew 25:1-13). Five were wise, and five were foolish. The five wise bridesmaids had oil in their lamps, while the five foolish ones did not. And when the cry went out that the bridegroom was coming, the five bridesmaids who were wise were ready to meet him. But the foolish bridesmaids were unprepared.

Jesus told this story to illustrate the fact that you can appear to be a Christian. You can sit in church next to other Christians. You can carry a Bible like everyone else. You can even believe in the soon-coming of Jesus Christ for His church. *But that doesn't necessarily mean that you know Him.*

If you truly have a relationship with Christ, then the truth that He could come back at any time should dramatically impact the way you live. The Bible says, "And everyone who has this hope in Him purifies himself, just as He is pure" (1 John 3:3).

In other words, if you really are a follower of Jesus Christ and believe He will soon return to earth, you will strongly desire to be a more godly person. You will truly want to live a life that is pleasing to the Lord, and you will hate the very idea of grieving or disappointing Him. You will want to avoid the things that would be wrong or sinful or spiritually detrimental, and you'll be doing your utmost to follow Him and grow in Him.

Does that sound like you? Are you ready for His return?

FOXHOLE CHRISTIANS

Give heed to the voice of my cry, my King and my God, for to You I will pray.
(Psalm 5:2)

Before I became a Christian, I thought I already was one. Whenever I was in trouble, I cried out to Jesus. I thought I must surely be a Christian because I was praying. But I didn't really understand what being a Christian was all about.

When the chips are down, most people do pray. It has been said, "There are no atheists in foxholes." If your life is on the line, you will pray. I think back on my own life and recognize that whenever trouble hit, I would call on God. I would pray, "God, if You get me out of this crisis, I promise I will serve You. I will do whatever You ask me to do." He would get me out of that one and I would say, "Thanks, God. See You the next time I'm in a jam." So in a sense, you could say that I "prayed." But my prayer life consisted of moments of crisis when I called out to God out of fear.

In the Book of Jonah, we find the story of a great storm that arose on the sea. We read that all the sailors on the ship with Jonah began to call on their gods. That's what people do in dreadful storms. They will call upon their gods or higher powers. But that doesn't mean necessarily mean they have a relationship with the true and living God. It's possible to pray and not even know the God you are praying to.

Christians pray, but praying doesn't necessarily mean you are a Christian. You need to have a personal relationship with God. You need to believe in Jesus Christ and follow Him.

LET GO AND TAKE HOLD

"For I, the Lord your God, will hold your right hand, saying to you,
'Fear not, I will help you.'" (Isaiah 41:13)

A man who fell over the side of a cliff was hanging on to a branch that was starting to give way. Recognizing it was only a matter of time before he would fall to his death, he shouted, "Is anybody up there? Somebody help me!"

Suddenly Jesus appeared, leaned over the edge, and said, "Young man, reach out and take my hand, and I will save you. But first, you must let go of that branch you're holding on to."

The man didn't want to let go of the branch.

Jesus told him, "You must take hold of My hand and let go of the branch, or I can't pull you up."

The man paused for a minute and said, "Is anybody *else* up there?"

A lot of us don't want to let go. We still want to hold on to a part of our old lives. But there has to be a moment in each of our lives in which we have recognized we are sinners and have asked for God's forgiveness. Then Jesus Christ comes in. But we have to let go. Some changes must take place.

The Bible says there is a spiritual blindness in all those who have not yet turned their lives over to Jesus Christ. So we must have our spiritual eyes opened, turning from darkness to light, and from the power of Satan to God (see Acts 26:18). As we yield to God and His will for our lives, we will receive the forgiveness of sins. Then we will see the incredible benefits of making those changes.

But we have to let go of our branch and take hold of His hand.

A CALL TO COURAGE

"I have told you all this so that you may have peace in me. Here on Earth you will have many trials and sorrows. But take heart, because I have overcome the world." (John 16:33, NLT)

Have you ever been afraid of the future? Maybe you feel as though you're in a rut, or maybe you are discouraged. Perhaps you feel that you will have to face the problems and challenges of life all alone.

If any of these things are true of you, then take heart, because you certainly aren't the first child of God to feel that way (nor will you be the last!). Jesus had a message for His disciples to give them hope as they faced an uncertain future, so they would not be afraid, but would be courageous.

During the last week of His life on Earth, Jesus knew His departure was at hand. So before He left His disciples, He wanted to encourage them. First, He warned them that they would face hardship and difficulty. But then He told them, "These things I have spoken to you, that in Me you may have peace. In the world you will have tribulation; but be of good cheer, I have overcome the world" (John 16:33, NKJV).

"Be of good cheer." Take heart! It was Christ's call to courage in the lives of His frightened disciples. Jesus wasn't simply saying, "Cheer up. Come on, put a smile on your face!" He was saying more than that. He was saying, "Be brave. Be courageous."

If you are courageous, cheerfulness will follow. Yes we will face trouble and heartaches in this broken world of ours. It's part of life on this side of heaven. But we also have the assurance that He has already overcome the world.

And that makes us overcomers, too.

ARISE AND WALK

Then behold, they brought to Him a paralytic lying on a bed. When Jesus saw their faith, He said to the paralytic, "Son, be of good cheer; your sins are forgiven you." (Matthew 9:2)

The Gospel of Mark gives us the account of a group of men who wanted to bring their paralyzed friend to Jesus for healing. Jesus was teaching in a home, and the men couldn't get in the door with their disabled friend because of the huge crowd. Undaunted, they climbed up on top of the house and dug through the roof to lower the paralyzed man inside…dropping him right in front of Jesus (see Mark 2:1-5).

When Jesus saw the faith of these men, he looked at their paralyzed friend and said, "Son, be of good cheer; your sins are forgiven you" (Matthew 9:2). Jesus was saying, "You no longer have to be afraid of the penalty for your sin. Your past is behind you. I am giving you another chance in life."

Jesus then told him to get up, pick up his bed, and go to his house (Matthew 9:6). This man had a choice. He could have stayed on his sickbed forever. He could have said, "I can't" or "I won't." He had a choice, and he decided to respond.

There are people today who don't want to change. They don't want to leave their lifestyle or turn from the choices they have made. They refuse to take hold of God's promises and provision and power.

If you want to change, if you want to break free from a vice that has you in its grip, a lifestyle you are trapped in, or an addiction that you can't seem to shake, then Christ has a word of encouragement to you: "Get up and walk. You can do it. Be of good cheer, and arise."

TAPPING INTO GOD'S POWER

*And He said to her, "Daughter, be of good cheer; your faith
has made you well. Go in peace." (Luke 8:48)*

As Jesus made His way to the home of Jairus, a ruler of the synagogue whose daughter was ill, there was a woman in the crowd
who had been sick for 12 years. It almost appears that Jesus was unaware
of her in the crowd. But in reality, He had been waiting for her.

This woman had spent all her money trying to find a cure for her disease.
She thought, *If I could just touch Him when He passes by, I know I will
be healed* (see Luke 8:43-48). So as Jesus passed by, she reached out and
touched the hem of His garment. And suddenly, instantaneously, right there
on the spot, she was healed.

When she touched Him, Jesus stopped and said, "Somebody touched
Me, for I perceived power going out from Me" (Luke 8:46). The word
"power" that Jesus used speaks of the dynamite power of God. It is the
Greek word from which we get the word "dynamite." So Jesus was essentially saying, "Someone just tapped into my dynamic, explosive power."

As the crowd parted, the woman fell down before Jesus. He assured her,
"Daughter, be of good cheer; your faith has made you well. Go in peace"
(Luke 8:48). In this woman's moment of need, His power healed her and
gave her courage.

The same power that impacted this woman can impact you today.
The same power came from the Holy Spirit to the disciples on the Day of
Pentecost, and they went out to turn their world upside down. And the same
power is available to every Christian, to give us courage to live the Christian
life and to share our faith.

Jesus specializes in empowering weak people who turn to Him for
strength.

WHY THE CROSS?

For the message of the cross is foolishness to those who are perishing, but to us who are being saved it is the power of God. (1 Corinthians 1:18)

A true story was reported about a couple visiting a jewelry store. As the jeweler showed them various cross necklaces, the woman commented, "I like these, but do you have any without this little man on them?"

That is what so many people want today: a cross without Jesus. They want a cross without any offense...one that will look cool with their outfits. But if we could travel back in time and see the cross in its original context, we would realize that it was a bloody and vile symbol. It would have been the worst picture imaginable to see someone hanging on a cross.

The Romans chose crucifixion because it was meant to be a slow, torturous way to die. It was designed not only to kill someone, but to utterly humiliate them as they died. Crucifixions outside Roman cities served as warnings to anyone who would dare oppose the rule of Rome.

If there was any other way, do you think that God would have allowed His Son to suffer like this? If there had been any other way we could have been forgiven, then God surely would have found it. If living a good moral life would get us to heaven, then Jesus never would have died for us. But He did, because there was and is no other way. He had to pay the price for our sin. At the Cross, Jesus purchased the salvation of the world.

If you were ever tempted to doubt God's love for you, even for a moment, then take a long, hard look at the Cross. Nails did not hold Jesus to that cross. His love did.

HEROES WANTED

*Be strong and of good courage, do not fear nor be afraid of them; for the Lord
your God, He is the One who goes with you. He will not leave you
nor forsake you. (Deuteronomy 31:6)*

The world has never been more advanced technologically, yet we
have never been in worse shape spiritually and morally. It can
be frightening to wonder what kind of world we will be facing in years to
come, and what kind of world our children and grandchildren will face as
they grow up.

We need courage to live in these days as followers of Jesus Christ. Yet
courage seems to be something that's in short supply today. Sometimes we
forget what real heroism and real courage really are. We wonder where all
the heroes are now.

I believe that anyone today who is a true follower of Jesus Christ and will
stand up for what he or she believes is a true hero. It takes courage to be a
follower of Jesus, to live an uncompromised life, to do the right thing, and
to proclaim the gospel. Those who do that are heroes in my book.

It takes courage for a young Christian to resist peer pressure and remain
sexually pure until marriage and then to be faithful in that marriage. It
takes courage for a family to stay together and to resist the temptation to
cave in at the first sight of a problem or a challenge to the vows they have
made to one another. It takes courage today to be honest and not cheat. It
takes courage to follow Jesus. It takes a real man and a real woman to be a
follower of Christ.

Is this a description of your life right now? Are you someone who fears
nothing but sin and desires nothing but God? Have courage. He is with you,
and He will not forsake you.

IN CONCLUSION...

"Vanity of vanities," says the Preacher; "Vanity of vanities, all is vanity."
(Ecclesiastes 1:2)

Before I became a Christian I was, like most young people, looking for purpose and meaning in life. The thinking of the day was that we, the young people, were going to change our world. The adult "establishment" didn't have the answers. Our faith in government was shattered. So we thought we would change things.

But after a little time, I began to realize that the youth movement had the same phony love and hypocrisy I had seen in the adult world. It was the same selfishness and emptiness of the generation that preceded it...and the generations that would follow. It was only a pale version of what can really be known in a relationship with God and as you walk with His people.

On my high school campus, there was a very outspoken group of Christians who weren't ashamed of the gospel. I went to one of their meetings, heard the gospel, and—much to my own surprise—gave my life to Christ. As I saw God's promises coming to literal fulfillment in my own life, in the days that followed my faith in Jesus Christ—His love and power—grew and grew.

Having lived in the world for seventeen years and having sampled many of the pleasures it had to offer, I knew the futility and emptiness of it all. I knew it was a dead-end street. I knew then that this world was empty.

And it still is. As Solomon said, "Everything is meaningless...utterly meaningless!" (Ecclesiastes 1:2, NLT).

So what's the answer? "Fear God and keep His commandments, for this is man's all" (Ecclesiastes 12:13). Without God, life is vain and empty. But experiencing the reality of His Holy Spirit living in the very core of our being gives life a dimension that defies all description.

A RADICAL DIFFERENCE

Who is he who overcomes the world, but he who believes that Jesus is the Son of God? (1 John 5:5)

The Book of Acts tells the story of a handful of men and women who, by the power of the Holy Spirit, did not leave their world the same way they found it. They were ordinary people whom God enabled to do extraordinary things. It was the beginning of a movement that continues to this very day.

On the Day of Pentecost, about 120 believers were gathered together when the Holy Spirit was poured out. Everywhere they went, they were ridiculed and opposed and persecuted and physically assaulted for their beliefs. Some were even put to death. Yet within a period of about 30 years, this original group of 120 and their converts came to be known as those who turned their world upside down. When we see their fearless proclamation of the Good News, their expectant prayers, and their full-hearted willingness to obey, these Christians almost seem radical.

But it isn't that they were radical; it is just that we're not radical enough. We are living a watered-down version of the Christian life. What we see in the Book of Acts is normal, New Testament Christianity.

Could what happened in Acts happen again? Could we see another great movement of the Holy Spirit? The answer is yes, we could. But it starts with you. It starts with me. Let me ask you this: What if everyone in the church behaved just as you do? How well would the church know the Bible? What kind of a prayer life would the church have? How many people would be giving a hand to the discouraged and needy? How many would be hearing the gospel? What kind of church would it be?

The church is made up of people like us. And we can make a radical difference.

PRACTICAL POWER

"But you shall receive power when the Holy Spirit has come upon you; and you shall be witnesses to Me in Jerusalem, and in all Judea and Samaria, and to the end of the Earth." (Acts 1:8)

Before He ascended into heaven, Jesus told His disciples that He had a job for them to do. He would come back and establish His kingdom (see Acts 1:6-8), but until then, He wanted them to go out and bring the gospel message to others, and see His kingdom established in their lives.

It was a daunting task, and the apostles were in no way ready for such a work. There were things they still didn't understand, and their faith was relatively weak. How could they be expected to stand up before thousands and proclaim the gospel?

The answer is that they could do this with a power they had never known...the power of God's own Holy Spirit.

Power is an exciting thing, isn't it? We always want a faster car or a more powerful computer. We work out to get stronger. God says, "I have power for you. It is power with purpose. It is practical power." The resurrection of Jesus Christ gives us power to live the Christian life.

It is impossible to live the Christian life successfully except by the power of the Holy Spirit. But the glorious thing about Christianity is that even though we can't measure up to God's standards, God will take residence in our hearts so we can live this life through His power. God's calling is God's enabling. He will enable us to do what He has called us to do.

PEACE AND VICTORY

> *"When you are reviled and persecuted and lied about because you are my followers—wonderful! Be happy about it! Be very glad! for a tremendous reward awaits you up in heaven. And remember, the ancient prophets were persecuted too." (Matthew 5:11-12, TLB)*

There are two primary sources of spiritual attack in the life of the Christian: outward and inward. While an inward attack comes in the form of infiltration, an outward attack is persecution. And for many, an outward attack takes them down.

Persecution is one of Satan's primary methods of attack in the life of the Christian. Jesus talked about persecution in the parable of the sower, in which the seed symbolizes the Word of God. He explained, "But he who received the seed on stony places, this is he who hears the word and immediately receives it with joy; yet he has no root in himself, but endures only for a while. For when tribulation or persecution arises because of the word, immediately he stumbles" (Matthew 13:20-21).

If you are going to be a true follower of Jesus Christ, then you *will* be persecuted. But Jesus said, "Blessed are you when they revile and persecute you, and say all kinds of evil against you falsely for My sake. Rejoice and be exceedingly glad, for great is your reward in heaven, for so they persecuted the prophets who were before you" (Matthew 5:11-12). You're in great company: the prophets were persecuted as well.

The apostle Peter, in his first letter, adds this important provision: "For it is commendable if a man bears up under the pain of unjust suffering because he is conscious of God. But how is it to your credit if you receive a beating for doing wrong and endure it? But if you suffer for doing good and you endure it, this is commendable before God. To this you were called, because Christ suffered for you, leaving you an example, that you should follow in his steps" (1 Peter 2:19, NIV).

Let's not be persecuted because we're acting like jerks and deserve it, but rather because we are like Jesus Christ and reflect Him to a lost world. And let's never forget that in Him we have peace and victory over persecution and tribulation.

THE FAITHFUL FOLLOWER

"But whoever denies Me before men, him I will also deny before My Father who is in heaven." (Matthew 10:33)

Near the end of his life, the apostle Paul wrote to the young pastor, Timothy, "I have fought the good fight, I have finished the race, I have kept the faith" (2 Timothy 4:7). A few sentences later, he referred to a man named Demas who had deserted him, "having loved this present world, and has departed for Thessalonica" (2 Timothy 4:10).

When it got too hard for Demas, he quit. He didn't want to be a follower of Jesus if it required anything of him, if it cost him anything, and certainly if it meant he would suffer persecution.

Jesus spoke of the same dilemma in the Parable of the Sower, in which He compared the Word of God entering the hearts of men and women to a farmer who scatters seed. Jesus explained, "He who received the seed on stony places, this is he who hears the word and immediately receives it with joy; yet he has no root in himself, but endures only for a while. For when tribulation or persecution arises because of the word, immediately he stumbles" (Matthew 13:20-21).

There are some who will abandon their Christian faith when trouble comes or persecution arises. They give up. They deny the Lord.

One way people do this is by simply saying, "I don't know Him." But another way is to simply turn away from every opportunity to confess your faith in Jesus Christ, refusing to speak up for Him when the opportunity arises.

Do people know that you're a Christian? Do your coworkers know you're a Christian? Do your family members know that you are a follower of Jesus Christ? Are you speaking up for Him?

As you take advantage of every opening (even the smallest ones) to speak about what God has done for you and what Jesus means to you, your faith will grow stronger…and you'll experience more joy than you thought possible.

USE WHAT YOU HAVE

Therefore, as through one man's offense judgment came to all men, resulting in
condemnation, even so through one Man's righteous act the free gift came
to all men, resulting in justification of life. (Romans 5:18)

When God released the children of Israel from bondage in Egypt, it took them a while to get to the Promised Land—a lot longer than it needed to. When they finally arrived, Moses had died, and Joshua had been appointed to lead the Israelites into this new land. God said to Joshua, "Moses My servant is dead. Now therefore, arise, go over this Jordan, you and all this people, to the land which I am giving to them—the children of Israel. Every place that the sole of your foot will tread upon I have given you..." (Joshua 1:2-3).

The Israelites could have stood at the border of the Promised Land and said, "Will you look at that? Wow. Isn't it nice?" But they had to *go in* and possess their possessions.

That's like you and me sometimes, isn't it? We stand around and admire something rather than really putting it to its intended use. It's like buying an SUV, but never actually taking it four-wheeling. In the same way, we can stand around and admire bedrock biblical principles like justification and say, "Isn't it great what God has given to us? Wow, it's just-as-if-I-had-never-sinned? This is wonderful."

But the fact is, we have to possess our possessions. Justification by faith isn't just a simple legal matter between God and us; it is a living relationship. For this reason, we don't have to pray *for* victory, we need to pray *from* victory. We don't fight *for* success, we fight *from* it. We don't need to go out to win the battle, the battle has already been won. So we need to walk into each new day in the authority and power of our Commander-in-Chief, Jesus Christ.

KEPT BY HIS LOVE

Nothing in all creation will ever be able to separate us from the love of God that is revealed in Christ Jesus our Lord. (Romans 8:39, NLT)

When you go to a place like Disneyland with your children, you know where they are. You don't leave the park and forget them, because you protect what you love.

In the same way, God never forgets what He loves. Writing to first-century believers, Jude addressed his letter, "to all who are called to live in the love of God the Father and the care of Jesus Christ (v. 1, NLT)." In the original language, the clear implication is, "You are *continually kept* by Jesus Christ."

Whatever your difficulties may be today, you need to know that you are preserved in Christ, and that He will maintain His investment, which He purchased at such a great cost at the Cross. He will protect you, preserve you, and keep you.

Yet the Bible also tells us to keep ourselves in the love of God (Jude 21). Is this a contradiction? No. It's merely two sides of the same coin. The Bible is teaching that God will keep us, but at the same time, we must keep ourselves in His love. We don't keep ourselves *saved*, but we keep ourselves *safe*.

There are things we must do on a daily basis to keep ourselves in a place where God can actively bless us, and to keep ourselves away from all that is unlike Him, and those things that would drag us down spiritually.

Attacks will come our way. Were it not for the preserving grace of God, none of us would make it. Clearly, we are preserved, protected, and kept by the power of heaven. Let's make sure we walk in that generous protection and covering of our God, putting it on like a garment—or body armor—every morning before our feet hit the floor.

IS MEEKNESS A WEAKNESS?

Therefore I, a prisoner for serving the Lord, beg you to lead a life worthy of your calling, for you have been called by God. Be humble and gentle. Be patient with each other, making allowance for each other's faults because of your love.
(Ephesians 4:1-2, NLT)

The ancient Greeks didn't put much stock in humility. In classical Greek, humility was a derogatory term suggesting low-mindedness and groveling servanthood. It was looked upon as an undesirable, negative trait. Sometimes humility doesn't fare much better in our culture, as evidenced by attitudes that say, "Look out for number one" and "What's in it for me?"

The Bible, however, makes it clear that God expects us to put the needs of others above our own. And in the language of Scripture, "meek" doesn't mean weak. The biblical term literally means "strength under constraint." Think of a mighty racehorse here, controlled by a bit in his mouth…or maybe a powerful car with a huge engine being driven ever-so-carefully in a school zone.

A person who is meek in the biblical sense may be a very strong individual with a high capacity to hurt you…but chooses not to.

Some through the years have described Jesus as "meek and mild." Was God's Son weak, then? Not on your life! In His great strength, however, He chose not to return insult for insult, blow for blow, wound for wound. He gave us an example to follow, the example of a powerful man who chose the path of humility, and dealt with others in gentleness.

To walk that path means humbling ourselves. Sometimes, it means going to a individual and saying, "I don't know if I have said or done something to harm you or offend you, but if I did, I'm truly sorry. Let's try to work it out." And it means saying these things even if you are convinced you're right and the other person was wrong from the get-go. That is where humility and meekness come in.

We need to get rid of any me-first, what's-in-it-for-me attitudes and start thinking biblically. And we need to be asking, *What can I do to help others? How can I learn to resolve conflicts?* It can change your life.

Jesus said, "Blessed are the meek, for they will inherit the Earth." They will also bring pleasure to the heart of God Himself, and that's about as good as it gets.

WHY WE NEED UNITY

*There is one body and one Spirit, just as you were called
in one hope of your calling. (Ephesians 4:4)*

When you put your faith in Jesus Christ, you became a part of the church. You are a part of the body of Christ. We are all together in this new family, and we should do nothing to unnecessarily disrupt it. In Ephesians 4, the apostle Paul likens the church, the body of believers, to the human body.

All the parts of the body need to work together. When I'm up on the platform speaking, for example, I might gesture with my hand. I don't think about my gestures ahead of time. But as I am saying a certain thing, my hand is gesturing, accentuating what I am saying verbally. My brain sends a signal to my hand, and my hand cooperates. But what if my hands suddenly decided to break loose and do their own thing while I was speaking? My gestures would look bizarre, and would actually distract or even contradict what I was trying to say. Or, what if I was apologizing for something when my eyes decided to do their own thing and start rolling? My eyes would be contradicting what my mouth was saying.

Just as we need cooperation in the human body, we also need it in the body of Christ, working together toward a common purpose. Now, Paul isn't talking about "unity at any price" here. He wasn't saying that it doesn't really matter what we believe, that as long as we're into "spirituality" and believe in a higher power, then we are all God's children. Sometimes in our desire for unity, we can end up embracing the wrong beliefs.

Paul has told us that we need to be unified, but this is all predicated on biblical truth. We build our unity on a foundation of the solid, undeniable truths of Scripture.

THE SOURCE OF HAPPINESS

You have turned for me my mourning into dancing; You have put off my sackcloth and clothed me with gladness. (Psalm 30:11)

It has been said that the best cure for hedonism is an attempt to practice it.

If you chase after pleasure, you will eventually come to the same conclusion as King Solomon: "I said to myself, 'Come now, be merry; enjoy yourself to the full.' But I found that this, too, was futile. For it is silly to be laughing all the time; what good does it do?" (Ecclesiastes 2:1-2, TLB).

The Bible tells us that if the driving desire of our lives is to please ourselves, that very quest will be the source of endless problems and heartaches. "What is causing the quarrels and fights among you? Isn't it the whole army of evil desires at war within you? You want what you don't have, so you scheme and kill to get it. You are jealous for what others have, and you can't possess it, so you fight and quarrel to take it away from them. And yet the reason you don't have what you want is that you don't ask God for it" (James 4:1-2, NLT).

It comes down to this: If you live for yourself and your own happiness and pleasure, then you will be a miserable person. It's ironic that the people who live for happiness never find it, while the people who live for God find happiness as a byproduct. The people who chase after pleasure never really experience it. They may find little bits here and there, but nothing to speak of. Certainly nothing enduring. Yet the people who live for God experience the ultimate pleasure—a joy that bubbles up from deep down in the inmost being.

Pleasure isn't in itself a bad thing, although you might get that impression from some Christians. I think the Christian life is the most pleasurable life around. Why? Because God is the creator of light and laughter and joy... beginning here and now, and stretching on into eternity. The Bible teaches, "You have made known to me the path of life; you will fill me with joy in your presence, with eternal pleasures at your right hand" (Psalm 16:11, NIV).

Cheap thrills are a dime a dozen. True and lasting happiness comes from the hand of God.

NEW AND IMPROVED

Therefore, if anyone is in Christ, he is a new creation; old things have passed away; behold, all things have become new. (2 Corinthians 5:17)

Madison Avenue discovered long ago that a good way to sell a product is to add the words "new and improved." The only thing that may be new and improved is the box or label, but we really want to believe the product is better. There is something in us that loves the newest and the latest.

But everything that is new soon becomes old. We purchase a new car, but then someone spills a cup of coffee in the back seat, or it gets dinged in the parking lot. We get a new gadget, but it breaks the day after the warranty expires. We buy new toys for our children, but they run out of batteries.

So we say, "If I just get a new wardrobe...if I get a new haircut...if I change my friends...if I change my house...if I change my career...that will make everything better." It may make things a little bit different (for awhile), but it won't make them better. It all will come down to the same old problems, because you still have to deal with the same old you inside. New surroundings or a new appearance aren't going to change us. We have to change.

God is the true Giver of new things—things that will last forever. When we come to Him through a new birth by faith in Christ, He gives us a new nature, a new heart, a new life, a new hope, and a new purpose. He takes ordinary people and makes them extraordinary.

OUR CHOICE IN LIFE

Do you not know that to whom you present yourselves slaves to obey, you are that one's slaves whom you obey, whether of sin leading to death, or of obedience leading to righteousness? (Romans 6:16)

As a guest on Larry King Live a few years ago, Billy Graham was asked to comment on the rash of violence on high school campuses, as well as other problems in our culture. He said, "One thing that is being missed by many people is that the devil is at work."

That is so true. The devil is at work. When you get down to it, it is the only logical and plausible explanation for the madness that humanity is capable of. Just as surely as there is a God in heaven who loves you, there is a devil from hell who hates you. Jesus summed it up succinctly when He said, speaking of Satan, "The thief does not come except to steal, and to kill, and to destroy. I have come that they may have life, and that they may have it more abundantly" (John 10:10). At the end of the day, our choice in life really boils down to belonging to the Lord, or belonging to Satan. There is no third, "independent" option.

A lot of people say they don't choose either. But in reality, by not choosing God, they choose the devil by default. There are no other choices. One of Satan's most brilliant strategies is to convince people he does not exist, when all the while, he is manipulating their lives. Humanity is basically bad. And it is the devil who works through the fallen nature of human beings, getting them to do the evil things that he does.

God gives us a choice in life. We aren't forced to choose Him. Nor are we forced to choose the devil. But God has given us something called free will. We can choose sin, which leads to death. Or we can choose obedience to God, which leads to righteousness.

UNDER GOD'S PROTECTION

No temptation has overtaken you except such as is common to man; but God is faithful, who will not allow you to be tempted beyond what you are able, but with the temptation will also make the way of escape, that you may be able to bear it. (1 Corinthians 10:13)

In the New Testament, we have the account of Jesus saying to Peter, "Simon, Simon! Indeed, Satan has asked for you, that he may sift you as wheat. But I have prayed for you, that your faith should not fail; and when you have returned to Me, strengthen your brethren" (Luke 22:31-32).

Put yourself in Peter's sandals. You're sitting near the Lord when He turns to you, looks you in the eyes, calls you by name, and says, "Satan has been asking excessively that you be taken out of the care and protection of God. The devil has been asking for you by name." I don't know about you, but if Jesus Christ, the Son of God, said that to me, it would be cause for great concern.

Peter was such a big fish that Satan himself went after him. I wonder if the Lord paused for effect: "Satan has been asking for you...by name....But I have good news, Peter. I have prayed for you."

It's a good reminder to us that when the devil comes knocking at our door, we should say, "Lord, would you mind getting that?" We are no match for the devil. But even though he is a powerful foe, he is still a created being, and certainly not as powerful as God. Even so, we don't want to tangle with him. We want to stand behind God's protection.

In spite of the devil's power and wicked agenda, he must first ask permission when it comes to attacking the children of God, because of the hedge of protection that God has placed around us.

God knows what you are ready for. And He won't give you more than you can handle.

THE LUST OF THE EYES

For all that is in the world—the lust of the flesh, the lust of the eyes, and the pride of life—is not of the Father but is of the world. (1 John 2:16)

Why do we get tempted in our minds? Because it is command central. It is here that we reason, think things through, contemplate, dream, and fantasize. The Bible tells us, "For though we walk in the flesh, we do not war according to the flesh. For the weapons of our warfare are not carnal but mighty in God for pulling down strongholds" (2 Corinthians 10:3-4).

Eve was tempted through the lust of the eyes: *Eve, check it out. Have you ever seen a piece of fruit like this?* Satan attacked Eve's mind. The lust of the eyes is mental temptation, temptation that comes through the realm of the thoughts.

As the apostle Paul wrote to the church at Corinth, "But I fear, lest somehow, as the serpent deceived Eve by his craftiness, so your minds may be corrupted from the simplicity that is in Christ" (2 Corinthians 11:3).

We can commit horrible mental sins, that no one else knows about, reaching into the past through our memories, and into the future through our imagination. Often, the devil will get us to just contemplate some sin, by saying, *You don't have to actually DO this. Just think about it. That's all. What's the harm? It doesn't have to go any further than this. You can handle it.*

But after a while, thinking and fantasizing about it isn't enough. We want to take it to the next level. So we start flirting. We start touching. We start tasting. We start playing with it. Then, the next thing we know, we're caught in it.

As Martin Luther once said about temptation, "You can't stop the birds from flying over your head, but only let them fly. Don't let them nest in your hair." In other words, temptation is all around us, but if we're walking in the counsel and strength of God's Spirit, we don't have to succumb to it.

RESPONSIBILITY

But He said, "More than that, blessed are those who hear
the word of God and keep it!" (Luke 11:28)

W hen Peter and John came before the priests, elders, and scribes
to answer for their preaching of the gospel, who was there?
Acts 4:6 says that Annas, the high priest Caiaphas, and others were gathered together in Jerusalem.

Annas and Caiaphas were the very men who were responsible for the
crucifixion of Jesus Christ. Caiaphas was the ruling high priest, and Annas
was his father-in-law, the former high priest. In those times, judicial and
religious responsibilities were intertwined. Caiaphas had great authority as
both a religious figure and a legal figure. This was a man who had dedicated
his life to the study of Scripture and the pursuit of God. He should have
known better. Yet he ended up becoming the man responsible for the
persecution and death of Jesus.

Pontius Pilate, the Roman governor, is the one who actually sent Christ
to His death. Pilate is the one who ordered Jesus Christ to be flogged, and
for spikes to be driven into His hands and feet. Yet Jesus said to him, "The
one who delivered Me to you is guilty of a greater sin" (John 19:11). How
can that be? Pilate was an ignorant nonbeliever. He didn't know any better.
But Caiaphas was a man who knew the Scriptures.

Knowledge brings responsibility. If you have heard the truth of God,
if you have been exposed to the gospel message, then God will hold you
accountable for what you know. *Blessed are those who hear the word of*
God and keep it! (See Luke 11:28.)

A WALKING LIGHT BULB

> *"Let your light so shine before men, that they may see your good works and glorify your Father in heaven." (Matthew 5:16)*

The religious leaders thought they had eliminated the problem when they crucified Jesus. But now, His disciples were preaching and performing miracles. It was as though Jesus had returned. And so He had—in the hearts and lives of His people.

This reminds us that one of the best arguments for the Christian faith is a transformed life. New believers are the best advertising God could have because their lifestyles change, their attitudes change, and even their countenances change. The greatest biography of Jesus is written in the words and actions of His people. Your godly lifestyle is a testimony, just as if you were a walking miracle, like the lame man whom Peter and John healed.

Jesus told us we are to be the light of the world and the salt of the earth. There is a place to let our lights shine and proclaim the truth of God. And there is a place for us to be salt.

Even if you don't tell people you are a Christian, they will sense something different about you, and they will watch you. As a representative of Christ, you're like a walking light bulb.

If you are being the kind of follower of Jesus that God wants you to be, if you are being a "salty" Christian, then your lifestyle will stimulate a thirst for God in others. The greatest compliment is when someone wants to know more, when he or she approaches you and says, "What is it about you?" That is your opportunity to...turn on the light.

One paraphrase of Scripture puts it this way: "Through thick and thin, keep your hearts at attention, in adoration before Christ, your Master. Be ready to speak up and tell anyone who asks why you're living the way you are, and always with the utmost courtesy" (1 Peter 3:15, The Message).

ABILITY VS. AVAILABILITY

But we have this treasure in earthen vessels, that the excellence of the power may be of God and not of us. (2 Corinthians 4:7)

When Peter and John were brought before the Sanhedrin, it was a source of complete amazement that these untrained laymen could be so well-versed in the Scriptures—and more importantly, in their understanding. They were ordinary fishermen, blue-collar, salt-of-the-earth-type people. This doesn't mean they were illiterate. But they hadn't attended the rabbinical schools or spent their lives in the study of the Scripture.

Acts 4:13 tells us that when these religious leaders "saw the boldness of Peter and John, and perceived that they were uneducated and untrained men, they marveled. And they realized that they had been with Jesus." These simple fishermen appeared to be better-equipped than the professionals were. How did this happen? The disciples had been with Jesus. They were boldly sharing their faith. They knew the Scriptures. They were men who prayed.

This should give hope and encouragement to those who think of themselves as ordinary people. Maybe God hasn't called you to be a pastor, a missionary, or to some professional ministry position. But God can use you, too. It's clear that He is looking for ordinary men and women to bring the gospel message to others.

God can use you where you are...and the opportunities are endless. There is a mission field where you work, where you go to school, and in your neighborhood. You are God's representative, and He is calling you to go into this world and speak up for Him. God isn't looking so much for ability as He is looking for availability. So make yourself available to Him.

DRAW YOUR SWORD

...The sword of the Spirit, which is the word of God. (Ephesians 6:17)

In the listing of a Christian's spiritual armor in Ephesians 6, the sword stands alone as an offensive weapon. When I go into battle, I don't beat my enemy with my shield or try to defeat him with my belt or chase him down with my sandal or throw my helmet at him. I pull my sword out of the sheath and I use it.

Ephesians 6:17 tells us to take up the sword of the Spirit. When we are tempted, the most effective weapon that God has given to us as believers is the sword of the Spirit, which is the Word of God.

Jesus modeled this so beautifully during His temptation in the wilderness. When the devil tried temptation after temptation against Him, Jesus used the sword of the Spirit (see Luke 4:1-13). The devil said, "Why don't You turn a rock into a piece of bread? I know You're hungry."

Jesus said, "It is written, 'Man shall not live by bread alone, but by every word that comes out of the mouth of God.'"

Then the devil said, "Why don't you worship me right now?"

Jesus responded, "It is written, 'You shall worship the Lord God only. Him only you shall serve.'"

"Why don't you cast yourself off of here, and the angels will catch you," Satan said, quoting Scripture out of context.

Jesus responded, bringing the Scripture back into context, "It has been said, 'You shall not tempt the Lord your God.'"

The sword of the Spirit...it is sharp, it is powerful, and the enemy cannot stand before it. So draw your sword, Christian.

TARES AMONG THE WHEAT

"Let both grow together until the harvest, and at the time of harvest I will say to the reapers, 'First gather together the tares and bind them in bundles to burn them, but gather the wheat into my barn.'" (Matthew 13:30)

In Acts 5, the Scripture gives us the sobering story of Ananias and Sapphira. At a time when many in the church were giving selflessly and sacrificially of their resources, this couple made a terrible choice...and paid for their deceit with their lives. Their choice? They could give sacrificially to the early church, or they could give a little. But what they chose to do was the worst thing possible: They decided to pretend they were "giving everything," when in reality they were holding a portion back for themselves. This was a sin of hypocrisy.

Ananias and Sapphira found out that you can't fool God. It's interesting that the name Ananias means "God is gracious," but he found out that God is also holy. The name Sapphira means "beautiful," but her heart was ugly with sin. It's easy for us to condemn Ananias and Sapphira for their dishonesty. But maybe we need to examine our own lives to see if our profession is backed up by our practice.

The devil loves to counterfeit the genuine. He appears to operate by the adage, "If you can't beat 'em, join 'em." He has his tares among the wheat. There are false Christians, false preachers, false teachers, false apostles, and false prophets. There are Ananiases and Sapphiras in our ranks. The Judas Iscariots are out there, too. They go to the same churches that we do, live in the same neighborhoods, and attend the same schools.

But one of these days God, who knows all hearts, will separate the wheat from the chaff and the true from the false. And that, by the way, is *His* job... not ours.

A MEANINGFUL LIFE

"Let your light so shine before men, that they may see your good works and glorify your Father in heaven." (Matthew 5:16)

How should I live my life on this earth? What purpose does God have in mind for me, now that I have received His Son Jesus Christ into my heart?

These are questions every believer should ask, because if you have no goals or purpose, you can waste your life. As I have often said, if you aim at nothing, you are bound to hit it.

Many people simply want to prolong their lives, rather than try to find their purpose in life. Certainly medical science is helping us live longer lives. We can add years to our lives, but we cannot add life to our years. Should our primary goal be to prolong our lives, or should it be to live life to its fullest?

Jim Elliot was fresh out of college when he felt the call of God to go to the mission field. Tragically, Jim and four other young missionaries lost their lives in the jungles of Ecuador in an attempt to reach others with the gospel. It might seem like a terrible waste of life for such a young man with so much promise. But after his death, this entry was found in one of his journals: "I seek not a long life, but a full one, like you, Lord Jesus."

That's a good goal: To live a full life, a life with meaning and purpose. We don't know how long we will live; that is up to God. But life is not merely a matter of years. It is a matter of how we live. It is not the years that count, but what you do with those years. What kind of life are you living right now?

FULLY GOD, FULLY MAN

Let this mind be in you which was also in Christ Jesus, who, being in the form of God, did not consider it robbery to be equal with God, but made Himself of no reputation, taking the form of a bondservant, and coming in the likeness of men." (Philippians 2:5-7)

Because Jesus was God, we might ask, did He have full knowledge of God as a little baby in the manger at Bethlehem? Or did this knowledge come to Him over a period of time? When Jesus was born, could He have turned to Mary and said, "I am God Almighty, the Messiah of Israel. I am God in human form. And by the way, Mary, the Earth is round. Some people are going to say that it is flat, but I am telling you it is round. I made it myself."

Jesus didn't do that. Instead, He squealed and giggled and made noises like any other baby. And He had a human mind. The Bible says of Jesus, "And the Child grew and became strong in spirit, filled with wisdom; and the grace of God was upon Him" (Luke 2:40). When Jesus was 12 years old, Mary and Joseph found Him in the temple after the Feast of the Passover, "sitting in the midst of the teachers, both listening to them and asking them questions" (verse 46).

Then in Luke 2:52, we read that "Jesus increased in wisdom and stature, and in favor with God and men." This would appear to be saying that Jesus went through a learning process like anyone else. Yet at the same time, He did not have the limitations that sin brings on one's life.

Jesus walked the earth in a human body and died like a man, in the sense that His body ceased to function just like ours do when we die. And though He was God, He emptied himself of the privileges of deity and walked among us as a man.

And because He was willing to become a Man, He has made it possible to be our great High Priest, who "understands our weaknesses since he had the same temptations we do, though he never once gave way to them and sinned. So let us come boldly to the very throne of God and stay there to receive his mercy and to find grace to help us in our times of need" (Hebrews 4:15-16, TLB).

GIVING GOD A MAKEOVER

> *Do not be idolaters, as some of them were; as it is written: "The people sat down to eat and drink and got up to indulge in pagan revelry."*
> *(1 Corinthians 10:7, NIV)*

At first glance, the sins that brought the children of Israel down in the wilderness don't seem to have any rhyme or reason. But a closer examination reveals that the root problem was a lack of relationship with the true and living God.

When Moses was temporarily taken out of the scene when he went to meet with God on Mt. Sinai, the people became antsy and impatient, wanting something to take his place. It was only a matter of time until they were bowing before a golden calf.

When you get down to it, Moses was their first idol, and the golden calf was their second. Moses was like God to them, so when Moses was gone, they created a god of their own making.

We do the same when we start remaking God in our own image. When we give God a 21st-century makeover, when we make God politically correct, when we start changing His Word to fit the perverted morals of our time, this becomes idolatry. We are remaking God because we aren't comfortable with what He says. We don't like His standards. So… if we can remake God in our image, we can live the way that we want to and do as we please.

In other words, we want a celestial salad bar where we can casually stroll up, choose the attributes of God that appeal to us most, and leave the rest behind. It's religion á la carte…but it is *not* New Testament Christianity.

When we mold God and His Word into our image, it's as much an act of idolatry as it was when the children of Israel worshiped the golden calf.

Let's bow low before the real God today, submitting to His full purposes and plans for our lives, and refusing to worship and serve any imitation—no matter how "comfortable" or politically correct it may seem at the time.

THE PERIL OF PRAYERLESSNESS

If you need wisdom, ask our generous God, and he will give it to you.
He will not rebuke you for asking. (James 1:5, NLT)

The Bible's gives us Jacob's first recorded prayer in Genesis 32:9-16. Up to this point, in seven chapters of the book of Genesis devoted to telling Jacob's life story, there had been no mention of him praying.

It makes me wonder if Jacob had ever prayed up to this point. It's possible, of course, but the Bible doesn't specifically mention it. It may have been Jacob's very lack of prayer and lack of dependence on God that made him feel as though he had to manipulate his circumstances.

It was commendable that Jacob was reaching out to God, and there are even some good things about his prayer. He acknowledged the God of Abraham and Isaac as the true God. He confessed his own unworthiness. He brought his petition to the Lord.

But it would have been better if he had simply said, *"Lord, what should I do now?"* Instead, he prayed and made his plans. In other words, he decided what he was going to do and then asked God to bless it.

Isn't that like us sometimes? We make our plans, and then ask God to bless them. But that's not really praying about a matter. Instead, we should pray along the lines of, "Lord, give me wisdom from your Word and from godly people who will guide me scripturally. Help me do the right thing."

But Jacob didn't do that. He wanted what was right, but he went about it in the wrong way.

We've all heard the old cliché, "God helps those who helps themselves." But the Bible shows us again and again that God helps those who *can't* help themselves. That's what Jacob needed to realize. Let's learn to seek out God's will rather than bypass it, consulting Him early and often. The sooner we commit our plans to Him, the sooner we'll enjoy heaven-sent success.

SURRENDER AT GETHSEMANE

Jesus went out as usual to the Mount of Olives, and his disciples followed him. On reaching the place, he said to them, "Pray that you will not fall into temptation." He withdrew about a stone's throw beyond them, knelt down and prayed, "Father, if you are willing, take this cup from me; yet not my will, but yours be done." An angel from heaven appeared to him and strengthened him. And being in anguish, he prayed more earnestly, and his sweat was like drops of blood falling to the ground. (Luke 22:39-44, NIV)

Have you ever felt lonely? Have you ever felt as though your friends and family had abandoned you? Have you ever felt like you were misunderstood? Have you ever had a hard time understanding or submitting to the will of God for your life?

If so, then you have an idea of what the Lord Jesus went through as He agonized at Gethsemane.

Hebrews tells us, "This High Priest of ours understands our weaknesses, for he faced all of the same testings we do, yet he did not sin. So let us come boldly to the throne of our gracious God. There we will receive his mercy, and we will find grace to help us when we need it most" (4:15-16, NLT).

Consider the fact that Jesus, who was God, was omniscient. He was all-knowing. Therefore, He was fully aware of the horrors of the crucifixion that awaited Him.

He knew His disciples would abandon him. He knew Judas Iscariot would betray Him. He knew that Simon Peter would deny Him. He knew they would rip His back open, press a crown of thorns into His head, beat Him, spit in His face, and crucify Him. Worst of all, He knew that all the sins of the world would be placed upon Him.

The Bible tells us that Jesus was "a man of sorrows, acquainted with deepest grief" (Isaiah 53:3, NLT). But the sorrow He experienced in Gethsemane on the night before His crucifixion seemed to be the culmination of all the sorrow He had ever known and would accelerate to a climax the following day. The ultimate triumph that was to take place at Calvary was first accomplished beneath the gnarled old olive trees of Gethsemane.

Jesus told Peter, James, and John, "My soul is exceedingly sorrowful, even to death. Stay here and watch" (Mark 14:34). Jesus' sorrow and anguish was so powerful, it threatened His very life.

In the face of this dreadful prospect of bearing God's full fury against sin, Jesus knelt to the ground and began to pray. This was not a quiet whisper of a prayer. Hebrews 5:7 tells us, "While Jesus was here on earth, he offered prayers and pleadings, with a loud cry and tears, to the one who could rescue him from death. And God heard his prayers because of his deep reverence for God" (NLT).

This is what God's Son faced in order to become our Savior and Redeemer. Take time to praise Him this day, for what He endured to save you and make you His child.

THE RIGHT WAY TO PRAY

"If you abide in Me, and My words abide in you, you will ask what you desire, and it shall be done for you." (John 15:7)

When it comes to prayer, people sometimes mistakenly think they can first come up with a plan and then get God to do what they want Him to do. They think that if they really pester God through prayer, He'll finally cave in.

Others would teach that if we have enough faith, we can speak something into existence. We can just say it, and it will be ours.

Of course, both concepts are false. The fact of the matter is that prayer is not for the purpose of moving God your way. It is for moving you God's way.

Do you want to know the key to answered prayer? Then line yourself up with the will of God and start praying for what God wants you to have.

A literal translation of the verse that begins today's devotional might read: "If you maintain a living communion with Me, and My Word is at home in you, you can ask at once for yourself whatever your heart desires and it will be yours."

When we hear this verse, we immediately gravitate toward the part about asking whatever our heart desires. But here's what it comes down to. If you are maintaining a living communion with God, and His words are at home with you, then your prayers will change. You won't be praying for self-indulgent things. Instead, you will be praying for the things God wants you to have.

This is what prayer is really all about. It's about getting our will into alignment with the will of God.

UNANSWERED PRAYERS

And He was withdrawn from them about a stone's throw, and He knelt down and prayed, saying, "Father, if it is Your will, take this cup away from Me; nevertheless not My will, but Yours, be done." (Luke 22:41-42)

I am so glad that God will overrule my prayers at times, because I have prayed for things fervently, believing they were the will of God, and they were flat-out wrong. I am so thankful that God said no to those prayers.

Yet I have actually heard some people say, "Never pray, 'Not my will, but Yours be done.' That is a lack of faith." Some have even said, "What you should really pray is, 'Not Your will, but mine be done.'" Let's just say that I don't want to be standing too close to those people when lightning strikes, because they have things turned around.

Never be afraid to pray, "Not my will, but Yours be done." By saying that, you are simply saying, "Lord, I don't know all the facts. I don't know everything there is to know. My knowledge is limited. My experience is limited. So if what I am praying is outside of Your will for any reason, please graciously overrule it." You won't always understand how you should pray. What it comes down to is telling God that you want His will more than your own.

I know this is hard at times. Sometimes you don't understand why God doesn't give you what you ask for. When you're young and single, you may see a handsome guy or beautiful girl and just know that person is the one for you. But as the lyrics to a country song say, "Sometimes I thank God for unanswered prayers."

As time passes, you will look back with 20/20 hindsight, and you will say, "Thank God He did not answer my prayers," or "Thank God He answered my prayers," whichever the case may be.

Finally...remember the words of Jesus: "Your heavenly Father already knows all your needs, and he will give you all you need from day to day if you live for him and make the Kingdom of God your primary concern" (Matthew 6:32-33, NLT).

ONE BITE AT A TIME

So be careful how you live. Don't live like fools, but like those who are wise.
(Ephesians 5:15, NLT)

Even Christians have the capacity to fall away from God into serious sin…but it doesn't happen overnight. It may appear that they do, but in reality, it doesn't happen that way.

For instance, you may have seen someone at church last week, only to discover that on the following Thursday they have gotten into some immoral lifestyle or are doing something they shouldn't be doing. You think, *I don't get it. I just saw them in church last week. They were doing fine.* I propose that compromise has been taking place over a long period of time in that person's life, and he or she finally just caved in.

It's like a massive tree in Colorado I heard about recently. The tree had stood for over four hundred years and then—suddenly—it came crashing to the ground. No one could understand why a tree of that size would just topple over like that. After all, this old giant had been struck by lightning on fourteen different occasions. It had weathered countless storms and had never fallen. But one day, without warning, it just crashed.

It turned out that the tree had been killed by beetles. Little insects had, over a prolonged period of time, chewed their way through its mighty fibers until it came crashing down.

That is how compromise works. The devil may be wicked, but he's not an idiot. He knows how to rip people off. He doesn't tell you what he's up to in the beginning. Instead, he comes to you with a little enticement. He will infiltrate through compromise and then take you down, one bite at a time.

The book of Hebrews warns us: "See to it, brothers, that none of you has a sinful, unbelieving heart that turns away from the living God. But encourage one another daily, as long as it is called Today, so that none of you may be hardened by sin's deceitfulness" (Hebrews 3:12-13, NIV).

That's where accountability with a close friend in the Lord can be so beneficial. We need someone who loves us, who will ask us the tough questions about our lives…and who won't be turned aside by vague answers!

COMING UP EMPTY

I said in my heart, "Come now, I will test you with mirth; therefore enjoy pleasure"; but surely, this also was vanity. (Ecclesiastes 2:1)

It's not that unusual to pick up a newspaper, read an article, or turn on the news and learn that another celebrity has checked into rehab or another rock star has overdosed or committed suicide.

We have a hard time understanding how these "beautiful people," these men and women who seem so perfect to us in their airbrushed photos and Tinseltown world, could be utterly miserable and bitterly unhappy. The truth is, many of them have the same problems that we do—even though they possess some of the material things we can only dream about. Yet many of them have discovered the emptiness and futility of living for "things" or for "celebrity."

The world offers a fleeting happiness that comes and goes…fast. Its happiness depends entirely on personal circumstances. If things are going well, then you're happy. If circumstances in your life have taken a bad turn, then you are miserable. But God offers you a happiness that will be there in spite of your circumstances. It's not a happiness that grows out of what you have, it comes from who you know. The Bible says, "Happy are the people whose God is the Lord!" (Psalm 144:15).

The world tells you to take drugs, party, and get drunk. That's where it's at, they say. But God says, "And do not be drunk with wine, in which is dissipation; but be filled with the Spirit" (Ephesians 5:18).

Have you been settling for a cheap substitute? If so, you have been coming up empty. Maybe, like Solomon, you will conclude that it is meaningless. Just so much emptiness, like a bubble that bursts or a wisp of a vapor. That's the conclusion everyone will eventually come to. So you can either take God's Word for it now…or you can learn it the hard way.

HEARING GOD

"Your word is a lamp to my feet and a light to my path." (Psalm 119:105)

There are a lot of people today who say they hear the voice of God telling them to do thus and so. But what we must remember is that God will never contradict His Word. He will *always* lead us according to what the Bible says.

Some people come up with some lame concepts, such as "We're not married, but God has told us it's okay to have sex." I can assure you that God did *not* say that, because He says in His Word, "You shall not commit adultery" (Exodus 20:14). God will not contradict His Word.

Let's say you were hoping for a letter from someone. You stand at the window, waiting for what seems like an eternity for the mail carrier to arrive. Finally, he drives up and you bolt over to your mailbox. You're looking for that letter. Maybe it's from someone you're in love with. Maybe it's an answer to a job application. Maybe it's something you ordered in the mail. Maybe you've won the sweepstakes.

But imagine this. What if you had a handwritten note from God to you? Would you carry it around in your pocket for a couple of weeks and open it when you got around to it? I doubt it. You probably would tear it open as you're thinking, "Wow, God spoke to me! What does He have to say?"

The Bible is a written letter from God. A lot of us carry it. We have it in different colors and sizes. We have it in different translations. But so many of us never read it.

One of the wonderful, supernatural aspects to reading God's Word is the way it will speak so directly to specific circumstances we may be dealing with in our lives. We can even be reading a portion of the Bible we've read many times before, when suddenly the words leap off the page at us with fresh meaning. No matter where you are in life right now, God has a personal message for you right now waiting in the pages of the Bible.

FINISHING WHAT WE START

You ran well. Who hindered you from obeying the truth? (Galatians 5:7)

I magine, for a moment, that you and I are competing in a race. When the starter's pistol is fired, we take off, and I leave you in my dust. I'm running really well. Let's say we're going for ten laps, and we are coming to the last one. I say to myself, "I am creaming the competition. I am going to go get a Krispy Kreme doughnut now." So I wander off the track. Let's say that you cross the finish line ten minutes later. Now, it's clear that I beat you, but if I didn't do the final lap and cross the finish line, then I have lost the race anyway. It doesn't matter if I led for nine out of ten laps. I had to finish the race I began.

In the same way, there are people who started off with a great burst of energy as they followed the Lord. Maybe you were one of those people. Maybe you came to Christ during the days of the Jesus Movement. Or perhaps you came more recently. That's great. But that was then and this is now. How you were running a year ago, or even a month ago, is no longer significant. The question is, *how are you running right now?* Are you keeping up the pace? Are you going to make it across the finish line? You can make it if you want to.

Some seasons of the Christian life will be very difficult— and you'll have to hold onto God's Word and the promise that He will complete the work He has begun in your life (see Philippians 1:6).

Keep running, my friend. The finish line is near.

THE QUEST

Hell and Destruction are never full; so the eyes of man are never satisfied.
(Proverbs 27:20)

I read about a convention where *Star Trek* memorabilia was auctioned off, including a half-filled glass of water that had been sipped by a cast member who had a virus. The item sold for $40. The person who bought it immediately drank it, because he or she wanted to get the same virus the cast member from *Star Trek* had.

"Bizarre" is one word that comes to mind after a story like that one. But is it really any more bizarre when you start thinking about the things that supposedly normal people dedicate their entire lives to? They will dedicate their lives to acquiring possessions...or to sexual conquests...or to heaping up academic degrees. But what they will find out eventually is that if in their pursuit of these things, they forget about God, it will result in emptiness.

Take it from the expert, Solomon, who penned the Book of Ecclesiastes. Solomon was the one person who could say, "Been there, done that, bought the T-shirt." He knew about these things firsthand. He went on a quest, deciding he was going to try everything this world had to offer. But he wisely concluded that just as death and destruction are never satisfied, so human desire is never satisfied.

When God created us, He wired us this way. The Bible says that He has placed eternity in our hearts (see Ecclesiastes 3:11), which simply means that in the heart of every man and woman, there is a sense that there is something more out there. It's almost as though we were born with a God-shaped blank inside.

But when you have Christ at the center of your very being, when you pursue a daily walk with the living God, that "blank" will fill to over-flowing with purpose, peace, and a passion for life.

DIVINE DEPOSITS

> *So teach us to number our days, that we may gain a heart of wisdom.*
> *(Psalm 90:12)*

Let's say that your phone rings tomorrow morning, and it's a call from the manager of your bank. He tells you, "I received a very unusual call the other day. Someone who loves you very much and is quite wealthy has given you a large sum of money. This anonymous donor will be depositing 86,400 cents into your account every single day."

"How is that again?" you ask.

"Every single day, this person will deposit 86,400 cents into your account."

Is that much money? you wonder at first. Then you get out your calculator and figure out that it amounts to $864 every day. *That's pretty good*, you're thinking.

"But there is one condition," the banker continues. "You have to spend it every single day. You can't save it up. You can't add it to the next day's balance. Every day, you must spend that money. What is not spent will be taken away. This person will do this each and every day, but the condition is that you must spend the money."

So you go back to your calculator and figure out that $864 times 7 equals $6,048 per week. That amount, multiplied by 52, comes to $314,496 per year. That's a pretty good deal. And that is also a fantasy.

So let's deal with reality. Someone who really does love you very much deposits into your bank of time 86,400 seconds every single day. That someone is God. And the condition is that you must spend it. You can't save up time today and apply it toward tomorrow—there's no such thing as a 27-hour day. Each and every day, you have the opportunity to invest your precious commodity of time.

GREEN LIGHTS AND BLUE SKIES

He will not let you stumble and fall; the one who watches over you will not sleep. Indeed, he who watches over Israel never tires and never sleeps. (Psalm 121:3-4, NLT)

If I decided how my day were to go, I would never write in "crisis." I would never write, "Get sick" here, or "Have my tire go flat" there, or "Have this unexpected disaster take place." I would just write in all the good stuff in life. I would plan for everything to go my way. There would be no traffic on the freeways. It would always be green lights and blue skies.

But we are not in charge of our lives. God is. And He will allow so-called "bad things" happen to us in the course of our days. But as time goes by, you will find that the significant things you learn in life didn't really come from the good times and the mountain-top experiences. They came from those times of crisis in which you were more dependent on God. Many of the most difficult days will, in retrospect, turn out to be unbelievably valuable, because it is through those so-called "bad times" that you will learn some of life's most important lessons.

The things we experience are not random events that float in and out of our lives. They are rather specific events that have been chosen by God and are timely and purposeful. This means the good things as well as the bad things. It means the wonderful, happy times of life as well as the dark, difficult days.

When you put your faith in Jesus Christ, you come under His protective care. God is fully aware of everything that happens to you, and thankfully He is never asleep on the job. He pays careful attention to the smallest details of your life and is in complete in control of all circumstances that surround you. He knows what's happening in your life right now—knows it better than you do. And His presence and provision will be all you need to make it through.

THE VOICE OF CIRCUMSTANCE

So Gideon said to God, "If You will save Israel by my hand as You have said—look, I shall put a fleece of wool on the threshing floor; if there is dew on the fleece only, and it is dry on all the ground, then I shall know that You will save Israel by my hand, as You have said." (Judges 6:36-37)

Not only does God speak to us through His Word, and not only will He never contradict His Word, but God also speaks through circumstances. Although I'm not one to base major life decisions on circumstances alone, there have clearly been times when I have sensed that something was the will of God, and then things would fall into place circumstantially. At other times, circumstances have made it obvious that God was saying "no."

A classic example of God communicating through circumstances was when God spoke to Gideon, who laid his fleece out on the ground, asking God to confirm His Word. And certainly, in the account of Jonah, we can see how that reluctant prophet got the right message when God brought his journey to an abrupt halt, and he found himself in the belly of a very large fish.

Of course, as a part of this process, God speaks to us through people. For example, there have been times when I have been listening to a someone preach or I've been talking with a friend, and suddenly what he is saying addresses the very situation I'm going through, even though he is completely unaware of my circumstances. It makes me realize that it is God Himself speaking to me through those individuals.

Maybe God has spoken to you through a pastor or a Christian friend. Or perhaps He has been speaking to you through circumstances. Listen carefully, keep committing your way and your path to the Lord in prayer, and remember that He will never contradict His Word.

FAITHFUL

His mother said to the servants, "Whatever He says to you, do it." (John 2:5)

When David was called by God to be king, he was out watching sheep, just being faithful. The day David killed Goliath, he didn't wake up that morning and hear God say, "David, today you are going to the valley of Elah. There will be a giant Philistine named Goliath, and you will kill him with a stone." No, at his dad's request, David was taking some cheese sandwiches to his brothers out on the front line…just being faithful on an errand for his dad.

What was Gideon doing when God called him? He was hiding from his enemies. He was terrified. But God saw his potential, and the next thing Gideon knew, he was leading troops into battle.

And what was Elisha doing when Elijah called him to carry on the work? He was out plowing in the field. Moses was watching a bunch of sheep in the desert when God called him to deliver the Israelites. Then there was Daniel, who was so faithful to the Lord that his enemies couldn't find one thing wrong with him. They had to make up lies about him so that he would be sentenced to death.

My point is this: They were faithfully doing what God had set before them. They weren't running around, looking for big, important things to accomplish. They were simply doing the little things.

Sometimes, we have great ideas of what God will do. But we have to wait on Him. What are your dreams right now? Maybe you want to do something for God, but you think it will never happen. Then again…maybe it will. Maybe it even will surpass your wildest dreams. Just be faithful to do what God has set before you right now.

COMMITTED TO LEARN

*Be diligent to present yourself approved to God, a worker who does not need
to be ashamed, rightly dividing the word of truth. (2 Timothy 2:15)*

Have you ever had one of those golden opportunities in life to
share the gospel, and you found that you just weren't prepared?
Or have you had someone fire some really hard questions at you, and you
were rendered speechless?

After I had been a Christian for two weeks, I felt I needed to get out and
do something with my faith. I was walking down the street, and who did I
run into but my very close friend from elementary school. I started wit-
nessing to him. He was listening, and he was open. It seemed as though
I was making some progress. I was getting excited.

I didn't notice, however, that someone else was eavesdropping on our
conversation. He walked up to me and said, "I have a few questions for
you."

I thought, *No problem. I've been a Christian for two weeks. I think
I can grapple with most theological issues at this point. Fire away.*

So he fired four or five pretty tough questions at me. I can't even
remember today what they were. All I remember is that I was dumbfounded.
I didn't even have a clue. I was ashamed. I was embarrassed. But worst of all,
I felt that I had let the Lord down.

I made a commitment that day—a commitment to study the Bible so
I would not be caught in that position again. Do I have "all the answers"
now, after all these years? Of course not. But back in those early days, I realized that I needed to prepare and equip myself as well as I knew how so
I could be an effective tool in God's hand.

That's pretty much what Paul had in mind when he wrote these words
to Timothy: "All scripture is inspired by God and is useful for teaching the
faith and correcting error, for re-setting the direction of a man's life and
training him in good living. The scriptures are the comprehensive equip-
ment of the man of God and fit him fully for all branches of his work"
(2 Timothy 3:16-17, Phillips).

TEMPORARY PLEASURES

"Yes, a person is a fool to store up earthly wealth but not have a rich relationship with God." (Luke 12:21, NLT)

There is a story in the Bible about a man named Esau who gave up everything for a little temporal pleasure. As the firstborn, Esau had been given the family birthright, which meant that he would one day be the spiritual leader of his family and would be in the ancestral line of the Messiah. But Esau didn't seem to care much about that.

One day, his brother Jacob came along and proposed a trade: Esau's birthright for some stew that Jacob was cooking. It sounded like a good deal to Esau at the time. Later, he realized how cheaply he had sold out. But it was too late.

In the book of Hebrews, we read: "Make sure that no one is immoral or godless like Esau, who traded his birthright as the oldest son for a single meal. You know that afterward, when he wanted his father's blessing, he was rejected. It was too late for repentance, even though he begged with bitter tears" (Hebrews 12:16-17, NLT).

Esau had no regard for spiritual things, and there are a lot of people like that today. They could care less about God until they find themselves in a bind—or until some tragedy hits. Then suddenly, miraculously, they have time for God. Then when the crisis is past, they return to their old ways.

Jesus spoke about a farmer whose crop had produced generously. The farmer decided to tear down his barns and build larger ones to store everything.

That way, he could say to himself, "And I'll sit back and say to myself, 'My friend, you have enough stored away for years to come. Now take it easy! Eat, drink, and be merry!' But God said to him, 'You fool! You will die this very night. Then who will get everything you worked for?'" (Luke 12:19-20, NLT).

Are things on this earth more important to you than treasures in heaven? Everything you may hold dear will be left behind one day. And the only thing that will matter is what is waiting in heaven for you.

A PICTURE OF COURAGE

"Blessed are you when they revile and persecute you, and say all kinds of evil against you falsely for My sake. Rejoice and be exceedingly glad, for great is your reward in heaven, for so they persecuted the prophets who were before you." (Matthew 5:11-12)

God not only gives us the right words to say in a given situation, but He also gives us the power to stand up for our faith—even if it means harassment, hardship, or persecution.

The apostle Peter wrote, "If you are reproached for the name of Christ, blessed are you, for the Spirit of glory and of God rests upon you..." (1 Peter 4:14). God will give us the strength that we need, just as He has strengthened His sons and daughters in the face of fierce persecution down through the centuries.

You may think you couldn't cope if people made fun of you. You don't know if you could handle it if your life was actually threatened for the sake of the gospel. But if God allowed you to be put into such a situation, He would give you the strength *in that moment* to face it. He would give you the necessary boldness and courage.

Throughout history, God has given special grace and courage to millions of Christians who were persecuted for the faith. Many were tortured. Some even lost their lives. But they were unwilling to renounce Christ, unwilling to deny the Lord who had so radically changed their lives.

That's the way it was with the church's very first martyr, Stephen. The Lord gave him so much grace that even in the face of danger and death, his face shone like the face of an angel. And even while he being stoned to death, dying on his knees, Stephen stood tall. He had lived like Christ. He had spoken like Christ. And he would die like Christ.

HIS ULTIMATE PURPOSE

*Moreover we know that to those who love God, who are called according
to his plan, everything that happens fits into a pattern for good.
(Romans 8:28, PHILLIPS)*

We must remember that God never tests us without a purpose or
a reason. You might wonder, Why does God allow His children to go through these trials? The answer is God's ultimate purpose
is that we might be conformed into the image of Jesus Christ.

There are many times in our lives when we will go through trials, and
things will work out really well. That's when we love to quote Romans 8:28:
"All things work together for good to those who love God, to those who are
the called according to His purpose." Many things that make no sense at
the time will work out in the end.

A classic example of this is Joseph. Talk about things really going wrong!
Joseph went out to visit his brothers on an errand for his father and the next
thing he knew, he was sold as a slave. But with God's providence, he was
elevated to a position of great authority. He was able to help his brothers
and his father and do much good.

Another reason God allows trials is so we will become strong spiritually.
James 1:2–3 says, "My brethren, count it all joy when you fall into various
trials, knowing that the testing of your faith produces patience." Different
translations say that testing produces "heroic endurance" or "fortitude."
James meant that trials will toughen us up and give us staying power. God
wants iron to enter our souls.

Temptation can be endured and overcome. Remember that God's
ultimate purpose in allowing trials in our lives is so that we might be conformed into the image of Jesus Christ.

A BURDEN FOR THE LOST

Then Philip went down to the city of Samaria and preached Christ to them.
(Acts 8:5)

Philip was a man God used to bring others to himself. But why was he so powerfully used by God? What was his secret?

Philip had a deep concern for lost people. This was evidenced by the fact that he went to Samaria and preached Christ. That may not mean a lot to us, but it meant a lot to the Samaritans. You see, the Jews and the Samaritans hadn't been on friendly terms for generations. In fact, they hated each other. For the most part, Jews had no contact with Samaritans—even avoiding walking across their territory if they could. Yet Philip, a Jew, went to Samaria and preached the gospel.

When God told Jonah to go to Nineveh and bring a message to them, Jonah went in the opposite direction. Why? Because Jonah hated the Ninevites, who were known for their cruelty and savagery. The Jews and the Ninevites had fought with each other on many occasions.

So when God told Jonah to go to his mortal enemies, the prophet basically said, "No way. I know You. I know the way that You are. You always forgive people. If I go to preach to them, they're going to repent. You will forgive them, and I don't want them to be forgiven. I want them to be judged."

Philip, however, was willing to go. He walked right out of his comfort zone and proclaimed the Good News to the Samaritans. As a result, "there was great joy in that city" (Acts 8:8).

Are you willing to step out of your comfort zone out of a deep concern for men and women outside of Jesus Christ? That's the starting point. And once you start moving in response to that concern and in obedience to the Lord, He can use you mightily.

ALTOGETHER DIFFERENT

What this means is that those who become Christians become new persons.
They are not the same anymore, for the old life is gone. A new life has begun!
(2 Corinthians 5:17, NLT)

The Ethiopian official's conversion in Acts 8 shows us what happens when someone becomes a Christian. He'd been bumping along down the desert road in his chariot, reading a scroll of the prophet Isaiah out loud, and not understanding what the prophet was saying. He knew he was missing something…but he didn't know what it was. But after Philip led him to Christ and baptized him, the Ethiopian "went on his way rejoicing" (Acts 8:39).

When someone becomes a Christian, the change that occurs defies description. Receiving the Lord Jesus as Lord and Savior doesn't improve a man or woman's life by a few degrees, it's a major life transformation. It changes an individual completely. Jesus described it as being born again.

What really happens behind the scenes when a true conversion takes place? According to the Bible, it means turning from darkness to light and from the power of the devil to God.

Many people experience God in a way they can feel profoundly, right away. But not everyone does. Others may have no idea how significant it is when they put their trust in Christ. When I asked Christ to come into my life, I felt no emotion whatsoever. And because of that, I was convinced that God had turned me down. It wasn't until later that I realized the significance of what I had done. It had nothing to do with my emotions.

Conversion isn't about a big emotional rush…it's about becoming a completely new person. You have new desires, new priorities, new hopes and dreams, and down the road, when this life is over and done, you have a new destination… eternal life in heaven. Those thoughts made that Ethiopian official one happy man…and they'll do the same for you and me.

LEARNING TO STAND

You adulterers! Don't you realize that friendship with this world makes you an
enemy of God? I say it again, that if your aim is to enjoy this world,
you can't be a friend of God. (James 4:4, NLT)

A person with conviction is hard to find in our culture today. Very few people will stand up and say, "This is what I believe...." And when you do stand up for your convictions as a Christian, people may laugh. They may even get mad. But I will tell you something else they will probably do. They will probably respect you. Don't be surprised if they give you a hard time in front of their friends. But then when everyone is gone, they may walk up and whisper, "Listen, the next time you are praying, put in a good word for me."

Make your stand, because if you think compromise works, if you think lowering your standards and diluting your biblical principles will help bring someone to Christ, then consider Lot, the nephew of Abraham. Lot lived a compromised life. The problem with Lot was that he wanted a friendship with God, but he also wanted to flirt with this world. But the Bible says, "Friendship with this world makes you an enemy of God" (James 4:4, NLT).

There are many people like Lot today. They want to know God, but there is a weakness in their faith and character. When they're around their Christian friends, they're fine. But the moment they get away from those believers, they immediately drop their standards in order to "blend in." Their faith is dependent on the faith of someone else.

Though there is great benefit in Christians fellowshipping together, we have to learn how to stand on our own, because many times temptation will hit us when we're alone. As it has been said, "Character is what you are when no one is looking."

BALAAM'S ERROR

What sorrow awaits them! For they follow in the footsteps of Cain, who killed his brother. Like Balaam, they deceive people for money. And like Korah, they perish in their rebellion. (Jude 1:11)

A Roman Catholic priest who had heard people confess every imaginable sin and crime—including murder and adultery—said that he had never heard anyone admit to being covetous. Yet coveting actually made God's Big Ten—The Ten Commandments.

The Bible tells the story of Balaam, a prophet who was greedy for gold. He was hired by the Moabites to bring a curse upon Israel. He seemed to be a prophet working for profit. But as Balaam was preparing to carry out his assignment, God spoke to him and said, "You shall not go with them; you shall not curse the people, for they are blessed" (Numbers 22:12).

Balaam ultimately ignored God's command. Then, as he was making his way in disobedience to God, the donkey he was riding refused to go further. So he began to beat the donkey. And when the two reached an impasse, God opened the donkey's mouth, who turned and said to Balaam, "Am I not your donkey on which you have ridden, ever since I became yours, to this day? Was I ever disposed to do this to you?"

The animal had more sense than her master did. The Lord opened Balaam's eyes spiritually, and standing in front of his donkey was an angel with his sword drawn. The angel essentially said, "It's a good thing for you that your donkey stopped. You were about to be killed."

Greed kept Balaam out of harmony with the love of God, and it can do the same with us. We can become so focused on material things that they become more important to us than anything else.

Don't let greed keep you out of harmony with the love of God.

LORD OF ALL

> *"A good tree cannot bear bad fruit, nor can a bad tree bear good fruit. Every tree that does not bear good fruit is cut down and thrown into the fire. Therefore by their fruits you will know them." (Matthew 7:18-20)*

There are people today who say, "I am a Christian," but they're out getting drunk. They say, "I am a Christian," but they're engaging in premarital sex or being unfaithful to their husband or wife. They say, "I am a Christian," but in their business, they lie to people every single day. They distort things. They take money that is not really theirs. There are a lot of people today who *think* they are Christians but are not, because they haven't really changed. They're not living according to what the Bible teaches.

Don't misunderstand me here. I'm not saying that a Christian doesn't sin or make some pretty big mistakes. But I am saying that there is a big difference between a person who slips up, sins, is sorry for it, and wants to change, and a person who lives in continual, willful, habitual sin.

The Bible says that if you live that way, you don't know God. Maybe the reason that some people have never really known the joy of the Lord is that they have never met the basic requirements of salvation. They think being a Christian is just having Jesus along for the ride. They don't realize that He wants to be their Lord and wants to lead and guide them. They don't realize that He has a distinct and unique plan and purpose for their lives.

Jesus Christ wants to be the Lord of every aspect of your life. He wants to be the Lord of your business, your free time, your relationships—the Lord of all.

It's hard for us to yield some things in our lives—old attitudes, old habits, old associations. Yet as the Holy Spirit makes us aware of these one by one, and we surrender them in obedience to God's Word, we will experience more and more heaven-sent peace and joy.

IMMORTALITY

These perishable bodies of ours are not able to live forever. But let me tell you a wonderful secret God has revealed to us. Not all of us will die, but we will all be transformed. (1 Corinthians 15:50-51, NLT)

When he reached the age of seventy, historian Will Durant said, "To live forever would be the greatest curse imaginable."

Will we live forever? The answer is "yes" and "no." Will our bodies live forever? No. Will our bodies cease to exist at one point? Absolutely. But the soul is immortal. Each one of us has a soul. It is the soul that gives each of us uniqueness and personality...and that part of us that will live forever.

Today, many people are searching for immortality, that elusive fountain of youth. Sometimes, it's hard for us to accept the fact that life is passing and death is approaching. One day, you will wake up and realize you have more life behind you than you have in front of you. But the question we should be asking is not, "Can I find immortality?" Rather, it should be, "Where will I spend my immortality?"

If you have put your faith in Jesus Christ and have asked Him to forgive you of your sin, the Bible teaches that you will go immediately into the presence of God in heaven when you die. That is God's promise to you.

But God not only promises life beyond the grave. He also promises life during life, not just an existence, but a life that's worth living. Jesus said, "My purpose is to give life in all its fullness" (John 10:10, NLT).

That is the hope and promise for all Christians. That is why the believer does not have to be afraid to die...or afraid to live.

COURAGE IN HIS PRESENCE

> *But immediately Jesus spoke to them, saying, "Be of good cheer!*
> *It is I; do not be afraid." (Matthew 14:27)*

Jesus had told His disciples to go over to the other side of the Sea of Galilee. They were in their little boat, rowing across, when a huge storm suddenly came out of nowhere (see Matthew 14:22-33). As the storm grew worse, they began to despair of their lives.

Now these men had their sea legs. They were seasoned sailors. But they were despairing of life, which tells us that this was no ordinary storm. It got darker and darker, and suddenly they saw Jesus walking toward them on the water. They were terrified and thought He was a ghost. "But immediately Jesus spoke to them, saying, 'Be of good cheer! It is I; do not be afraid'" (Matthew 14:27). So for the disciples in the storm, His presence brought courage.

One of the most frightening and difficult things in life is having to face your problems alone. We can be a lot braver when we know someone is standing with us. It's good to know that others are standing by us in our hardships. And it's even better to know that God is standing with us. Whatever we're facing, we can be encouraged and find courage because Jesus is there with us.

Keep in mind that Jesus had sent the disciples to the other side. He didn't promise them smooth sailing, but He promised them safe arrival. The Christian life is not one that guarantees we will have smooth sailing. But I can promise you this: it will be exciting. There will be a lot of joy, a lot of blessings, and a lot of changes. And I assure you, you will get to your destination safely.

Be of good cheer. He is with you.

Tuesday

ATTENTION WITH INTENTION

And He said to them, "He who has ears to hear, let him hear!" (Mark 4:9)

It is possible to hear God's Word with our ears, but not with our hearts. Jesus knew that we can often hear without understanding. That is why He would so often say, "He who has ears to hear, let him hear!" If we were to paraphrase that in our modern language, Jesus would be saying, "Pay attention to what I'm saying. Listen carefully to what I am telling you right now." *He who has ears to hear, let him hear....*It is attention with intention.

I do quite a bit of traveling. When I get on a plane and take my seat, I hear the safety message that the flight attendants give before every single flight. They have a long list of information to give out, pointing out the exits and the location of the oxygen masks and life vests. But often I don't pay attention. I may look at a magazine instead. Because I have heard it so many times, I think I don't need to listen.

But what if a few minutes after takeoff the pilot came on the intercom again and said something like this? "We are currently experiencing some technical difficulties, and the flight attendant is going to go through that safety message for you one more time," I can guarantee you that I would be listening. Why? Because my life would depend on it. I would want to know where those exits are. I would want to know what steps I needed to take. I would like to survive in an emergency.

And that is precisely how we should read the Word of God. We need to listen carefully. It is attention with intention, listening with the desire to apply what we have read to our own daily situations, because so much depends on that infusion of wisdom and life. Probably more than we'll ever know.

QUICK TO LISTEN, SLOW TO SPEAK

*Whoever has no rule over his own spirit is like a city
broken down, without walls. (Proverbs 25:28)*

In this day of instant information, we can get our news so fast that we
don't have to wait for the evening news anymore. We don't have to wait
for the newspaper. We can go out on the Internet and get our news in real
time.

I think this makes it hard for us to slow down and listen, especially to
God. Many of us are like Martha in Luke's Gospel, running around in our
little self-made circles of activity, instead of calmly sitting at His feet and
listening like Mary did.

But James 1:19 tells us, "So then, my beloved brethren, let every man
be swift to hear, slow to speak, slow to wrath." We ought to post that verse
where we can see it every day. How different our lives would be if we heeded
its admonition.

James tells us we should be swift to listen, but we also should be slow to
speak. How many times have you blurted out something, only to regret it
the moment it left your lips? Jesus said, "But I say to you that for every idle
word men may speak, they will give account of it in the day of judgment.
For by your words you will be justified, and by your words you will be
condemned" (Matthew 12:36-37).

We should be slow to anger. How easy it is to rationalize our outbursts
of rage (especially when we are driving). But Proverbs 29:11, (NLT) says, "A
fool gives full vent to anger, but a wise person quietly holds it back."

How much better our lives and our witness would be if we were swift
to hear, slow to speak, and slow to wrath!

A MILLSTONE OR A MILESTONE?

But he who looks into the perfect law of liberty and continues in it, and is not a forgetful hearer but a doer of the work, this one will be blessed in what he does. (James 1:25)

Some people see the Christian life as rules and regulations and hardships, but God's law is the law of *liberty*...which means that it's not a list of do's and don'ts, but rather wills and won'ts. Unless God's Word has made a change in our lives, it hasn't really entered our lives. God's Word becomes a millstone if we don't make it a milestone. In James 1, we find three tests that can help us determine whether we are truly spiritual.

First, a truly spiritual person will control his or her tongue (see verses 19-20). We may take pride in the fact that we aren't immoral or violent, but we can inflict pain on others by wounding them with our words. David wrote, "I will guard my ways, lest I sin with my tongue; I will restrain my mouth with a muzzle, while the wicked are before me" (Psalm 39:1).

Second, a truly spiritual person will care about others (James 1:27). Jesus said that when we give a drink to strangers, invite them into our homes, clothe them, or visit them when they are sick or in prison, we are doing it for Him and even to Him (see Matthew 25:34-40).

Third, a truly spiritual person will not be polluted by the world (James 1:27). As 1 John 2:16 says, "For all that is in the world—the lust of the flesh, the lust of the eyes, and the pride of life—is not of the Father but is of the world." We want to keep ourselves from being corrupted by this world.

If we are truly spiritual men and women, then our good works will be clearly evident.

JUDGE NOT?

> *For what have I to do with judging those also who are outside? Do you not judge those who are inside? But those who are outside God judges. Therefore "put away from yourselves the evil person." (1 Corinthians 5:12-13)*

*J*udge not, lest you be judged....We've all heard it. It's in the Bible, in Matthew 7:1, where Jesus said, "Judge not, that you be not judged." But let's understand these words in their proper context. A better translation of the statement would be, "Condemn not, that you be not condemned." In other words, God is the final judge. He decides who gets into heaven and who does not. Greg Laurie doesn't decide that. You don't decide that. No one else decides that. We are not to condemn, meaning to pass final judgment.

But we are to judge, in the sense of making evaluations—even corrections when necessary—regarding fellow believers. Paul addresses this very subject in 1 Corinthians 5:

"I wrote to you in my epistle not to keep company with sexually immoral people. Yet I certainly did not mean with the sexually immoral people of this world, or with the covetous, or extortioners, or idolaters, since then you would need to go out of the world....For what have I to do with judging those also who are outside? Do you not judge those who are inside?" (verses 9-10, 12).

Paul was saying that it is our job to judge those inside the church. But a lot of believers ignore this. They say, "Oh, no. Just be loving." But I would respond that they don't really know what love is. Love cares enough to confront.

We are so into loving everyone—not even understanding what the word means— that we have lost our sense of discernment in standing up for what is right. When we do take such a stand, we should do it with compassion, concern, and humility. But sometimes love means making the hard choice, and taking the hard stand.

THE VOICE OF PEACE

"For you shall go out with joy, and be led out with peace...." (Isaiah 55:12)

Not only does God speak to us through His Word, and not only does He speak to us through people and circumstances, but God also speaks to us through His peace. Colossians says, "Let the peace of God rule in your hearts, to which also you were called in one body; and be thankful" (3:15). Another way to translate that verse is, "Let God's peace act as an umpire in your lives, settling with finality all matters that arise."

God's peace can settle with finality what you should do. Here's how it works. Maybe you think that something is the will of God. The circumstances of the situation have fallen into place. You begin to proceed, but then you have a complete lack of peace. Something inside of you is saying, "Don't do it."

The Old Testament tells the story of a clever group of individuals known as Gibeonites, who lived in Canaan. God had instructed Joshua not to make any deals with the inhabitants of the land. So the Gibeonites put on old shoes and clothes and pretended as though they had come from a distant country. They told Joshua they had come to enter into an agreement with him. Joshua unknowingly struck a deal with his enemies because he failed to consult the Lord.

Things can look good outwardly. Everything can seem right. Be careful! Learn to listen to that still, small voice. Learn to pay attention to that peace, or lack of it, in your life because that is one of the ways God will lead you. When you're in the will of God, you will have His peace.

And there is nothing in all of life as wonderful as that.

BEAUTY FOR ASHES

> *To all who mourn in Israel, he will give a crown of beauty for ashes, a joyous blessing instead of mourning, festive praise instead of despair.*
> *(Isaiah 61:3, NLT)*

I have been amazed at the testimonies of some people when they tell me the way they used to be. I've looked at them and thought, *There is no way they used to be that way.* Jesus Christ has so radically changed them.

Isaiah 61:3-4 (NLT) promises that God "will give a crown of beauty for ashes, a joyous blessing instead of mourning, festive praise instead of despair. In their righteousness, they will be like great oaks that the Lord has planted for his own glory. They will rebuild the ancient ruins, repairing cities destroyed long ago...."

For the person who has made a mess of his or her life—a pile of ashes, so to speak—God says, "I will bring beauty." For those who mourn because of the wrongs they have done and the sins they have committed, God says, "I will bring joy out of it."

Only God can take a tangled mess of a life, turn it around, and transform it in such a way that you wouldn't even know that individual used to be a very different person. Not only that, but such a transformation gives hope to others who may still despair over the condition of their lives.

If you come to Christ and say, "Lord, here I am. Forgive me of my sin," He can transform you and change you. He can take your mistakes and your sins, turn them around, and even use them for His glory. When you commit your life to Christ, putting the broken, stained, twisted pieces into His hand, He will transform it into a thing of beauty.

THE SECRET OF LIVING

*The secret of the Lord is with those who fear Him, and He
will show them His covenant. (Psalm 25:14)*

Have you ever been semi-listening in on someone's conversation? Not intentionally, of course, because you would never do that. Maybe you were in a restaurant and your table was right next to someone else's. And then (even though you didn't mean to hear) someone said, "What I'm about to tell you now is a secret. I need you to hold this in complete confidence…."

What did you do? Did you put your hands over your ears? No. If you're like most people, you listened more carefully. We all love to hear secrets! We all want to know the inside story. Even if someone is a complete stranger, we're still interested and intrigued by what his or her secret might be.

God has a secret that He wants to declare to you. The Bible says, "The secret of the Lord is with those who fear Him" (Psalm 25:14). In many ways, this isn't really a secret, because it is plainly declared in Scripture. Unfortunately, because so few people have opened up the Bible to see what it says, they have missed out.

This is the secret of making life more full and meaningful. It is a secret that can help you avoid untold misery and heartache. You might even say it's the secret of living. Solomon said much the same in the concluding chapter of Ecclesiastes: "Let us hear the conclusion of the whole matter: Fear God and keep His commandments, for this is man's all" (Ecclesiastes 12:13)

That's what it all comes down to. A deep reverence for God and His Word, and a desire to walk that particular path He has marked out for your life.

FOR OUR GOOD

> *For this is the love of God, that we keep His commandments.*
> *And His commandments are not burdensome. (1 John 5:3)*

A lot of us don't like commandments, because we see them as restrictive. CNN founder Ted Turner once made this statement about the Ten Commandments: "We're living with outmoded rules.... Today, the commandments wouldn't go over. Nobody around likes to be commanded."

I agree with Turner that people don't like to be commanded. But if we want to live lives that are full, we have to recognize there is structure, there are parameters, and there are absolutes.

It would be like someone saying, "I don't like traffic laws. I'm not into stoplights. I don't believe in speed zones. And by the way, I think I should be able to drive on whatever side of the road I feel like driving on. I want my freedom." Now there's a freedom that might be…short lived! Those traffic laws and rules of the road are there for our protection. Those stoplights and traffic lanes are there so we can get to where we need to go.

The Bible does indeed command us not to do certain things or act in certain ways. But it also tells us what we ought to do—what will bless our lives and bring grace and goodness into the lives of others. When it tells us to stay away from one thing, it tells us to do another thing in its place.

For example, the Bible says, "And do not be drunk with wine" (Ephesians 5:18). There is the don't. But here is the do: "But be filled with the Spirit, speaking to one another in psalms and hymns and spiritual songs, singing and making melody in your heart to the Lord" (verses 18-19). God says, "Don't do this, but do this instead."

God's plan is always better. Sure, He tells us to stay away from certain things. But it's for our own good. And as the apostle John reminds us in today's opening verse…God's commands are not burdensome. And the pleasure and benefit that flows from walking in His love makes the requirements seem even lighter still.

Thursday

COUNTING THE COST

"And whoever does not bear his cross and come after Me cannot be My disciple. For which of you, intending to build a tower, does not sit down first and count the cost, whether he has enough to finish it...." (Luke 14:27-28)

When Jesus was in Jerusalem during the Passover, John's Gospel tells us that many believed in His name after they saw the signs He did. But Jesus did not entrust himself to them, because "He knew all men, and had no need that anyone should testify of man, for He knew what was in man" (John 2:24-25).

To put it simply, many believed in Him, but He did not believe in them. Many believed in Him, but their faith was superficial. It was shallow. It was based on the moment, not on a real commitment. For this reason, Christ did not commit Himself to them.

There are many people who say they want to follow Jesus. And that's good. But that commitment will be challenged. We must decide to follow Jesus not because our best friend is, not because our boyfriend or girlfriend is, not because our parents are, but because we have chosen in our own heart of hearts to follow Christ.

Many of us can get caught up in the moment. It's like watching an Olympic medal ceremony. We see someone representing their nation standing up on that pedestal. As the gold medal is placed around the athlete's neck and the flag of his or her country is raised while the national anthem plays, we say, "I want to be an Olympic athlete. That is what I want to do." But do we realize the hours, days, months, and years these athletes dedicate to one competition?

We get excited about the medal ceremonies. But are we willing to go through the training? Are we willing to count the cost? Is our commitment to Him and Him alone? Are we willing to be real followers of Jesus?

TOO BUSY TO SERVE?

*Then another of His disciples said to Him, "Lord, let me first go and bury my
father." But Jesus said to him, "Follow Me, and let the dead
bury their own dead." (Matthew 8:21-22)*

Everyone who serves the Lord is busy. We all have a long list of
things to accomplish. But I thank God for every volunteer in the
ministries that we so often take for granted. When you go to church, there
are people who will help you find a seat, minister to your children, and
maybe even show you where to park. All of these people are volunteers.
And they are doing these things because they love Jesus.

Maybe the Lord has spoken to you about getting involved in a ministry.
And maybe you have been resistant, saying, "This is a busy season of life. I
have other things to do."

That's what one man said when Jesus called him to service. He
responded, "Lord, let me first go and bury my father" (Matthew 8:21).
Now, this man's father was not actually dead. What he was actually
employing here was a Near Eastern figure of speech, a common expression
that described a son's responsibility to help his father in the family business
until the father died and the inheritance was distributed. In other words,
this man was saying, "Lord, not now. I'll do it later. I would like to go and
preach the kingdom, but I'm busy right now."

The same can happen to us. God might speak to our hearts about
serving Him more. And we respond, "Lord, I love You. I check in every
Sunday. I put a little something in the offering. But I just don't have time
to go out and do that extra stuff."

If you haven't discovered the joy of serving God, then frankly, you're
missing out! There is something for every one of us to accomplish in His
service. The One who created you and put you together knows more about
what fulfills your life than anyone in this whole wide world...even yourself.

CREATING FRICTION

"Do not think that I came to bring peace on Earth. I did not come to bring peace but a sword." (Matthew 10:34)

Following Jesus Christ is the best life possible on Planet Earth... but it doesn't mean that it will be friction-free. Jesus Himself made a very radical statement on this subject: "...For I have come to 'set a man against his father, a daughter against her mother, and a daughter-in-law against her mother-in-law'; and 'a man's enemies will be those of his own household'" (Matthew 10:35-36).

Wow. We may think the Lord came to bring harmony so we can all "just get along." Ultimately, that is true. But temporarily, there may be some division and opposition ahead of us. As a Christian, your life will create friction. People will laugh at you or even get upset with you. When they're telling a dirty joke and you walk in just as they're getting to the punch line, you spoil all their fun, because the joke will need to be continued later.

You bring friction, but it is a *good* friction, because it reminds unbelievers of their lack of relationship with God. Your commitment to Jesus Christ makes them uncomfortable, and sometimes...they'd rather not have you around. Even so, that temporary friction can bring about the ultimate unity when the unbelievers in your life put their faith in Jesus Christ.

Jesus was saying, "Do you think that I have come to bring peace on Earth? No, I'm telling you that I have come to bring strife and division." Sometimes this means saying goodbye to friends. It means saying goodbye to things that would hold you back. It means no longer trying to agree with everyone, with a foot in both worlds.

The truth is, straddling a fence is one of the most uncomfortable positions I can think of.

THE DEITY OF JESUS

That at the name of Jesus every knee should bow, of those in heaven, and of those on Earth, and of those under the Earth, and that every tongue should confess that Jesus Christ is Lord, to the glory of God the Father.
(Philippians 2:10-11)

There are people today who say that Jesus never claimed to be God; it is just something people dreamed up. But that is a lie. Jesus indeed claimed to be God. And any group who says that Jesus is not God is not a Christian group, no matter how big their Bibles may be or how much they might look like Christians.

Jesus made clear claims to deity. He said, "For if you do not believe that I am He, you will die in your sins" (John 8:24). When Moses saw the burning bush and walked up to it, he heard a voice speaking to him that said, "Do not draw near this place. Take your sandals off your feet, for the place where you stand is holy ground....I am the God of your father—the God of Abraham, the God of Isaac, and the God of Jacob" (Exodus 3:5, 6). It was a claim to deity. So when Jesus said, "Unless you believe that I am He, you will die in your sins," it means that Jesus claimed to be God.

To suggest that Jesus never claimed to be God is ludicrous. We know, for instance, that on many occasions He accepted worship, something absolutely reserved for God alone. He said to Satan during the temptation in the wilderness, "'You shall worship the Lord your God, and Him only you shall serve'" (Matthew 4:10). Yet on other occasions, Jesus personally accepted worship.

When Thomas saw the risen Lord, he fell down before Him and said, "My Lord and my God!" (John 20:28). Jesus accepted that, because He is indeed the Lord and God.

IS THERE A CATFISH
IN YOUR TANK?

Do not marvel, my brethren, if the world hates you. (1 John 3:13)

I heard a story about some fish suppliers who were having problems shipping codfish from the East Coast. By the time the fish reached the West coast, they were spoiled. They froze them, but by the time the fish arrived, they were mushy. So the seafood company decided to send them alive…but the fish arrived dead. On their third try, they once more shipped the fish alive, but with one difference. They included a catfish in each tank. You see, the catfish is the natural enemy of the codfish. By the time the codfish arrived, they were alive and well, because they had spent their trip fleeing the catfish.

Could it be that God in His wisdom has put a catfish in your tank to keep you alive and well spiritually? Maybe there's a person at work who always has eight hardball questions for you every Monday morning regarding spiritual things. Maybe it's that neighbor who constantly gives you a hard time about your faith in Jesus. Maybe it's a spouse or family member who doesn't believe. And you begin to wonder, "Why is this happening to me?"

It's just that catfish in your life…keeping you spiritually alert and on your toes.

Shortly before His crucifixion, Jesus told the disciples, "If you were of the world, the world would love its own. Yet because you are not of the world, but I chose you out of the world, therefore the world hates you" (John 15:19).

God will allow persecution in the life of the believer. If you're experiencing persecution—whether subtle or out front and in the open—here are two things to remember:

1. Persecution confirms that you are a child of God.
2. Persecution causes you to cling closer to Jesus.

When you endure persecution for your faith, remember that this world is not your home.

As far as I know, there are no catfish in heaven.

JUST OUR NATURE

But each one is tempted when he is drawn away by his own desires and enticed.
(James 1:14)

We all know what it's like to be tempted. But where does temptation come from?

It does not come from God.

James 1:13-14 says, "Let no one say when he is tempted, 'I am tempted by God'; for God cannot be tempted by evil, nor does He Himself tempt anyone. But each one is tempted when he is drawn away by his own desires and enticed." We play a key role in our own temptation.

It is like the scorpion who wanted to cross a pond. Scorpions can't swim, of course, so he needed a ride. He walked up to a rather unsuspecting turtle and said, "I was wondering if you might give me a lift across this little pond?"

The turtle said, "Are you joking? You will sting me, and we will both drown."

The scorpion said, "My dear turtle, if I were to sting you, I would go down with you. Where would the logic be in that?"

As they made their way across the little pond, however, the scorpion pulled out his stinger and gave the turtle a mighty sting. As they both sank to the bottom, the turtle turned to the scorpion and said, "There was no logic in stinging me. Why did you do it?"

The scorpion replied, "It has nothing to do with logic. It's just my nature."

This is a good point. When we give in to temptation, it has nothing to do with logic. It's just our nature. We like to say, "The devil made me do it" or "Circumstances overwhelmed me" or "I couldn't control myself." But in reality, it's just our sinful nature.

Let's not give in to the enticement of our own desires. As the Scripture says, "Rather, clothe yourselves with the Lord Jesus Christ, and do not think about how to gratify the desires of the sinful nature" (Romans 13:14, NIV).

ENEMY STRATEGIES

*Teach me to do your will, for you are my God; may your good Spirit
lead me on level ground. (Psalm 143:10, NIV)*

On a trip to Alaska some years ago, I went fishing for king salmon. In one spot, our group used bright orange salmon eggs as bait. But in another place, we used another type of lure.

In the same way, the devil uses different kinds of bait, different lures to pull us in. And he works with two close allies in our temptation: the world and the flesh. Every temptation falls under one of three categories: the world, the flesh, and the devil. The Bible says, "For all that is in the world— the lust of the flesh, the lust of the eyes, and the pride of life—is not of the Father but is of the world" (1 John 2:16).

When Eve was tempted by the devil at the tree of the knowledge of good and evil, she faced all these temptations. "So when the woman saw that the tree was *good for food*, that it was *pleasant to the eyes*, and a tree *desirable to make one wise*, she took of its fruit and ate. She also gave to her husband with her, and he ate" (Genesis 3:6, emphasis mine).

The lust of the flesh is the gratification of physical desires. Eve saw that the tree was good for food. The lust of the eyes is mental temptation; Eve saw that it was pleasant to the eyes. The pride of life is a craving for honor; Eve took note that it was desirable to make one wise.

It's good to recognize that these are the temptation strategies, or bait, the enemy uses in our lives. It helps to know what our enemy is up to, because then we can avoid his lures…and swim right by every disguised hook.

AN OPPORTUNE TIME

Now when the devil had ended every temptation, he departed
from Him until an opportune time. (Luke 4:13)

In a broad sense, temptation can come to us at any time. Of course, it often happens after times of great blessing. Jesus was tested, or tempted, in the wilderness for 40 days and nights, right after His baptism in the Jordan River when the Spirit of God came upon Him in the form of a dove. After the dove came the devil. After the blessing came the attack. Often after great times of blessing, the enemy will be there, wanting to rob us of what God has done.

Maybe you have experienced a great time of blessing in your life recently. Enjoy it, but keep your guard up. The enemy will be there. He will attack you, and he will tempt you. He waits for the opportune time to confront us, and we are often the most vulnerable when we think we are the strongest.

If you think that weak believers had better be careful, then I have a thought for you: Strong believers had better be careful, too. The Bible says, "Therefore let him who thinks he stands take heed lest he fall" (1 Corinthians 10:12).

Many times temptation can come when we're relaxing. Take David for example. He was tempted when he was up on the rooftop taking a little rest and relaxation, at the time when kings usually go out to battle. He noticed the beautiful Bathsheba as she was bathing on her rooftop, he lowered his guard, and we know the rest of that story.

There is no rest from the spiritual battle. Always keep your guard up, because the moment you think, *It won't hit me here,* that is where it will hit you. The enemy is just waiting. He is looking for an opportunity. So keep your armor on.

FOCUSED ATTACKS

"And these are the ones by the wayside where the word is sown. When they hear, Satan comes immediately and takes away the word that was sown in their hearts." (Mark 4:15)

Temptation comes to everyone, but the enemy focuses many of his attacks on those who are young in the faith—and those who are making a difference in the kingdom.

Right after we make a decision to follow Jesus Christ, the devil shows up, tempting us to doubt our own salvation. He whispers in our ears, "You think Christ really came into your life? Are you crazy?" This is a tactic the enemy keeps recycling again and again. (And why not? He'll use it as long as it works!)

The Bible warns us that when we are young in the faith, we are especially vulnerable. We see in the parable of the sower that young believers are immediately attacked. Jesus said, "And these are the ones by the wayside where the word is sown. When they hear, Satan comes immediately and takes away the word that was sown in their hearts" (Mark 4:15). The evil one is there to pounce upon those who are young in the faith.

Temptation also comes to those who are making a difference in the kingdom of God. First of all, Satan doesn't want you to come to Christ. But once you have made that commitment, his next strategy is to immobilize you, to get you to compromise yourself and be ineffective. He doesn't want you to be a threat to his kingdom.

If you want to make a difference, if you want to reach people who don't know the Lord, then don't expect a standing ovation in hell. The enemy won't take it lightly. He will attack you. You had better expect it and brace yourself for it. And while you're at it, pray for other believers, whether new in the faith or already making a difference.

BETWEEN TWO WORLDS

And I, brethren, could not speak to you as to spiritual men, but as to men of flesh, as to infants in Christ. (1 Corinthians 3:1, NASB)

The Bible mentions a category of Christians who are described as "fleshly," or "carnal." These are people in an arrested state of spiritual development. They have never really grown up. They're caught between two worlds: they have too much of the Lord to be happy in the world, but too much of the world to be happy in the Lord. They're the most miserable people around.

Many of us realize that this world doesn't have the answers and can't be trusted. But at the same time, we don't trust God either. We haven't made a stand.

The time has come to say, "I believe in Jesus Christ...*period*." It's time to stand for our principles and not just blend into the woodwork.

So often in our attempts to gain credibility, we lose our integrity. In our attempts to relate to people, we lose any power we will have in relating to them, because we have compromised our principles.

The Bible gives us many examples of people who stood up for what was right at the risk of losing something important, even their lives. One such person was Daniel, who held a position of great influence in Nebuchadnezzar's court. Even so, he would not compromise his principles.

Maybe you're afraid to stand up for Jesus Christ. You're afraid that it could hurt your career, or a relationship or something else. But there comes a moment when we have to stand for what we know is true. You may be criticized, and might even lose something important to you. But whatever you lose, God will make it up to you...a thousand times over. He will bless you for standing for what is right.

IT'S ALL RELATIVE

But what things were gain to me, these I have counted loss for Christ.
(Philippians 3:7)

When you become a Christian, one of the more notable changes is that you will give up many of the things you once did. Of course, this depends on your lifestyle prior to your conversion. But for many of us, a dramatic change will take place.

I have heard people share their stories of how they came to Christ and the great sacrifices they made to follow Him, saying things like, "I had a great life...I went to parties...I had so much fun...But I gave it all up for Jesus Christ, hallelujah! I left it all for the glory of God!"

When I hear statements like that, I feel like asking, "What in the world are you talking about? *You gave it all up?* What did you give up?"

If they were to look at those things honestly and realistically, they would come to the same conclusion that Paul did. He said, "But what things were gain to me, these I have counted loss for Christ. Yet indeed I also count all things loss for the excellence of the knowledge of Christ Jesus my Lord..." (Philippians 3:7-8).

Paul was saying that the stuff that used to be so important, the stuff he once valued so highly, meant *nothing* to him now in comparison with the awesome privilege and value of belonging to Jesus.

We might do well to bring certain activities or habits in our lives under the same scrutiny. It's a good idea to periodically ask ourselves, "Is this thing that I am doing slowing me down or speeding me along in my walk with God? Is it building me up spiritually or is it tearing me down?"

The conclusion has to be the same: If anything is keeping you from an intimate, open-hearted relationship with God through Jesus Christ, whatever that thing may be, you must count it as a *loss*.

THE ULTIMATE PRIZE

Therefore we also, since we are surrounded by so great a cloud of witnesses, let us lay aside every weight, and the sin which so easily ensnares us, and let us run with endurance the race that is set before us. (Hebrews 12:1)

When I was a kid, I had all kinds of ribbons on my walls for races I had run, but not one of them was blue. Not one of them had the words "first place." They were all purple. Purple represented "honorable mention." An honorable mention is not first, second, third, or fourth place. It means "also ran." In other words, "We don't want him to feel bad, so we'll give him a purple ribbon."

Of course, everyone wants first place. Everyone wants to win the gold medal. That's where the prestige is.

But let me say this. I am running this race of life, and the Bible tells me that one day in heaven there will be a reward waiting for me. It won't be based on how much I have done or how much recognition I have gained in the course of my life. It will be based on how faithful I was to what God called me to do. The same is true for you. Your reward will be based on how faithful you are to the calling you have received from God.

Let me also say that I am not running this race for the reward. Nor am I running it for other people or to score points. I am running this race for Jesus. He is the One we all should be running for.

The apostle Paul presents the same principle in Philippians 3:10: "That I may know Him and the power of His resurrection, and the fellowship of His sufferings, being conformed to His death...." Paul was saying, "This is why I am doing it—my purpose for running this race is to know Jesus Christ." That is what mattered to him. And that is what should matter to us.

Thursday

ONE THING

One thing I have desired of the Lord, that will I seek: that I may dwell in the house of the Lord all the days of my life, to behold the beauty of the Lord, and to inquire in His temple. (Psalm 27:4)

David wrote, "*One thing* I have desired of the Lord, that will I seek…." He was saying that one thing that really excited him was spending time in the presence of God.

Mary knew this one thing, too, when Jesus came to visit her and her sister Martha in the little village of Bethany. She sat down at His feet, absolutely riveted by everything He had to say.

Martha, a hardworking woman, wanted to impress the Lord with the fine meal she was preparing. That is an understandable thing if you had a guest like Jesus. Can you imagine Jesus showing up at your house? You would want to offer Him your best, right? You wouldn't give Him a microwave dinner or reheated food from last night. You would want to prepare a special meal.

As Martha was working away, she undoubtedly kept looking for Mary. *Where is Mary? I can't believe she's not in here.* Finally in frustration, she came out—probably with her hands on her hips—and said, "Lord, do You not care that my sister has left me to serve alone? Therefore tell her to help me."

Jesus replied, "Martha, Martha, you are worried and troubled about many things. But one thing is needed, and Mary has chosen that good part, which will not be taken away from her" (Luke 10:41-42).

Mary figured out one thing, and that was the importance of sitting at Jesus' feet. What is your "one thing"?

FORGET THE PAST

*Not that I have already obtained all this, or have already been made perfect,
but I press on to take hold of that for which Christ Jesus took hold of me.
Brothers, I do not consider myself yet to have taken hold of it. But one thing I
do: Forgetting what is behind and straining toward what is ahead, I press on
toward the goal to win the prize for which God has called me
heavenward in Christ Jesus. (Philippians 3:14, NIV)*

Everyone who has run a race knows that you can break your stride by looking over your shoulder to check out how your opponents are doing. Many races have been lost when the leader looked back. When you see that finish line, that's the time to give it everything you've got… because sometimes it's mere inches that separate one runner from another. You must stay focused.

This is the idea behind Paul's statement in Philippians 3:13. The apostle was saying, "Don't look back. Don't look behind you."

When God promises, "I, even I, am He who blots out your transgressions for My own sake; and I will not remember your sins" (Isaiah 43:25), He is not predicting a lapse in His memory. God is saying. "I will no longer hold your sin against you, because my Son has paid for it at the cross."

Therefore, we need to do what God does: forget our past. Yes, we certainly need to learn from our mistakes and remember some of the bitter lessons we have learned. But we no longer need to be *controlled* by our past.

That is what Paul meant by "forgetting what is behind…." Think about the horrible things Paul had done. He shared responsibility for the death of Stephen, and had to carry that in his conscience until his final day. He knew that he was responsible for terrible deeds. But he was able to put his past in the past. And we need to do the same.

So Far to Go

I don't mean to say I am perfect. I haven't learned all I should even yet, but I keep working toward that day when I will finally be all that Christ saved me for and wants me to be. (Philippians 3:12, TLB)

There is a sign along an airport runway that says, "Keep moving. If you stop, you are in danger and a danger to those who are flying." The same could be said of Christians. We always need to keep moving forward spiritually. We cannot rest on our laurels.

Even the apostle Paul said he could not live off his past experiences. He needed to maintain his forward momentum. Here was one of the greatest Christians of all time saying that he still didn't have the Christian life wired. He was saying, "I haven't arrived at some higher supernatural plane, unattainable to other believers. I have so far to go."

If anybody ever knew God, it was the apostle Paul. He had led countless people to faith. He had established churches. He had written much of our New Testament. Yet he said of himself that he had so much to learn and so far to go.

Imagine Paul sitting around with a group of Christians. One person might say, "God inspired me to say something to someone today. It was wonderful." Another might say, "I heard God speak to my heart once."

Paul could say, "God gave me inspired letters to write that will make up half the Bible. Also, I've actually died and gone to heaven, and then I was sent back to Earth again."

Who could top that? If anyone could boast, it was Paul. Yet he did not boast. He said, "It's been a long road and a bumpy road, and I've still got a long ways to go."

GOD'S ROAD CREW

While Annas and Caiaphas were high priests, the word of God came to John the
son of Zacharias in the wilderness. And he went into all the region around the
Jordan, preaching a baptism of repentance for the remission of sins.
(Luke 3:2-3)

Sometimes people on road crews aren't very popular. I appreciate
the work these crews do, but it seems they always do it at the worst
time...like during rush hour. What I have never understood is why they
have to close lanes miles before the work site. They block off the entire freeway while they're way over on the other side doing their work. Some people
get rather angry with them.

John the Baptist was on God's road crew. The Bible describes him as
"The voice of one crying in the wilderness: 'Prepare the way of the Lord;
make His paths straight. Every valley shall be filled and every mountain and
hill brought low; the crooked places shall be made straight and the rough
ways smooth'" (Luke 3:4-5).

The word for "crying" could also be translated "howling." John was
wasn't known for subtlety. He had a task to perform, and he realized that he
had a relatively short period of time to do it. His job was much like that of a
herald who went ahead of a royal procession.

John was there to prepare the way for the Lord. He was on God's road
crew, leveling the mountains, bringing up the low places. It was his task
to prepare the nation for the Messiah and then to present the Messiah to
them—and he wasn't very popular for it.

In a sense, that is our job as Christians as well. We need to realize that
like John, our time is limited. We have to make every moment and every
opportunity count. By our words, our actions, and our example, we prepare
the way for God to work in the hearts of men and women. It may mean we
won't win any popularity contests along the way, but there's no better job in
all the world than being on the Lord's full-time road crew.

TRUE REPENTANCE

"Therefore bear fruits worthy of repentance, and do not begin to say to yourselves, 'We have Abraham as our father.' For I say to you that God is able to raise up children to Abraham from these stones." (Luke 3:8)

What do you think of when you hear the word "repent"? Maybe you think of someone wearing a sandwich board with flames on it, who is yelling, "Repent!" It's a word we don't hear very much today.

You might be surprised to know that the first word to fall from the lips of Jesus Christ after He began His public ministry was "repent" (see Matthew 4:17).

The word "repent" means more than mere regret or sorrow. You can be sorry for something and not be repentant. You can feel regret over a certain sin, especially if you reap the consequences of it. The person who gets caught in a lie is sorry. The criminal who gets caught is sorry. But the question is whether that sorrow leads to change. It might not. The liar might just be more careful. The criminal may plot his next crime with more foresight. There are people who are sorry for reaping the consequences of what they have done, but they have never made any changes in their lives.

Real sorrow, according to the Bible, will lead to repentance and change. John the Baptist preached to the multitudes, "Therefore bear fruits worthy of repentance..." (Luke 3:8). Many people have never really repented of their sins. They have never really brought forth fruit in keeping with repentance. But this is absolutely necessary if you want to be forgiven of your sin. Recognition of personal sin is always the first step in receiving forgiveness.

It's important to remember, however, that repentance and sorrow over our sins are means to an end, meant to take us from one circumstance of life to another. God doesn't want us to walk in constant sorrow. He wants us to change the direction that was bringing harm to our lives and walk under His blessing and protection.

A Chip off the Rock

For whom He foreknew, He also predestined to be conformed to the image of His Son, that He might be the firstborn among many brethren. (Romans 8:29)

W hen two people have been married a while, they start becoming like each other. This has happened with my wife and me. We know each other so well that I can start a sentence, and she can finish it. She knows what I'm thinking even when I'm not saying it. I am just amazed at her intuition. But I can read her as well. Having been married for more than three decades now, we've spent a long time together.

This is even more the case when we have been spending time with Jesus Christ. We become like Him, "a chip off of the ol' Rock," we might say. This is God's ultimate plan for every Christian—to make us like Jesus.

We see this in the life of Peter. He was burned by the enemy's fire when he denied the Lord. But when touched with fire at Pentecost, he became the new-and-improved Peter. The same thing that happened to him can happen to you. The same power is available to every believer. That's because when someone has been with Jesus—and by that I mean when they spend time in the Lord's presence and spend time growing spiritually—they will become more like Him.

Before you ever made your appearance on Earth, God chose you. God knew there would come a day when you would put your faith in Him, and He chose you before you chose Him. And what is His goal for you? His goal is that you might become like Jesus.

GENUINE SALVATION

"Enter by the narrow gate; for wide is the gate and broad is the way that leads to destruction, and there are many who go in by it. Because narrow is the gate and difficult is the way which leads to life, and there are few who find it."
(Matthew 7:13-14)

Many people today have essentially believed a watered-down gospel that deletes the message of repentance. They believe in an all-caring, nonjudgmental God who requires no repentance or a change in their lifestyle. They will say things like, "I believe in Jesus Christ, but my God is not judgmental. My God would never send a person to hell."

The thing is, you can't have it both ways. You can't make up your Christian faith as you go.

There are many people, even in the church, who hold to a watered-down belief. This diluted gospel may be the most dangerous plague facing the church today, because it gives a sense of false assurance to the person who believes it.

The Bible speaks of false prophets who give false assurance. In Jeremiah 6:14, God says, "They have also healed the hurt of My people slightly, saying, 'Peace, peace!' when there is no peace."

It would be like going to the doctor when you're having a heart attack, and having the doctor tell you, "Oh, you're fine. You're being so dramatic! You'll be okay. Just live with it."

There are ministers today who say, "God loves you and everything is fine. You can do whatever you want and live however you please. Let's just love one another and have a great time."

But that is a false gospel. Yes, God loves us. Yes, God receives any person who comes to Him. But He asks us to repent, to turn from our sins. If we are not willing to do so, then we are not experiencing biblical faith. As a result, we won't receive what the Bible describes as genuine salvation.

DIVINE DISCIPLINE

God blesses those who patiently endure testing and temptation. Afterward they will receive the crown of life that God has promised to those who love him.
(James 1:12, NLT)

W hy does God bring tests into our lives? Is it because He wants to give us a hard time or embarrass us? No. It's because God wants us to *learn*. He wants us to mature spiritually, learning to trust Him even when we don't understand Him. He wants us to be patient with Him, even when He doesn't work according to our schedules.

The Bible says, "For whom the Lord loves He chastens...." (Hebrews 12:6). Although God will discipline you when necessary, the word *chasten* also means "to train." God wants to teach you, to grow you. He loves you so much that He will bring a series of tests and lessons into your life to whip you into shape. Those very tests, difficulties, and obstacles can all be indications of God's love for you.

When you start to cross the line and do something you shouldn't, God's Holy Spirit will be there to convict you. When you try to do something that you know is wrong and God puts an obstacle in your path, it's because He loves you.

The times you should be concerned about are when you can do things that you know are wrong and feel no remorse. But when you know something is wrong and struggle with it, that's a sign you are a child of God and He loves you enough to show you when you're going astray. Instead of seeing God's discipline as an intrusion in your life, welcome it. And be thankful He is looking out for you.

RESISTING TEMPTATION

Your word I have hidden in my heart, that I might not sin against You.
(Psalm 119:11)

Not only do many of us in the United States have more than one Bible, but we have them in every color and every translation. The question is do we read them? We need to read God's Word and commit it to memory. While it's a good idea to carry the Bible in your briefcase or purse, the best place to carry the Bible is in your heart.

I would be embarrassed to admit how many dumb songs I know. I haven't even attempted to memorize them—I've just heard them so many times that they simply get into my brain. We should be using our memory banks for the memorization of Scripture. That way, when the enemy attacks, we'll have the Word of God to call upon and to give us the strength that we need.

After all, one of the best tools to use when temptation comes knocking at our door is the Word of God. He modeled that for us when Jesus was tempted in the wilderness. Again and again, He answered the temptation with, "It is written..." (see Matthew 4).

What shape is your sword in? Is it polished from daily use as you study the Scripture on a daily basis? Has it been sharpened on the anvil of experience as you have applied and obeyed its truth in your life? Or, is your sword rusty from lack of preparation? Is it dulled by disobedience?

Sin will keep us from the Word of God. But if we apply the teaching of God's Word, it will keep us from sin.

HOT WATER

Happy is the man who doesn't give in and do wrong when he is tempted, for afterwards he will get as his reward the crown of life that God has promised those who love him. (James 1:12-13, TLB)

Have you ever had the bottom drop out of your life? Things had been going along reasonably well. The birds were singing. The sun was shining. Then without warning, the storm clouds began to gather... and it started to rain on your parade. A calamity hit. A tragedy struck, and suddenly you felt lower than you had ever felt before. What was it all about?

Or have you ever had one of those times where you were walking with God, trying to do all the things that should build you up in your Christian faith, when, out of nowhere, you were hit with a heavy-duty, intense temptation? Sometimes it happens at the most unbelievable times...like when you're in prayer or in church. And you ask yourself, *Why is this happening to me? Why me? Why now? Why this?*

What is the purpose of trials and temptations in the life of the Christian? Is there anything we can do to move them along a little more quickly?

Of course, none of us enjoy trials. None of us enjoy being tested and tempted, but there are some valuable lessons that come through these times God allows in our lives.

One of the worst aspects of enduring hardships and difficult seasons in our lives is that inevitable feeling that our lives are spinning out of control. And that tends to add the element of fear to our struggle and frustration. That's why I like this passage in James so much, where the apostle says: "My brethren, count it all joy when you fall into various trials, knowing that the testing of your faith produces patience. But let patience have its perfect work, that you may be perfect and complete, lacking nothing" (James 1:2-4).

We can be patient, and even joyful, knowing that our lives are not out of control...they're in His control. No matter how hot it may get for us, the hand on the thermostat is that of our Lord and Savior, who loves us more than we could begin to understand.

Tuesday

OUR GREAT PHYSICIAN

When Jesus heard it, He said to them, "Those who are well have no need of a physician, but those who are sick. I did not come to call the righteous, but sinners, to repentance." (Mark 2:17)

It's worth noting that every person Jesus had conversations or contact with was in a different situation, and He dealt with each one differently. This is because He recognized that even though we all share many of the same problems and basic needs, every man, woman, and child is a unique individual, with unique needs.

In His encounters with people, Jesus was like a physician. He basically said, "I want to let you know that I did not come to bring the righteous to repentance, but I came to bring sinners, because those who are whole do not need a physician."

I think the hard thing about being a doctor must be seeing people, for the most part, only when they are sick! They usually don't have their patients stop by and say, "Hey, Doc, I'm feeling good and I just wanted to tell you that. Want to go to lunch?" You don't usually call your doctor when you're feeling at the top of your game. You call when you are feeling sick, and your doctor will have you come in to his or her office, examine you, and apply the specific remedy to the area of need.

Jesus is the Great Physician. He came to heal the brokenhearted, to preach deliverance to the captives, give sight to the blind, and freedom to the oppressed. He has already determined your precise areas of need, whatever they may be, and he will minister to you as an individual.

THE ULTIMATE SACRIFICE

"For God so loved the world that he gave his only Son, so that everyone who believes in him will not perish but have eternal life." (John 3:16)

I heard a true story about a man who operated a drawbridge. At a certain time every afternoon, he raised the bridge for a ferryboat to go by, and then lowered it in time for a passenger train to cross over. He performed this task precisely, according to the clock.

One day, he brought his son to work so he could watch. As his father raised the bridge, the boy got excited and wanted to take a closer look. His father realized his son was missing and began looking for him. To his horror, his son had come dangerously close to the bridge's gears. Frantic, he wanted to go rescue him, but if he left the controls, he would not be back in time to lower the bridge for the approaching passenger train.

He faced a dilemma. If he lowered the bridge, his son would be killed. If he left it raised, hundreds of others would die. He knew what he had to do. With tears streaming down his face, he watched the passenger train roll by. On board, two women chatted over tea. Others were reading newspapers. All were totally unaware of what had just transpired. The man cried out, "Don't you realize that I just gave my son for you?" But they just continued on their way.

This story is a picture of what happened at the Cross. God gave up His beloved Son so that we might live. But most people don't give it a second thought. How about you? Are you conscious of the ultimate sacrifice God made on your behalf? Will you be sure to thank Him?

NOT JUST SPECTACULAR

Now when He was in Jerusalem at the Passover, during the feast, many believed in His name when they saw the signs which He did. (John 2:23)

Jesus attracted crowds. And what really fascinated the multitudes was that He did something that none of the religious leaders or so-called prophets of the day could do. He performed miracles. As a result, His fame spread throughout the land. And as you might expect, all those who were afflicted with various physical maladies began to follow Jesus, not so much to hear His teaching, but to be delivered from their sickness.

There are many people today who are looking for the spectacular, for something exciting. And it's true, the Christian life can be exciting. It can bubble over with hope, peace, and joy. But here's the problem: Sometimes life is just "daily." We won't always have the fireworks, the emotional highs, spiritual goose-bumps, or get a front row seat to God's supernatural workings. Much of life in Christ is simply walking in trust and obedience day by day.

If we build our faith on the emotional plane and on the spectacular, we will quickly fall away, because God never promised a continual feast for our feelings. After we have initially come to Him, we need to grow beyond emotional experiences and get down to the reality of what it means to be a believer. Like the believer in Psalm 1, we need to send our roots deep into the soil of His Word. "Planted by the rivers of water…" we will bring forth "fruit in its season," and our "leaf also shall not wither."

THE SOURCE OF OUR PROBLEMS

But the Lord is faithful, who will establish you and guard you from the evil one.
(2 Thessalonians 3:3)

W e are living in a time when we love to blame someone or
something else for the things we do. It's convenient to have a
scapegoat, especially when no one likes to take responsibility for their own
actions anymore. We can make a million excuses for our wrong behavior, but we never seem to say, "The problem is looking back at me in the
mirror...I'm responsible for my actions" or "I have sinned against God."

Tragically, even in the church today, psychology is in many cases placed
on the same level as the Bible (and sometimes above it). Many in the church
know more about self-esteem than they do about self-denial. They know
more about inner healing than they do about outward obedience.

But is low self-esteem the source of our problems today? Is it the fault of
others? Is it our family? Our culture or upbringing? Global warming? Our
excuses are legion.

James gives us the answer, telling bluntly and accurately the source of
our problems: "Where do wars and fights come from among you? Do they
not come from your desires for pleasure that war in your members? You lust
and do not have. You murder and covet and cannot obtain. You fight and
war. Yet you do not have because you do not ask" (James 4:1-2).

James was saying, "Your problems come from your desire for pleasure
that battles within you." The Bible isn't saying that pleasure in and of itself
is necessarily wrong. There are certain pleasures that have been given to us
by God Himself.

James is warning us about possessing a pleasure-mad mentality...of
making pleasure number one in our lives. He is saying that the source of
our problems lies in a selfish pursuit of pleasure.

A PROUD LOOK

A man's pride will bring him low, but the humble in spirit will retain honor.
(Proverbs 29:23)

God hates a proud look. That is interesting to me. I would expect God to start the list of things He hates with "hands that shed innocent blood" or adultery, maybe. But no. Number one on His list is *a proud look* (see Proverbs 6:16-19).

Why is this such a big deal? After all, in our culture today, pride is seen as a virtue. Be proud of your heritage, we're told. Be proud of who you are.

But the Bible says that God hates a proud look. What does this mean? Well, a proud look speaks of a person who would want his or her will above the will of God and the will of others. It speaks of people who are arrogant and full of themselves.

Did you know that pride was the first sin ever committed? Even before Adam and Eve ate the forbidden fruit, the sin of pride was committed by Lucifer. He wasn't satisfied to be an angel serving the Lord. He wanted to be God. And God banished him because of his pride.

So what did he do? He tempted Eve with the forbidden fruit. He basically said, "Go ahead and eat of it, Eve, because when you eat of it, you will be as a god, knowing good and evil. You will know more than everyone else" (see Genesis 3:5). What was he appealing to? Her pride. And she gave in.

You see, pride is probably at the root of most of the problems in our culture today. It is probably at the root of so many of our sins today. When we say, "I don't need to live God's way. I will do what I want to do when I want to do it," that is pride.

God hates a proud look. So let's not put our will above the will of God.

FRIENDSHIP WITH THE WORLD

And do not be conformed to this world, but be transformed by the renewing of your mind, that you may prove what is that good and acceptable and perfect will of God. (Romans 12:2)

When we come across the term "world" in the Bible, it isn't necessarily speaking of the Earth, per se. Rather, it is often speaking of a system, a mentality, or a way of thinking. This system, this mentality, is controlled by "the god of this world," also known as Satan.

A serious enemy the Christian faces today is the world. The Bible warns, "Adulterers and adulteresses! Do you not know that friendship with the world is enmity with God? Whoever therefore wants to be a friend of the world makes himself an enemy of God" (James 4:4, NLT). In the original language, the term "friendship" in this verse appears only in the New Testament and speaks of a strong emotional attachment, to love, to have an affection for, or even to kiss.

The Christian who turns from Christ and His church to seek pleasure and satisfaction from this world has put other gods in His place. That is the message God gave Jeremiah for His wayward people: "For My people have committed two evils: they have forsaken Me, the fountain of living waters, and hewn themselves cisterns—broken cisterns that can hold no water" (Jeremiah 2:13).

A cistern is a large well or pool carved in a rock. A broken cistern has sprung a leak and can't hold water. God is saying, "If you go out there to the world and drink from that well, it is not going to satisfy you."

So what are we to do when we are surrounded by this mentality, this world system that is so contrary to what the Word of God teaches? The only way to counteract this world's message is to saturate ourselves with the things of God.

Tuesday

YOUR BEST DEFENSE

Therefore submit to God. Resist the devil and he will flee from you. (James 4:7)

Whand the Bible tells us to "submit to God," and to "resist the devil" (James 4:7), it doesn't mean we are to go out and attack the devil. The devil will do the attacking. The word "resist" is essentially a defensive word meaning "to withstand an attack."

Nor does the Bible say to "converse with the devil and he will flee from us" or to "consider all of the temptations the devil offers, then resist him, and he will flee from us." Once you start messing with sin and with the devil, it is only a matter of time before you get hooked. It is like the free samples you're offered when you walk though the store or the mall. You are given just enough to whet your appetite, but not enough to satisfy it.

The devil has been at this for a long time. He is no idiot; he will not necessarily present his full agenda. Instead, he will say, "Take just a little nibble. Just have a taste for the fun of it. It won't hurt you. Just this one little time." And you know the rest of that story. This is why the Bible tells us to resist the devil. Keep as much distance from him as possible.

So where do we find the resolve and strength to resist? We need to submit to God as we resist the devil. "Submit" is a word used to describe a soldier under the authority of a commander and speaks of a willing, conscious submission to God's authority. It means to completely surrender yourself to the Word and will of God. That is your best defense.

HIS WAY OR YOUR WAY?

Come now, you who say, "Today or tomorrow we will go to such and such a city, spend a year there, buy and sell, and make a profit"; whereas you do not know what will happen tomorrow. For what is your life? It is even a vapor that appears for a little time and then vanishes away. (James 4:13-14)

The Bible doesn't condemn the person who makes plans for the future. Rather, it criticizes the person who makes those plans with no thought whatsoever for the will of God. That is a dangerous thing to do. God will not share His glory with another.

There is nothing wrong with making plans. Paul told the believers in Ephesus that he would return for renewed ministry among them, "God willing" (Acts 18:21). He wrote to the Corinthians that he planned another visit "if the Lord wills" (1 Corinthians 4:19). On other occasions, Paul spoke of his plans to do certain things and how the Lord changed his plans. We have our plans. We have our purposes. We have our agendas. But the Lord may redirect us.

Jesus taught us to pray, "Your will be done" (Luke 11:2). Our prayers will be effective and successful when we align our will with the will of God and pray accordingly. Prayer is not getting our will in heaven; it is getting God's will on Earth. It is not moving God our way; it is moving ourselves His way. We need to remember that His will may be different from ours. And we must be willing to accept that.

The God who knows you inside out also knows what lies ahead for you in life. We can always fall back on the simple promise of Jeremiah 29:11: "For I know the thoughts that I think toward you, says the Lord, thoughts of peace and not of evil, to give you a future and a hope."

God's plans for you are better than any plans you have for yourself. So don't be afraid of God's will, even if it is different from yours.

A CHANGED LIFE

And everyone who has this hope in Him purifies himself, just as He is pure.
(1 John 3:3)

Most Christians would readily agree with the simple truth that Jesus Christ is coming back again. But here is the question: If we believe that, how should it affect the way we live? We should be interested in taking the great truths of the Christian life and applying them to the way that we live. James 5:8 tells us, "You also be patient. Establish your hearts, for the coming of the Lord is at hand."

It is important to remember that God did not give us the prophecies of Scripture to entertain or tantalize us. Rather, these truths were given to us for a number of reasons. One of them is to motivate us toward personal godliness and bold evangelism. The truth of the soon return of Christ should cause us to want to live a holy life, and it should have a purifying effect on us. It should keep us on our toes spiritually.

It is interesting that when God points out what is wrong with a nation spiritually, He doesn't point His finger at the government; He points His finger at the church. God says that when a nation is sick, it is because there is a problem in His church. But He also tells us how to fix it: "If My people who are called by My name will humble themselves, and pray and seek My face, and turn from their wicked ways, then I will hear from heaven, and will forgive their sin and heal their land" (2 Chronicles 7:14).

What it comes down to is how the teaching that Christ is coming back affects you. Don't worry about the rest of the world. Don't even worry about your Christian friends. How does this truth affect you?

PREPARING WITH PATIENCE

Therefore be patient, brethren, until the coming of the Lord. See how the farmer waits for the precious fruit of the Earth, waiting patiently for it until it receives the early and latter rain. (James 5:7)

The early rains in Israel would usually come in late October or early November. These were anxiously awaited by the farmer, because they would soften the hard-baked soil for plowing. The latter rains would come in late April or May. These were essential to the maturing of the crops. If the farmer were to rush out and harvest his crops before their time, he would destroy them. So he had to wait.

As today's opening verse demonstrates, James knew that patience was also an important factor in awaiting the Lord's return. No crop appears overnight. Like farmers, we need to be patient and recognize that it takes time for growth to happen in our lives. However, the word "patience" does not speak of a passive resignation, but of an expectant waiting for the Lord. This is not a casual, nonchalant approach. Rather, it is an excited expectancy, a readiness.

Some believers don't live this way. They just passively bide their time. But the Bible tells us we should be actively preparing as we await the return of Christ: "And do this, knowing the time, that now it is high time to awake out of sleep; for now our salvation is nearer than when we first believed. The night is far spent, the day is at hand" (Romans 13:11-12).

Let's be sure we are living in a holy manner as we patiently wait for Christ's return.

AT THE RIGHT TIME

The Lord is not slack concerning His promise, as some count slackness,
but is longsuffering toward us, not willing that any should perish
but that all should come to repentance. (2 Peter 3:9)

As we look at this world we are living in, as we look at the way our culture is going, we say, "Lord, come back. Return soon." But God has His own schedule: He is not late, and He is not early. He will be right on time.

When Jesus came to Earth the first time, it was according to God's perfect plan: "But when the fullness of the time had come, God sent forth His Son, born of a woman, born under the law, to redeem those who were under the law, that we might receive the adoption as sons" (Galatians 4:4-5). I love that. When the time was just right, at the appointed hour, Jesus Christ—the Son of God—fulfilled the prophecies of Scripture and was born in a stable in Bethlehem. And when the time is just right, Jesus Christ, the Son of God, will return to the Earth.

Yet God has a plan He wants to accomplish in the interim. The Bible tells us, "The Lord is not slack concerning His promise, as some count slackness, but is longsuffering toward us, not willing that any should perish but that all should come to repentance" (2 Peter 3:9). The Lord is waiting for those last people to come into His kingdom and put their faith in Him. Can you imagine if you knew the one person whom God was waiting for? Wouldn't you be tempted to put a little pressure on that individual?

We need to remember that as Christians, our numbers are relatively small. But the task is immense. And the time is short.

A FRIEND IN NEED

So they sat down with him on the ground seven days and seven nights, and no one spoke a word to him, for they saw that his grief was very great. (Job 2:13)

Job certainly stands out as a shining example of someone who was patient in adversity. He went through incredible difficulties. You probably remember his story: It started out in heaven, with God telling Satan about the faithfulness of His servant Job. We can almost imagine God beaming and pulling on His suspenders as He spoke of His servant Job. But then He allowed hardship to fall on Job.

If it is true that into every life a little rain must fall, then Job was hit by a tsunami. In one day, he lost his flocks, his servants, all his children, and his health.

Then Job's friends came to visit. They could hardly recognize their friend, because he was in such sad shape.

One of the best things you can do for people who are hurting is to just be there for them. The Bible says we should "weep with those who weep" (Romans 12:15). You don't have to give them a sermon. You don't need to have all the answers. You simply need to be there.

I have been a pastor for many years, and I have come to realize that I don't have all the answers. Sometimes the best thing I can do for a person who is hurting, for someone who has lost a loved one, for the one who is facing a horrible sickness, is to be there and pray for him or her. By simply being there, you can be of great comfort to a friend in need.

READY TO GO?

Denying ungodliness and worldly lusts, we should live soberly, righteously, and godly in the present age, looking for the blessed hope and glorious appearing of our great God and Savior Jesus Christ. (Titus 2:12-13)

If the rapture happened today, would you be ready to go? The Bible says that Christ is coming for those who are watching and waiting. Does the thought that Jesus could come back today make your heart leap? Or does it make your heart sink?

Any person who is right with God should be excited about the imminent return of Jesus. It is a good litmus test of where you are spiritually. If the thought of His return brings joy to your heart, then that would indicate to me that you are walking with God. But if it causes fear, then that would be an indication that something isn't right spiritually.

As Jesus spoke to His disciples about end times events, He closed His teaching with a personal exhortation: "But take heed to yourselves, lest your hearts be weighed down with carousing, drunkenness, and cares of this life, and that Day come on you unexpectedly. For it will come as a snare on all those who dwell on the face of the whole earth" (Luke 21:34-35).

As followers of Christ, we need to be living in such a way that we are ready for His return. We need to be living in such a way that every moment counts. One day, each of us will be held accountable for how we spent our time, our resources, and our lives. Let's not waste them. Let's allow the anticipation of the Lord's imminent return to keep us on our toes spiritually. Let's allow it to motivate us to live godly lives.

THE ACCEPTABLE TIME

> *Behold, now is the accepted time; behold, now is the day of salvation.*
> *(2 Corinthians 6:2)*

Some people will say the reason they are not Christians is that it is just not their time yet. They don't think they are ready.

That would be like someone who is drowning in the middle of the ocean saying to the lifeguard, "I am not ready yet." What part of dead do they not understand? I would say that if you are drowning, then you are ready for salvation.

Unbelievers are in a worse state than a person who is drowning, because they are separated from God by their sin. If they are wondering when they should come to Jesus Christ, the time is right now. Not tomorrow. Not next week. Not next month. As today's opening verse declares, it's right now. God says, "Now is the accepted time; behold, now is the day of salvation."

This is the acceptable time. We don't know how long it will last. There is coming a day when Jesus Christ will return to this Earth for His people. There is coming a day when He will catch all true believers up into heaven with Him. We call it the rapture of the church. It is that moment that we look forward to as Christians, when we will go to be with the Lord. It is described in Scripture as happening "in a moment, in the twinkling of an eye, at the last trumpet. For the trumpet will sound, and the dead will be raised incorruptible, and we shall be changed" (1 Corinthians 15:52).

Now is the time when God is looking in grace upon those who are separated from Him by sin, and the gospel is going out to them. Now is the day of salvation.

SPIRITUAL BLINDNESS

"I will deliver you from the Jewish people, as well as from the Gentiles, to whom I now send you, to open their eyes, in order to turn them from darkness to light, and from the power of Satan to God, that they may receive forgiveness of sins and an inheritance among those who are sanctified by faith in Me."
(Acts 26:17-19)

Before I was a Christian, I had heard the gospel and even had a respect for it. But I didn't understand it. Christians would come up to me and give me tracts to read—even little red Bibles. They would thrust these things in my direction, say, "Read this," and then back off. I would take whatever they handed me and stuff it into my pocket. Meanwhile I was thinking, *I wish one of these people would just talk to me about God.* But no one did.

At home, I kept a drawer filled with all the materials people gave me. I had everything you could think of in that drawer. I wanted to know God, but I couldn't figure it out. Every once in awhile, I would take the drawer, empty it on my bed, read all that stuff, and try to make rhyme or reason of it.

The problem was that I was spiritually blind. I didn't get it yet. But then one day, it just clicked for me. God opened my eyes, which has to take place before a person can be converted. The Bible teaches that before we are Christians, we are blind to spiritual truth: "But even if our gospel is veiled, it is veiled to those who are perishing, whose minds the god of this age has blinded, who do not believe, lest the light of the gospel of the glory of Christ, who is the image of God, should shine on them" (2 Corinthians 4:3-4).

If you have unbelieving friends and loved ones, then you need to ask God to open their eyes and help them to see for themselves their own need for Him.

AT THE APPOINTED TIME

"Therefore My Father loves Me, because I lay down My life that I may take it again. No one takes it from Me, but I lay it down of Myself. I have power to lay it down, and I have power to take it again. This command I have received from My Father." (John 10:17-18)

At one point in Jesus' ministry, the people in His own hometown of Nazareth tried to kill Him. They had taken Him to the edge of a cliff to push Him off, but the Bible tells us that Jesus passed through their midst and went on His way (see Luke 4:30). This just goes to show that no one ever took the life of Jesus.

It is almost laughable to read the biblical account of soldiers—led by Judas Iscariot through the Garden of Gethsemane—coming to arrest God with their swords and spears, coming to supposedly take "against His will" the one who holds the solar system in the span of His hand.

The reason the people of Nazareth couldn't kill Jesus was because His hour had not yet come. He often used that phrase throughout His ministry. But His hour finally did come when He willingly went to the cross of Calvary.

Jesus said that He came to give His life as a ransom for many (see Mark 10:45). He came to lay His life down on the cross of Calvary. And at the appointed time, that is exactly what He did. At the appointed time, He was born in the manger in Bethlehem. At the appointed time, He was crucified on the cross of Calvary. At the appointed time, He rose again from the dead. At the appointed time, He will come again to this Earth. God keeps His appointments. And He is always right on time.

THE QUESTION OF HIS RETURN

"The Spirit of the Lord is upon Me, because He has anointed Me to preach the gospel to the poor; He has sent Me to heal the brokenhearted, to proclaim liberty to the captives and recovery of sight to the blind, to set at liberty those who are oppressed; to proclaim the acceptable year of the Lord."
(Luke 4:18-19)

In 1999, as the world prepared to enter a new millennium, there were some who claimed to have somehow deciphered a biblical code, secret messages, and an understanding of the original language of Scripture that revealed that Christ would come back in the year 2000. Of course, there is no Scripture whatsoever to support this kind of idea. And, of course, Christ did not come back in 2000. The fact is that we don't know when He will return. He could come back today. Or He could come back in 10 years. We really don't know.

Jesus said, "But of that day and hour no one knows, not even the angels of heaven, but My Father only" (Matthew 24:36). If you were to translate that from the original language, it would say something like this: "No one knows the day or the hour when the Son of Man will come back." God said what He meant, and He meant what He said. He will return when He is ready. He will return at the appointed time.

The purpose of Jesus' first coming was to preach "the acceptable year of the Lord," in other words, that salvation is available to all. But the purpose of His second coming will be to execute the vengeance of God.

If you are an unbeliever, you ought to come to Him now, since now is "the acceptable year of the Lord." Come to know His grace and love and invite Him into your heart and life. Don't wait until He comes with judgment for a sin–sick world.

POP QUIZZES

> *Show me Your ways, O Lord; teach me Your paths. (Psalm 25:4)*

One of the first things that often comes to mind when we go through difficulties is, *What have I done to deserve such a thing?* But it is important for us to know that God does have lessons He wants to teach us during trials. I definitely want to learn what He is trying to teach so that He doesn't have to repeat the lesson later on.

Remember in school when the teacher would announce, "Class, today I am going to give you a pop quiz"? Those who hadn't studied weren't ready for the test.

God gives pop quizzes too. There are times when He will bring certain tests into our lives. We find a good example of this in a test Jesus gave His disciples. The multitudes came wanting to hear Him, and they were all hungry. John 6:5-6 tells us, "Then Jesus lifted up His eyes, and seeing a great multitude coming toward Him, He said to Philip, 'Where shall we buy bread, that these may eat?' But this He said to test him, for He Himself knew what He would do." Jesus wanted to see if His disciples were learning anything. Jesus wanted them to say, "Lord, you are the Creator of the universe. You have a plan. We trust You."

God will test you because He wants you to grow up. He wants you to mature. He wants you to develop a walk with Him that is not based on your fluctuating emotions, but on your commitment to Him as you learn to walk by faith. When a crisis hits, you will see how much faith you really have.

GOD'S WAY

To the faithful you show yourself faithful; to those with integrity you show integrity. To the pure you show yourself pure, but to the wicked you show yourself hostile. (Psalm 18:25-26, NLT)

It's interesting how God approached different people in the Bible. To Abraham, God came as a traveler. Abraham was outside his tent when three messengers arrived. Two were angels, while one was God himself. We know that Jesus said, "Your ancestor Abraham rejoiced as he looked forward to my coming. He saw it and was glad" (John 8:56). Why did the Lord come to Abraham as a sojourner? Because that is exactly what Abraham was.

The night before Israel began their siege of Jericho, God came to Joshua, the commander of Israel's armies, as Commander of the Lord's army.

When God came to Jacob, He came as a wrestler, and Jacob wrestled with Him. Why? Because Jacob was always fighting, conniving, resisting, and wrestling to get what he wanted.

Maybe you can relate to Jacob. Maybe there is something you want from God, even a good thing, like the salvation of a husband or wife. Maybe you are tired of being single and want to get married. Or maybe you want to serve God in a ministry.

Don't resort to conniving, because you may get what you want…but at a great cost. Jacob got what he wanted and paid dearly for it. I believe that if he had waited on God, he would have received what he needed and what God had promised.

God wants to do His will in our lives in His way and in His time. If you need something from God, be patient and wait on Him. God will meet you wherever you are to lift you to where He wants you to be.

A CHANGE OF DIRECTION

"For we must all appear before the judgment seat of Christ, that each one may receive the things done in the body, according to what he has done, whether good or bad." (2 Corinthians 5:10)

One morning as Alfred Nobel was reading the newspaper, he was shocked to find his name listed in the obituary column. It was a mistake of course, but nonetheless, there it was. He was stunned to see that he was primarily remembered as the man who invented dynamite. At that time in history, dynamite was used in great effect for warfare. It distressed Nobel to think that all he would be known for was inventing dynamite—something that was used to take the lives of others.

As a result of reading this mistaken obituary, Nobel decided to change the course of his life. He committed himself to world peace and established what we know today as the Nobel Peace Prize. When the name Alfred Nobel is mentioned today, dynamite is rarely the first thing that comes to mind. Rather, we think of the prize that bears his name. It's all because Alfred Nobel decided to change the course his life was taking.

Another man, living centuries earlier, also changed the negative course of his life. His name was Paul, formerly known as Saul of Tarsus. Known as a relentless persecutor of the early church, he was determined to stop the spread of Christianity. But after a dramatic conversion on the Damascus Road, Paul devoted the rest of his life to preaching the gospel and building the church. Today we remember him as a missionary, church planter, and author of 13 New Testament epistles.

If you were to read your own obituary today, what do you think people would remember you for? It isn't too late to change your direction!

REVIVE US AGAIN!

Will You not revive us again, that Your people may rejoice in You? (Psalm 85:6)

Has it ever seemed as if you were out there all alone as a Christian? Sometimes it feels like you're the only one who is serving the Lord or speaking up for Him at your workplace or school. You know others who are Christians, but they seem reluctant (or afraid) to stand up and be counted as such.

As dark as things may become at times in your life, remember this. Isaiah 59:19 says: "When the enemy comes in like a flood, the Spirit of the LORD will raise up a standard against him." So here is the good news: when things are really wicked, when things are really dark, you can anticipate that God will do something.

That is why, as I look at the way things are going in our culture these days, I am praying and hoping for a work of God in our generation. When you look back at the great revivals in history, biblical and otherwise, you find five traits that are true of every revival:

1. All revivals began during a time of national depression and deep moral distress.
2. Revivals usually began with an individual, someone whom God would work on or work through. It may have been someone who would pray or someone who would preach.
3. Every revival was built on the Word of God being preached, taught boldly, and obeyed.
4. Every revival brought about an awareness of sin and the need to repent of it.
5. Every revival brought about a change in the moral climate; something happened in the culture as a result.

When God is forgotten, a moral breakdown soon will follow. But when we are really doing what God wants us to do, it will have an impact on our culture.

As much as we need spiritual renewal in our nation or in our city, however, it really begins with how I respond to the Lord's call on my life *today*. Take time today to draw near to Him, and seek His fresh perspective and guidance for your life. Let the revival fire begin in your own heart.

SALT AND LIGHT

"You are the salt of the earth. But what good is salt if it has lost its flavor?...
You are the light of the world—like a city on a hilltop that cannot be hidden."
(Matthew 5:13-14, NLT)

I think that we Christians are sometimes tempted to isolate ourselves. We want to submerge ourselves in a Christian subculture of our own making and not get too involved in the world.

But Jesus said, "You are the salt of the earth." When He made that statement to His disciples so long ago, they understood the significance of what He was saying. It can be lost on us today because we don't know it what it means.

In those days, salt was considered to be very valuable. In fact, the Romans considered salt more important than the sun itself. Roman soldiers would even be paid with salt.

So when Jesus said, "You are the salt of the earth," He was saying in a sense, "You're valuable. You're important. You're significant. You can make a difference."

Stop and think about salt. It really can do a lot. A little salt on a bland piece of meat can make all the difference. Have you ever had someone put salt in your water when you weren't looking? You immediately noticed the change. A little pinch of salt can alter the flavor of something, just as one Christian in a situation can effect change.

Have you ever been in a dark room and someone turned on a flashlight? The light wasn't hard to find, was it? In the same way, one believer who lets his or her light shine can really make a difference.

God has singled you out to make a difference—a strategic difference. And don't imagine you have to accomplish something great and dramatic to make an impact for the Lord. Remember that very large doors can turn on very small hinges. The God who created you, saved you, and equipped you knows how to use you in the most effective way...if you are completely yielded to His control.

RIGHT WHERE YOU ARE

The ravens brought him bread and meat in the morning, and bread and meat in the evening; and he drank from the brook. (1 Kings 17:6)

When the Bible says that ravens brought the prophet Elijah food in his exile, it doesn't mean they took his order, flew through the local fast food restaurant, and then delivered his meal. Ravens are scavengers. They would've brought little bits of meat and bread to Elijah. What's more, the water in the brook from which he drank probably would have been dirty and somewhat polluted. It wasn't an easy situation.

How easily Elijah could have said, "Well, Lord, I don't really want to be in this crummy little place. I kind of like being in front of people. I like the limelight." But the Lord was preparing Elijah for something beyond his wildest dreams. Not long after this, Elijah would be standing on Mt. Carmel in that great showdown with the false prophets (see 1 Kings 18:20-39). And the whole nation would be watching.

Sometimes, we don't like where God has put us. We say, "Lord, I don't like this situation. I don't like where I am. I want to do something great for You. I want to make a difference in my world." Maybe (for now) the Lord wants you to be effective right where you are. Maybe He wants you to take advantage of the opportunities in front of you and be faithful in the little things. Who knows what God has in store for you?

If God has you by some muddy little brook, so to speak, just hang in there. Be faithful, do what He has already told you, and wait on Him and His timing. God will do something wonderful for you or with you. Just be available and open to do what He would have you to do.

ON THE OFFENSIVE

Then at last they will reverence and glorify the name of God from west to east.
For he will come like a flood tide driven by Jehovah's breath. He will come
as a Redeemer to those in Zion who have turned away from sin.
(Isaiah 59:19-20, TLB)

I remember reading a story about one of the battles between General Robert E. Lee and General Ulysses S. Grant during the Civil War. General Lee was, of course, the head of the Confederate forces and was known for his brilliant tactics in doing a lot with a little. He didn't have the manpower or the organization of the Union army, but he was able to move in an effective way and foil his enemies on a number of occasions. His exploits had become so legendary that the Union soldiers were terrified of him.

One night, some Union soldiers were standing around the campfire talking about General Lee. They said, "What if General Lee does this? What are we going to do?"

General Grant was standing a few feet away. He walked over and said to the soldiers, "The way you boys are talking, you would think that General Lee is going to do a somersault and land in the middle of our camp. Stop talking about what he's going to do, and let him worry about what we're going to do."

Sometimes I see the same thing happening in the church: *Oh, the devil is doing this. The devil is doing that. Did you hear about this wicked thing that happened?* I think we should stop focusing so much on what the devil is doing and stop worrying so much about what he will do and instead let him worry about what we Christians will do.

Rather than trembling in fear about what our enemy is doing, we can rejoice in the power that God has given us to live victoriously and effectively for Him.

CREATED FOR A PURPOSE

"You are worthy, O Lord, to receive glory and honor and power; for You created all things, and by Your will they exist and were created." (Revelation 4:11)

Years ago, one of my sons asked me, "Dad, why did God put us here on the Earth?" I said, "God put us here on the Earth so that we might worship Him and glorify Him and know the God who created us."

Our ultimate purpose in life is not to attain success, fame, or even happiness. It should be to know the God who made us. In fact, the Bible says there are those in heaven singing, *"You are worthy, O Lord, to receive glory and honor and power...."* We were created to worship God.

Everybody worships. Certainly, we don't all worship the true God in heaven. But everyone, no matter who they are, worships someone or something. What do they worship? That all depends. Some worship the true and living God. Others worship a god of their own making. Some people worship people. They worship sports heroes or actors or musicians. Some people worship possessions. Some people even worship themselves. But when you get down to it, every person everywhere worships. And the reason for this is that God created us with an inner drive. We are created with a sense that there is something more to life than what we experience on this Earth.

You can worship a false god—a god of your own making, a god that you have brought out of your own imagination—and ultimately be disappointed. Or you can worship the true God. The true God—the living God, the only God, the God of the Bible—is the one to worship. He is the one to bow down to.

BECAUSE HE IS WORTHY

Oh come, let us worship and bow down; let us kneel before the Lord our Maker. For He is our God, and we are the people of His pasture, and the sheep of His hand. (Psalm 95:6-7)

Worship can turn the most miserable circumstances into a wonderful time. But our reason for worshiping should not be because we are in a good mood and feel like it. Nor should we refrain from worship because we are not in a good mood. We should worship because God is worthy. No matter what we are going through, no matter what our circumstances, God merits our worship. God is pleased when we worship Him with a proper heart.

I will share a little secret with you: Sometimes when you worship, your problems don't go away, but they won't seem as significant because you reevaluate things. You see, before you begin to worship, your problems can seem very big. But as you worship God and think about His glory, His power, His splendor, and His love, you come away with the realization that God is great and mighty, and your problems are tiny. You see Him in perspective.

The Book of Acts tells the story of Paul and Silas, who were beaten and imprisoned for preaching the gospel. The Bible tells us that at midnight, they worshiped God (see Acts 16:25). As they sang and worshiped, an earthquake came and the whole prison fell apart. It's wonderful when you can be lifted above your circumstances like Paul and Silas were. I'm not talking about mind over matter; I'm talking about faith over circumstances, about honoring the true God who is still on the throne, no matter what you are going through.

God may deliver you immediately from your situation, like He did with Paul and Silas. Sometimes God will change your circumstances. Sometimes He won't. But in all our circumstances, He is worthy of our worship.

A LIFE OF WORSHIP

And whatever you do, do it heartily, as to the Lord and not to men.
(Colossians 3:23)

Some people come to church with great expectations. They expect something profound to happen in the church service, and then they don't see it happen. The question is, did they ever stop and think the problem might be with them? If they have not been worshiping God for the last six days, they cannot effectively worship Him on Sunday. The worship in the sanctuary is largely meaningless unless it is preceded and prepared for by a life of worship.

The word *worship* comes from an old English word that means "worthship." It means to worship something because it merits your worship. But worship is not just when we sing a song.

Living a life of worship means that we live to glorify God in all we say and do. Classical guitarist Christopher Parkening has said there are two things he can do well: fish and play the guitar. Now you might not fish or play the guitar. Well, what can you do? *I can program a computer.* Good. *I can frame a house.* Great. *I can cook a good meal.* Very good. *I have artistic ability.* Great. You can take whatever you have and do it for the glory of God. Whatever you do, you can honor the Lord with it. God can use you in whatever vocation you are in. One paraphrase of Scripture quotes the apostle Paul saying, "And don't just do the minimum that will get you by. Do your best. Work from the heart for your real Master, for God, confident that you'll get paid in full when you come into your inheritance. Keep in mind always that the ultimate Master you're serving is Christ." (Colossians 3:22-24, The Message).

You can do your job well and effectively as a testimony and a witness for Jesus. You can live a life of worship.

HALF-HEARTED COMMITMENT

"I know all the things you do, that you are neither hot nor cold. I wish that you were one or the other! But since you are like lukewarm water... I will spit you out of my mouth!" (Revelation 3:15-16, NLT)

Milk is great cold. There's nothing quite like a cold glass of milk with some cookies. Milk is also good hot. With a little chocolate syrup, you've got yourself a terrific beverage. But lukewarm milk? The thought of it is sickening. It just doesn't cut it.

In Revelation 3, Jesus spoke of lukewarm individuals. He said, "I know all the things you do, that you are neither hot nor cold. I wish you were one or the other!" (verse 15). It's interesting that Jesus said He would prefer either hot or cold. You would think He would have said, "I would rather you be hot. But if lukewarm is all I can get, it's better than nothing."

You would think that lukewarm would be more acceptable to Him, because it's somewhat close to hot. But Jesus was saying, "I don't want lukewarm. I don't want half-hearted commitments. I want you to decide. I want you in or I would rather you were out."

Here's why. If you're hot, you're in. If you're on fire, if you're walking with God, then you're where God wants you to be. But if you're cold, hopefully you will at least realize you're cold and one day realize your need for Christ and come to Him.

But the lukewarm person is in the worst state of all because he is self-deceived. The lukewarm person says, "I go to church. I read the Bible sometimes. I kind of believe in God—when it's convenient." That's the worst state of all.

What is your spiritual temperature today?

HEAVEN'S AWARDS CEREMONY

For no other foundation can anyone lay than that which is laid,
which is Jesus Christ. (1 Corinthians 3:11)

Each year, millions of people watch the Academy Awards. They tune in to see what the celebrities are wearing and who will win the Oscars.

Now when it comes to that future day of rewards in heaven called the Judgment Seat of Christ, it is not going to be quite like the Academy Awards. We think the names of certain people will be called out, great men and women of the faith that we have heard of, and that they will get all of the awards. But it depends on what their motives were. It depends on why they did what they did. We don't really know who will receive what.

But I do know this: God will judge us on the quality of what we did rather than on the quantity. He will look at the motive. That is what matters.

Paul said of this judgment, "Now if anyone builds on this foundation with gold, silver, precious stones, wood, hay, straw, each one's work will become clear; for the Day will declare it, because it will be revealed by fire; and the fire will test each one's work, of what sort it is. If anyone's work which he has built on it endures, he will receive a reward" (1 Corinthians 3:12-14).

The wood, hay, or straw that burns quickly does not speak of gross sin as much as it does speak of putting more importance on the passing things of this life than on the things of God.

But if you have built your life on the right foundation, if you have done the things of God with the right motive for His glory, then you will receive a reward.

HIS REPRESENTATIVE

"If they persecuted me, they will also persecute you...." (John 15:20)

It's difficult for many new believers to understand how their friends and family could suddenly turn against them. People they have been close to for years suddenly become hostile, simply because they have said they were now following Jesus Christ.

I am amazed at how parents have turned against children. I've heard teens and young adults tell me how they were strung out on drugs, or living sexually permissive lives, or getting in trouble with the law all the time. Then they found Christ and their lives changed. They began living moral lives. Their parents were angry with them for coming to faith when, in fact, they should have been elated by the change.

Sometimes, even parents won't understand what the Lord is doing in your life. Sometimes your children won't understand. Sometimes, your husband or wife—or friends and coworkers won't understand.

Remember when Saul, later to become the apostle Paul, was striking out against Christians? One day on the Damascus Road, he met none other than Jesus Christ Himself who said, "Saul, Saul, why are you persecuting Me?" (Acts 9:4). Saul thought his fight was with the Christians. But it wasn't. It was with Christ Himself.

People take their hostilities out on you because you are God's representative. I have spoken with people who discover I'm a pastor and suddenly begin dumping everything they have against God on me. I have come to realize this happens because I am a representative of God, just as all believers are.

It's a great honor to be His representative. But with that honor comes responsibility. Be careful. Never, never turn someone who is seeking the Lord away from Him, because You have misrepresented Him. And if you're criticized, attacked, or ostracized simply for the name of Jesus, consider it a badge of honor. Because that's exactly what it is.

Tuesday

WORTH WAITING FOR

"Blessed are you when they revile and persecute you, and say all kinds of evil against you falsely for My sake. Rejoice and be exceedingly glad, for great is your reward in heaven, for so they persecuted the prophets who were before you." (Matthew 5:11-12)

You may have given up many things to follow Jesus Christ. You may have lost friends, even family, to be His servant. You may have resisted many temptations. Perhaps there have been hardships that you have endured because of your faith. God promises you a special reward in heaven.

There are many who have suffered much worse, those throughout church history who have laid down their lives—men and women who were put to death for their faith in Christ, men and women who, if they would have denied the Lord, could have walked away, but would not make that compromise. They have a special reward waiting for them in heaven.

James 1:12 says, "Blessed is the man who endures temptation; for when he has been approved, he will receive the crown of life which the Lord has promised to those who love Him."

If you have suffered the loss of something like a friendship, if you have taken ridicule and persecution, know that God will reward you (see Matthew 5:11-12). Whatever you gave up, He will make it up to you.

Sure, we give up a few things to follow Christ. Sometimes we may think, *I know it's wrong, but it looks kind of fun. I kind of wish I could do it.* But we know we shouldn't. So we resist. As time passes, you will look back at the fallout, the repercussions, and say, "I'm glad I avoided that." And ultimately, in that final day, God will give you a reward.

AFTER THE DOVE

Therefore let him who thinks he stands take heed lest he fall.
(1 Corinthians 10:12)

Often after great victories, some of the most intense challenges and temptations of the Christian life will come our way. I have found that after great blessings in my life, after God works in a powerful way, the devil will be there to challenge it.

Think about it. After God had powerfully worked through Elijah on Mount Carmel, the prophet became so discouraged that he wanted to die. After Jesus was transfigured, He came down from the mountain to find a demon-possessed person waiting for them.

Or recall how Jesus was baptized in the Jordan River and the Holy Spirit came upon Him in the form of a dove and God said, "This is my beloved Son, and I am fully pleased with him" (Matthew 3:17). Immediately after what must have been a glorious, affirming moment, Jesus was led into the wilderness to be tempted by the devil.

After the dove came the devil.

The devil will always be there to challenge whatever God has done. It may come after church, after God has blessed you and spoken to you. You leave the parking lot and get into a petty argument with a family member— or you're hit with a heavy-duty temptation.

You wonder how that could happen. But that's just the devil's way. He wants to make your life miserable. Most importantly, he wants to steal anything that God has done in your life.

The devil is watching us and he's looking for vulnerabilities. That is why we need to pray for any person whom we know that God is using. And that is why we need to brace ourselves. The more you step out to be used by the Lord, the more you can expect opposition from the devil.

Thursday

TRUE WORSHIPERS

Give unto the Lord, O you mighty ones, give unto the Lord glory and strength.
Give unto the Lord the glory due to His name; worship the Lord
in the beauty of holiness. (Psalm 29:1-2)

King Herod was a shrewd and clever tyrant, and he was a great builder. Today, some 2000 years later, the remains of his incredible structures, including his fortress of Masada, are still visible in Israel. He built Masada because he was afraid that someone would try to take his kingdom. He even had his own sons executed because he perceived them as a threat to his kingdom. It was said in Herod's day, "Better to be one of Herod's pigs than his sons."

When wise men from the East came to Jerusalem asking, "Where is He who has been born King of the Jews?" (Matthew 2:2), Herod suddenly realized there was another king in town. The Bible says Herod was troubled. He told them, "When you have found Him, bring back word to me, that I may come and worship Him also" (Matthew 2:8). Just as the wise men were true worshipers, Herod was a false one. He was hostile toward God, yet he masqueraded as a worshiper of Him.

Herods by the dozens sit in the pews of many churches today. Outwardly, they appear devout and deeply religious, but inwardly they are living a lie. They don't know God. They don't have a relationship with Him. They may sing the songs and give to the offering. They may do all the right things, but it doesn't mean they are true worshipers, because God looks on the heart.

If your life is not right with God when you come to worship Him, not only does it fail to please God, but it is offensive to Him. What does God see in your heart? There are plenty of false worshipers today. Are you a true one?

HOUSECLEANING

If we confess our sins, He is faithful and just to forgive us our sins and to cleanse us from all unrighteousness. (1 John 1:9)

Spring means many things to us. But one of the most notable things that comes with spring is spring cleaning, when we go through our houses and take care of all the messes that have built up over the months.

I heard about an interesting custom in Italy for New Year's Eve. At midnight, the windows of every house open and everyone pitches out whatever they absolutely hate—furniture, clothes, dishes—they all come crashing to the ground. Now I would call that serious housecleaning.

I don't know about you, but I am not the tidiest person on the face of the Earth. Ironically, I like to be in tidy surroundings. But in contrast, my wife Cathe is Mrs. Clean. She just loves to clean. And she does it all the time.

Now I would like to apply this to our spiritual lives. There are some of us who allow problems to develop. We allow things to get really out of control. And when we reap the inevitable results of sin or when some crisis hits, we turn to God and say, "Lord, I need Your help to get me out of this mess."

And then there are others who live their spiritual lives the same way that my wife cleans house. They are always maintaining their relationship with the Lord, always cultivating it, and constantly confessing their sins before God. That is the way to live.

You need to be cleansed from your sin on a daily basis. How much better it is to ask for that on a regular basis than to allow a major problem to develop in your life.

We need a professional. Essentially, we need God himself to come and clean house.

ANGERING GOD

The Lord is gracious and full of compassion, slow to anger and great in mercy.
(Psalm 145:8)

I'm the kind of person who is relatively even-tempered. But certain things can really get under my skin and make me mad. Most of those things seem to happen when I'm driving. I don't know why it is, but I take everything personally.

Have you ever had one of those times when you are driving along and you need to get into an exit lane off the freeway? There is an opening in the lane next to you. You politely turn your signal on. Then another driver speeds up, cuts you off, and you miss your off-ramp. When that happens, I am angry.

I'm so glad that God doesn't lose His temper, aren't you? Isn't that a frightening prospect? If God were in a really bad mood one day, what would He do? Would He start throwing planets around? Would He speak people out of existence?

I don't know about you, but I am very interested in what God both loves and hates. If God says He hates something, then I want to make sure I don't do that thing. Don't you feel the same way? I don't want to incur His wrath.

There is a passage of Scripture that specifically identifies seven things the Lord hates:

These six things the Lord hates, yes, seven are an abomination to Him: a proud look, a lying tongue, hands that shed innocent blood, a heart that devises wicked plans, feet that are swift in running to evil, a false witness who speaks lies, and one who sows discord among brethren.
(Proverbs 6:16-19)

We should look over this list of things that God hates and make sure we are not doing them. And if we are, let's make sure we stop.

DISSENSION AMONG BROTHERS

> *Brethren, if a man is overtaken in any trespass, you who are spiritual restore*
> *such a one in a spirit of gentleness, considering yourself*
> *lest you also be tempted. (Galatians 6:1)*

God hates a man who stirs up dissention among brothers, a person who intentionally divides other Christians. The amazing thing is that God places this sin of causing discord among brothers right up there along with murder, lying, and perjuring (see Proverbs 6:16-19).

One of the things that stirs up dissension is gossip. We hear something about someone. *They did what? With whom?* We are so anxious to tell someone else. What is it with us that we would actually rejoice in a weakness or problem in another Christian's life? The first thing we should do is pray for that person. And then we should seek to restore him or her, because it could be us next time.

But what do we tend to do? We don't talk to God about them, we talk to others about them—people who often aren't part of the problem or the solution. You would think by the actions of some people today that the Bible says, "If a brother or a sister is overtaken in a fault, you who are spiritual, go and tell as many people as humanly possible." Rather, it says, "You who are spiritual restore such a one in a spirit of gentleness."

God hates division and gossip. So if you have a problem or an offense to settle with a brother or sister, pray for them. Seek to restore them. Read Matthew 18, and take the proper biblical steps. Gossiping and talking about it will never resolve it. God hates this kind of thing.

Instead, let's seek to gently restore our brothers and sisters in Christ.

GLORIFY GOD

For you are the temple of the living God. (2 Corinthians 6:16)

God wants to clean your house, cleanse your temple. Under the old covenant, the temple was either a tabernacle in the wilderness or a great building in Jerusalem where the high priest, representing the people, met God.

But ever since the crucifixion and resurrection of Jesus, God doesn't live in a temple. John wrote in Revelation 21:3,

And I heard a loud voice from heaven saying, "Behold, the tabernacle of God is with men, and He will dwell with them, and they shall be His people. God Himself will be with them and be their God."

Under the new covenant, God lives in the hearts and lives of His own people.

We are so careful about cleaning the outside of our bodies. But what about the inside? Is there something that needs to be cleansed inside? The Bible tells us,

Or do you not know that your body is the temple of the Holy Spirit who is in you, whom you have from God, and you are not your own? For you were bought at a price; therefore glorify God in your body and in your spirit, which are God's.
(1 Corinthians 6:19-20)

When we give our lives to Christ and put our trust in Him, He comes in and cleans house. He throws out old clothes, old furniture, even the old food in the refrigerator. Then He lays down beautiful new carpet. He puts in new furniture. He fills the refrigerator with the finest gourmet foods. And we realize that He took the old things away only to put something better in their place.

God wants to clean house. Let Him do that. Invite the Spirit of the living God to do whatever He needs to do to make your life—your inner temple—a place where He will feel at home.

ONLY ONE ORIGINAL

Another parable He put forth to them, saying: "The kingdom of heaven is like a man who sowed good seed in his field; but while men slept, his enemy came and sowed tares among the wheat and went his way." (Matthew 13:24-25)

Y ou know something is popular when you start seeing its imitations everywhere. When someone comes up with a new design for something, it isn't long before everyone has created a version of it.

In the same way, we can look at so-called religions today and see imitations of the real thing. Whenever there is a genuine work of the Holy Spirit of God, we can always expect to see the devil's cheap knock-off. If there is a revival sent from God, there will be a false revival. If there are miracles from heaven, there will be miracles from hell. If you begin to see the movement of God in a certain area, then you will also see the movement of the devil.

Jesus told the story of the wheat and the tares, in which a man went out and planted a field of wheat. But in the night, his enemy came and planted tares among the wheat. The tares, also known as darnel, actually resembled wheat in the early stages of growth. If you were to see the two plants side by side, you wouldn't be able to notice a difference. But after a period of time, the darnel would show itself for what it really was…a useless weed. Eventually, it would actually uproot the wheat.

The devil has flooded the world with imitations, if you will. And that fact alone confirms there is an original! You cannot have imitations without the real thing.

It is by immersing ourselves in the Word of God that we will gain the discernment to distinguish between the true and genuine work of God and the copycat—and eventually destructive—work of the enemy.

Thursday

Make Your Choice

And Elijah came to all the people and said, "How long will you falter between two opinions? If the Lord is God, follow Him." (1 Kings 18:21)

Have you ever had one of those indecisive days? Usually I'm a decisive sort of guy. But then sometimes, I get into a mood where I can't seem to decide on anything! I can be at the window of a take-out place and suddenly be stricken with indecision. That's not so tragic at a take-out window. But when people are indecisive with God, it's a serious problem.

That's how it was with Israel in Elijah's day. For eighty-five years, the nation had gone back and forth between false gods and the true God. Not wanting to be responsible or live under absolutes, they would follow some other god—some exotic, foreign god, with all the evil practices associated with such worship. Then they would reap the painful results of following that god and would scurry back to the Lord and say they were sorry until their problems went away. Then they would go back like wayward children and do the same thing all over again.

Every time they were on the brink of destruction, God would be merciful and forgive them. One day, Elijah basically said to them, "Enough is enough. Make a choice. Which side are you on?"

Moses posed a similar question to Israel when they fell before the golden calf. He said, "Whoever is on the Lord's side—come to me!" (Exodus 32:26). His successor Joshua challenged Israel to "Choose for yourselves this day whom you will serve" (Joshua 24:15). And in Matthew 12:30, Jesus said, "He who is not with Me is against Me, and he who does not gather with Me scatters abroad."

Following Jesus demands a response. In the gospel of Luke, He declares, "If anyone would come after me, he must deny himself and take up his cross daily and follow me. For whoever wants to save his life will lose it, but whoever loses his life for me will save it" (Luke 9:23-24, NIV).

It's a decision we must make every day. Will you follow Him? Choose *this day* whom you will serve.

NO BROWNIE POINTS

For by grace you have been saved through faith, and that not of yourselves; it is the gift of God, not of works, lest anyone should boast. (Ephesians 2:8-9)

Some years ago a poll conducted by a major news magazine found that most Americans were sure they were going to heaven, but most didn't expect to see their friends there. A majority of those polled anticipated that Mother Theresa would make the cut, and others also cited certain celebrities and politicians whom they thought would qualify.

Sadly, this shows the confusion and the flawed reasoning that go into the most important decision we will ever make in life: the decision regarding where we will spend eternity.

Though this may come as a surprise to many people, Mother Theresa, as wonderful of a humanitarian as she was, did not have any better odds of making it into heaven than anyone else. Why? Because our entrance into heaven is not on the basis of what we have done for God; it is on the basis of what God has done for us. That's what it comes down to.

The lowest of the low, if they repent and ask God to forgive them, in spite of what they have done, will be admitted into heaven. And the best of the best, in spite of all of the good they have done, will not necessarily get in if they have not put their faith in Christ as their Savior. It doesn't matter what we have done, as commendable as it may be. Our entrance into heaven has nothing to do with good deeds or bad deeds. But it has everything to do with what Jesus did on the cross and our recognition that we cannot meet God on our own merit.

THE CHOICE YOU MUST MAKE

He who is not with Me is against Me, and he who does not gather with Me scatters abroad. (Matthew 12:30)

At one of the Harvest Crusades a few years ago, a Christian woman brought her unbelieving husband to the event. Throughout the evening, she was praying that he would come to Christ. At the end, when the invitation was being given, he said, "Come on. I want to go. Let's get out now before all the people leave."

She was heartbroken. As hundreds of people walked down to the field, they were going up the stairs to leave the stadium. On their way out, she saw one of the resource tables and said, "Honey, I want to get a Harvest T-shirt. Let me get this—quick."

As she made her way to the table, her husband walked over to an opening where he could see down to the field. He was struggling with indecision. As he watched, he happened to look up at one of the large video screens and, to his shock, saw his own face. The camera operator caught him standing there in his moment of indecision. Something triggered inside, and he thought, *I have to do this*. So he walked down to the field to give his life to Christ.

Meanwhile, his wife was wondering where her husband went. She happened to look up at the screen just in time to see him walking down the stairs, all the way to the field. So she walked down and joined her husband on the field as he made his commitment to Christ.

The fact is, there may be people around you right now who are that close to making a decision about their eternal destiny. What a great motivation to walk in the discernment and direction of the Holy Spirit, and "always be ready to give a defense to everyone who asks you a reason for the hope that is in you" (1 Peter 3:15).

DISCARDED LIVES

But she who lives in pleasure is dead while she lives. (1 Timothy 5:6)

On more than one occasion in the Bible, hell is compared to a big garbage dump. In fact, the very word that is used for hell in many New Testament passages is the Greek word *gehenna*.

Gehenna was a word used to describe a garbage dump outside Jerusalem during the time of the New Testament. Not only was garbage placed in this dump, but there were corpses as well. It burned day and night. There was always fire and smoke billowing from this horrid, stinking place known as Gehenna.

So Gehenna was a term the people would be familiar with in Jesus' day. He used this word on a number of occasions to describe hell, to depict its horrors, and to imply that the real place was far worse than even a place like Gehenna.

Now when you go to a dump, you will see things that are no longer of value to people. First of all, you will notice that it smells. There is all kinds of junk piled up that probably had been quite valuable at one time: old TV sets...stereo systems ...pieces of clothing...shoes. A lot of items that may have been of value at one time simply have been discarded.

Just stop and think of a life that has been wasted on the pursuit of sin, a life that has been wasted on the pursuit of pleasure, a life that has been lived without God. It is a life that ends up just being thrown away—a life that ends up in a garbage dump. That's what we do with our lives when we ignore God and live only for ourselves.

Tuesday

THE TIME TO RUN

Now behold, two of them were traveling that same day to a village called Emmaus, which was seven miles from Jerusalem. And they talked together of all these things which had happened. (Luke 24:13-14)

I find, as a Christian, that I need to be reminded of things that I sometimes forget. Have you noticed that you don't always know as much as you think you know? I've found that I often forget what I ought to remember, and remember what I ought to forget.

In Luke 24, we find the story of two men who had forgotten some things they should have remembered. At one time, they had been passionate followers of Christ, but now their dreams had been destroyed as they watched Him die on a Roman cross. Even as He hung there, they were hoping for a last-minute miracle. But no miracle came. They felt discouraged and let down. So they decided to leave town.

Now, Jesus had clearly stated that He would be crucified, and after three days, would rise again. He spoke of it often. But they had forgotten. Now, in their crushing disappointment, they wanted to put as much distance between them and the cross as possible.

We need to remember that every step away from the cross is a step in the wrong direction. When we are hurting or have failed spiritually, that is not the time to run away from the cross. That is the time to run to it.

Maybe something has happened in your life and you feel as though God has let you down. Maybe some tragedy has occurred. But God has neither failed you nor forgotten you. Now is the time to run back to the cross. Now is the time to remember His Word and the promises it holds for you.

EMPTY NET SYNDROME

Simon Peter said, "I'm going fishing." "We'll come, too," they all said. So they went out in the boat, but they caught nothing all night. (John 21:3)

I t was *déjà vu* time for the disciples. They had been fishing all night on the Sea of Galilee and hadn't caught anything. The Lord had risen, and had already appeared to some of the disciples. But since there were no clear marching orders, they thought they'd go back to what they knew how to do: fish.

Early in the morning, while it was probably still dark, they saw a figure standing on the shore. He called out, "Friends, have you caught any fish?"

Throughout the Bible, God often asked probing questions when He wanted a confession. In the same way, Jesus was asking His disciples, "Did you catch anything? Have you been successful? Have things gone the way you had hoped they would go? Are you satisfied?"

Why did Jesus want them to admit their failure? So He could bring them to the place where they needed to be.

When they cast the net on the right side of the boat, as Jesus told them to, their net became so heavy with fish that they couldn't pull it in. The Lord was teaching the disciples an important lesson: Failure often can be the doorway to real success.

We need to come to that point in our lives as well. We need to come and say, "Lord, I'm not satisfied with the way my life is going. I'm tired of doing it my way. I want to do it Your way." If you will come to God like that, He will extend His forgiveness to you. Then He will take your life and transform it in ways you couldn't imagine.

WHAT LOVE LOOKS LIKE

My little children, let us not love in word or in tongue, but in deed and in truth.
(1 John 3:18)

Have you ever felt like a spiritual failure? If so, then you're in good company. Even the apostle Peter felt that way after he had denied the Lord.

When Jesus told the disciples they would abandon Him in His hour of need, Peter insisted that *he* never would. But Jesus said that Peter would deny Him three times before the rooster crowed that day. And he did.

One of the results of that betrayal was that Peter found himself in a very awkward moment after Christ had risen from the dead. Jesus had appeared to them at the Sea of Galilee. Before they knew it, Jesus was cooking breakfast for everyone with the fish He had just helped them catch. Maybe as they ate, Peter was remembering when, not all that long ago, he denied the Lord by the glow of another fire.

Eventually, the Lord broke the silence, asking Peter a series of questions, each with the same phrase: "Do you love Me?"

Peter had learned his lesson. Instead of boasting of his love for the Lord, he simply answered, "Yes Lord; You know that I love you" (John 21:15-17). In the original language, the word Peter used for "love" was *phileo*. It could be translated, "have an affection for."

At least Peter was being honest. We can talk all day about how much we love God, but never act on it. Peter eventually proved his love for the Lord. A leader in the early church and the writer of two New Testament letters, he reportedly was crucified upside-down as a martyr for his faith.

How about you? Is your love for the Lord expressed more by your words than your actions?

JUST CUT IT LOOSE

Jesus said to him, "If you want to be perfect, go, sell what you have and give to the poor, and you will have treasure in heaven; and come, follow Me."
(Matthew 19:21)

When Jesus told the rich young ruler to sell what he had, give it to the poor, and follow Him, some have misunderstood this to be a blanket condemnation of believers having wealth—or of any person having wealth for that matter. Yet Jesus did not make this statement to any other wealthy person He encountered.

Nicodemus, who came to Jesus at night, was a wealthy man. We also know that Lazarus was a man of means. Yet Jesus did not require this of them. Why? Because Jesus looked into the young ruler's heart and saw that he did not possess possessions, but that possessions possessed him. What Jesus wanted from this young man wasn't his money, but his *heart*. Jesus didn't say, "Give your money to Me." Rather, He said, "Get rid of it and follow Me."

Jesus might have required a career or a relationship from someone else. But He was basically asking this man to dethrone his wealth and enthrone the Savior. Yet the man was essentially saying, "Lord, you can be second place, but my possessions are first."

What is holding you back from following Him? Is it an immoral relationship? Is it a group of friends who are having a bad influence on you? Is it alcohol or drugs?

Jesus is saying, "Turn your back on that and follow Me." He wants you to have His gift of eternal life. But if something is in the way of your accepting it, then you need to cut it loose. And until you do, you won't even want what He has to offer.

NO SECRETS

[Jesus] had no need that anyone should testify of man,
for He knew what was in man. (John 2:25)

I remember when my son Christopher was a little boy, he would try to hide something from me. He would say, "Dad, guess which hand it is in," as he held his hands in front of me.

I would say, "Buddy, you should put your hands behind you," because I could see his secret sticking out of his hand.

That's how we are with God: *God, I bet You can't find this sin. I bet You don't know this about me.* But God sees it as clearly as I saw what was going on with my son. He sees right through us. When God looks at us, we are transparent to Him. We have no secrets from God.

John's Gospel tells us, "Now when He was in Jerusalem at the Passover, during the feast, many believed in His name when they saw the signs which He did. But Jesus did not commit Himself to them, because He knew all men, and had no need that anyone should testify of man, for He knew what was in man" (John 2:23-25). He knows what is in you, and He knows what is in me.

It all comes down to the sincerity of our hearts. God wants you to be honest. He wants you to tell the truth. He knows everything about you—whether you're sincere, playing a religious game, or just fooling around. We might even fool ourselves in some of these matters, but we will never deceive Him.

By the same token, if you hunger for God to reveal Himself to you…if you long for His presence in your life…if you want more than anything else for Him to use you, then He sees that, too. And He will reveal Himself to you in wonderful and surprising ways.

GOD IS GOOD

> *Therefore consider the goodness and severity of God: on those who fell, severity; but toward you, goodness, if you continue in His goodness.*
> *(Romans 11:22)*

❝ If God is so good, why does He allow evil?" This always tops the list of questions about God, along with, "Why does God allow war or tragedy or injustice?" These very questions have a flawed premise: that we can determine what is good or not good about God. By asking these questions, we are really passing judgment on God.

Let's just take the basic question that presumes that if God is all-powerful, then He isn't loving. Or, maybe God is loving, but He isn't all-powerful. These assumptions place all responsibility for evil on God.

Yes, God could have made a world with no suffering, a world with no pain, a world in which we are all robots. But that is not what God wanted. He wanted us to make the choice ourselves whether to love Him, so He gave us free will.

When we look at many of the problems in our world today, we can place the blame not on God, but on man. God gave us standards to follow. He gave us laws to govern a society. But what does humanity do? It says we don't need God. And when we inevitably reap what we sow, we say that God blew it. But we really brought it on ourselves.

In spite of it all, we know that God answers prayer. Sometimes God can use our problems to bring us to Him. God can even use suffering in our lives.

The great hope we have as Christians is that one day, we will be in heaven with Him. So whatever suffering or trials you are facing right now, know that if you are a Christian, God has something good—something better than you could ever imagine or dream—beyond this life for you.

Tuesday

FORTY DAYS

While he was blessing them, he left them and was taken up to heaven. They worshiped him and then returned to Jerusalem filled with great joy.
(Luke 24:51-52, NLT)

During the forty days from His resurrection to His ascension to heaven, Jesus was constantly appearing and vanishing before the disciples. I think He was getting the disciples accustomed to the fact that even when He was not visible physically, He still would be present and available spiritually.

Before this time, the disciples had expected the Messiah of Israel to come and establish His kingdom, and that they would reign with Him at His side. There had been no doubt in their minds that Jesus was the Messiah. But when He was crucified, it seemed like a colossal blunder. Now in the days following the resurrection, they began to realize that this had been His plan all along. They understood that the Scriptures predicted that the Messiah would first suffer and later would come and rule in glory on Earth.

In the meantime, Jesus told them they were to "go and make disciples of all the nations, baptizing them in the name of the Father and the Son and the Holy Spirit," and to "teach these new disciples to obey all the commands I have given you" (Matthew 28:19-20, NLT).

After instructing them to wait in Jerusalem, where they would receive the promise of the Holy Spirit, Jesus led the disciples to Bethany and blessed them. Then, before their eyes, He was taken up to heaven.

The Father's promise, the Son's plans, and the Holy Spirit's power united in making these unlearned disciples the most invincible weapons ever to be held by the hand of God.

The disciples worshiped Him. They witnessed for Him. They would wait for Him until He returned. We should do the same.

TRUE BELIEVERS

Those who have been born into God's family do not sin, because God's life is in
them. So they can't keep on sinning, because they have been born of God.
(1 John 3:9, NLT)

Of the twelve disciples, we envision Judas Iscariot as the one with shifty eyes, lurking in the shadows. While the other disciples wore white, Judas would have worn black. He was the one you would have immediately recognized as the bad apple.

But I think Judas Iscariot was the very opposite: a phenomenal actor who came across as an upright man, devout in his faith. As one of the Twelve, Judas had been handpicked by the Lord Himself, but eventually betrayed Him for a few pieces of silver.

Judas made the choice to do the wrong thing, even though he had been exposed to so much truth. With his own ears, Judas heard Jesus deliver the Sermon on the Mount. With his own eyes, Judas saw Jesus walk on water. He saw Lazarus raised from the dead. He saw the multitudes fed with the loaves and fishes. He saw the blind receive their sight. He saw it all. Heard it all. Yet he became more hardened in his unbelief.

Judas could go deeper into sin because he really never knew Jesus. If you are a true follower of Christ and begin to compromise in some area of your Christian walk, you will sense the conviction of the Holy Spirit. But if you can sin without any remorse, then one must question if you really know God. The true child of God, though still a sinner, simply won't live in a pattern of sin.

If you find yourself, as a follower of Christ, immediately experiencing conviction when you start to sin, then rejoice. It is a reminder that you belong to the Lord.

A SON ISSUE

The people who walked in darkness have seen a great light. (Isaiah 9:2)

What is the real reason people don't come to Christ? The reason people don't come to the light is because they don't want their darkness, their sin, to be exposed. "For everyone practicing evil hates the light and does not come to the light, lest his deeds should be exposed" (John 3:20).

What is the worst sin you can commit? Murder? Adultery? Stealing? Lying? No. The worst sin you can commit is to say no to God's offer of forgiveness. Because when you stand before God Almighty on that final day, it's not going to be the sin question, it will be the Son question. By that I mean, God is not going to say, "You did a really great job. I am going to let you in to heaven." God is not going to say, "You went over your sin quota, and because of that, I'm not going to let you in." That's not it at all.

You may have committed sins your entire life and have been a wicked person, but if in the end you were to come to your senses and say, "Jesus Christ, come into my heart and forgive me," then God would let you into heaven. Because the big issue will be what you did with Jesus Christ.

The only way that we will get into heaven is because of what Jesus Christ did for us. Think of the greatest men and women of God that you know. They are not going to go to heaven because of their accomplishments or because of their gifts. They will walk through heaven's gate for one reason and one reason only: because they accepted what God did for them when His blood was shed at the cross.

We all go to heaven in the same way. And it will be the Son issue in that final day. Have you taken time recently to praise God for your eternal salvation, purchased at such a terrible cost? Why not find a place where you can be alone for a few minutes, and just pour out your heart in gratitude to Him for purchasing you entrance into heaven and eternal life.

SOMEONE'S WATCHING

The eyes of the Lord are in every place, keeping watch on the evil and the good.
(Proverbs 15:3)

A little boy was always getting into trouble in his Sunday School class, so in exasperation, his teacher said to him, "I want you to know that God is watching you all the time. Even when I can't keep my eyes on you, God has His eyes on you. He is watching you. So you'd better straighten up."

The boy was terrified by the thought of God watching him all the time. After Sunday School, he told his parents, "The teacher said that God is watching me all the time." They could see that the thought terrified their son rather than bringing comfort to his heart. So his parents put it into proper context for him. They said, "Yes, it's true that God is always watching you. But the reason is because He loves you so much that He can't take His eyes off you."

Many times when we think of God watching us, what comes to mind are the surveillance cameras we have in public places today. I knew someone who worked in a department store and showed me how these work. They are hidden in places where we tend to never look, and they can pretty much watch everyone. People don't even realize a camera is turning around and following them wherever they go.

So when we consider the fact that God is watching us, we might think, *That is terrifying.* But it all depends. If we are rebelling against the Lord, then the thought of it can be more than a little frightening.

But if our hearts are right with Him, then…what an incredible comfort! He never loses track of us, never misplaces our file, never takes His loving attention from us for even one moment. God is watching us, but He loves us so much that He can't take His eyes off us. We may lose sight of God, but He never loses sight of us.

WHAT'S IN A NAME?

He who dwells in the secret place of the Most High shall abide under the shadow of the Almighty. I will say of the LORD, "He is my refuge and my fortress; my God, in Him I will trust." (Psalm 91:1-2)

To show us different facets of His nature, God gives us different names for himself. The words used in Psalm 91:1-2 include *'Elyôwn, Shaddai, Jehovah*, and *'Elohîm*. First, we have "the Most High:" "He who dwells in the shelter of the Most High…." The Hebrew word used here for Most High, *'Elyôwn*, speaks of possession. It is the idea of owning something. It simply reminds us that God owns and possesses everything, and that includes you and me.

Then there is the word "Almighty:" "He who dwells in the secret place of the Most High shall abide in the shadow of the Almighty…." That is the word *Shaddai*. The thought here is of provision. It is wonderful to know that God owns everything. But it also wonderful to know that He wants to provide for us. Not only is He a living God, but He also is a giving God.

Then we have "the LORD:" "I will say of the LORD…." That phrase "the LORD" is *Jehovah*, a unique name God called Himself before His own people, the Jews. It speaks of covenant and His promise to them.

Finally, there is "My God:" "My God, in whom I trust." That is the Hebrew word *'Elohîm*, which tells us there is one God who is triune, or three in one: the Father, Son, and Holy Spirit. It also reminds us of the power of God.

So when we put it all together, we see that the all-knowing, all-powerful God who possesses heaven and Earth, who has entered into a special covenant with us, wants to provide for our needs. I want to know more about this God, don't you?

THE HEART OF THE MATTER

When Jesus had raised Himself up and saw no one but the woman, He said to her, "Woman, where are those accusers of yours? Has no one condemned you?" She said, "No one, Lord." And Jesus said to her, "Neither do I condemn you; go and sin no more." (John 8:10-11)

Throughout His earthly ministry, Jesus saved His most scathing words not for the sinners of the day, but for the self-righteous, religious hypocrites. When the religious elite brought the woman caught in the act of adultery before Him and pointed out that the law required death by stoning (John 8:5), Jesus stooped down and began to write something on the ground. We don't know what He wrote. But whatever it was, they all left quickly, from the oldest to the youngest.

When Jesus asked the woman where her accusers were and if anyone had condemned her, she told Him, "No one, Lord." So Jesus said, "Neither do I condemn you; go and sin no more."

Does this mean that Jesus approved of the way she lived? Far from it. He was getting to the heart of the matter. He knew the real problem was a heart issue—a heart captured by sin and estranged from God. If He could win her heart, it would change her lifestyle, too.

Sometimes I wonder if we in the church spend too much time protesting what unbelievers do and not enough time giving them the answer to their problems. Listen, I expect the world to be worldly. I expect sinners to behave sinfully. I don't expect them to live according to Christian standards.

There is a place to take a stand for righteousness and say what we are against. But the bottom line is that people are empty and need to hear the gospel of Jesus Christ. Let's expend our primary energy getting to the heart of the matter instead of dealing with the symptoms, because the heart of the matter is that people are lost. They need Christ. And we need to take that message to them.

OFFENDING GOD

"How terrible it will be for you teachers of religious law and you Pharisees. Hypocrites! You are so careful to clean the outside of the cup and the dish, but inside you are filthy—full of greed and self-indulgence!" (Matthew 23:26, NLT)

It was Cicero who said, "Of all forms of injustice, none is more flagrant than that of the hypocrite who, at the very moment when he is most false, makes it his business to appear virtuous."

Jesus had some harsh words for the Pharisees, the hypocrites of His day, because they pretended to be something they were not. They pretended to be holy when they were unholy. They pretended to be committed when they were uncommitted. And God doesn't like that. He would rather that we be honest and say, "I am a sinner. I am living the wrong way, but this is the way I choose to live," instead of saying, "I am a Christian," when all the while, we are living a secret life and think we're somehow hiding that fact from the Lord. How absurd. Hiding from an all-seeing, all-powerful, everywhere-present Creator? It didn't work for Adam when he tried to hide in the bushes in the Garden of Eden, and it won't work for us, either.

Jesus said to the Pharisees—and to all who would live this way—"Woe to you, scribes and Pharisees, hypocrites! For you are like whitewashed tombs which indeed appear beautiful outwardly, but inside are full of dead men's bones and all uncleanness. Even so you also outwardly appear righteous to men, but inside you are full of hypocrisy and lawlessness" (Matthew 23:27-28).

Don't pretend to be a holy man or a holy woman if you don't really want to be one. This is offensive to God. I'm not saying that it's better to be a sinner. What I am saying is that it's worse to pretend to be holy when you really don't want to be. Because then the only person you are actually fooling is yourself.

The bottom line to all this? Come to the Lord and open your heart before Him. Ask Him to forgive you, restore you, and fill you with His presence and joy once again. There's no need to hide from someone who loves you that much!

FACING THE MUSIC

"That to Me every knee shall bow, every tongue shall take an oath."
(Isaiah 45:23)

I once read that the expression "face the music" originated in Japan with the Imperial Orchestra. It was very prestigious to belong to this particular orchestra, and there was a certain man who desperately wanted to join. He wanted to play for the emperor, but had no musical talent. This man happened to be very wealthy, however, so he offered the conductor a large amount of money if he would allow him to join the prominent orchestra.

The conductor accepted the man's offer and gave him a flute. He told him that when the orchestra played, he was to simply hold the flute to his lips and move his fingers so he would convince people that he was playing. So the man became a member of the Imperial Orchestra. He pretended to play his flute, everyone thought he was a great musician, and his dream of performing before the emperor had been fulfilled.

But one day, a new conductor took over. He wanted to find out how good the musicians were, so he announced he would be auditioning every musician in the Imperial Orchestra. The man was terrified, because he couldn't play a single note. His pretending had caught up with him, and he was forced to admit he was a fake. He couldn't "face the music."

A day will come when we will stand before God himself. And though certain people may have done a brilliant job of fooling other people, they will have to face the music. The Bible tells us that all our life works will be tried by fire. In that day, the true motives of our heart will be laid bare, and the Lord will evaluate our entire lives. What was done with a true heart will endure, and be rewarded. What was done to impress others or burnish our own reputations will not survive the flame. We will be saved, the Scripture says, "but only as one escaping through the flames" (1 Corinthians 3:15, NLT).

Let's pray the prayer of David in Psalm 139: 23-24: "Search me, O God, and know my heart; Try me, and know my anxieties; And see if there is any wicked way in me, And lead me in the way everlasting." Let's make sure that those moments of evaluation in His holy presence will be joyful ones.

WANTED: DISCIPLES

"Then Jesus said to His disciples, 'If anyone desires to come after Me, let him deny himself, and take up his cross, and follow Me.'" (Matthew 16:24)

The great English preacher John Wesley once said, "Give me a hundred men who fear nothing but sin and desire nothing but God, and I do not care if they be clergymen or laymen. Such men alone will shake the gates of hell and set up the kingdom of heaven on earth." I don't know if Wesley ever found such men. But I know that Jesus did.

Jesus called these men to be His disciples. In the Book of Acts, they were described as "these who have turned the world upside down" (Acts 17:6). When that statement was initially given, it was not meant as a compliment. In fact, it was more of a criticism. But in a sense, that statement was a supreme compliment, because it acknowledged the impact these men were making.

If there was ever a time in history when the world needed to be turned upside down or, should I say, right side up, the time is now. But if it is going to happen, then it will need to be through committed believers like the ones John Wesley was looking for: people who fear nothing but sin and desire nothing but God. No fair-weather followers need apply. God is looking for disciples.

So what does it mean to be a disciple? It simply means that you take your plans, your goals, and your aspirations and place them at the feet of Jesus. It simply means saying, "Not my will, but Yours be done."

Let's commit ourselves to being men and women like that. Not mere fair-weather followers, but authentic disciples of our Savior and Lord.

LOVE, JOY, AND PEACE

But when the Holy Spirit controls our lives, he will produce this kind of fruit in us: love, joy, peace, patience, kindness, goodness, faithfulness, gentleness, and self-control. (Galatians 5:22-23, NLT)

The future is something we all should be thinking about, because we need to plan ahead. Not only do we need to think about what we will do in this life, but also what we will do for all eternity.

An extensive survey conducted in the United States by a leading polling agency distributed questionnaires to people of various ages and occupations, asking, "What are you looking for most in life?" When the results were compiled, the analysts were surprised. Most expected those who were polled to say they wanted to achieve certain materialistic goals. But the top three things that people wanted in life were love, joy, and peace—in that order.

Isn't that amazing...those just happen to be the first three qualities of life mentioned in Paul's description of the fruits of the Spirit. Right off the top, *love, joy, and peace.* In other words, the very things people are looking for today can be found in a relationship with God. Yet some have given up on these things. They say, "Love, joy, and peace? That's a pipe dream of flower children. Give me a break. You are not going to find things like that in the real world."

Would that describe how you feel right now? That isn't the way life ought to be. In a relationship with God through Jesus Christ, we are promised not only life beyond the grave, but a life that is full and rich and worth living on this Earth. Jesus gives us life with purpose and, of course, life with the hope of heaven.

DON'T QUIT NOW

Do you not know that those who run in a race all run, but one receives the prize? Run in such a way that you may obtain it. (1 Corinthians 9:24)

There are some events in the Olympics that don't interest me at all. But the series of events that I personally enjoy is track and field. I love to watch the relay races, the long distant runs, and the short sprints. And that is probably because I was into track and field when I was in high school.

During a recent Olympics, I was watching one of the long distance runs. One of the runners started off in the back. Then he moved up toward the middle. With about four laps to go, he suddenly broke ahead and took the lead. I thought, *Is he going to make it? Could he possibly win?* But it wasn't to be. In those last laps he fell back. The next thing I knew, he was in second place, third place, fourth place, fifth place. He didn't even win a medal.

I know what it's like to be in the last lap of a race. You are giving it your all, but your arms and your legs feel like rubber. It's like you have no control over them. They feel like they are burning inside. It's so hard to keep running.

In the Bible, the Christian life is often compared to running a race. The apostle Paul often used athletic terms to describe what it is to be a Christian. In today's opening passage, He wrote about running in such a way as to receive the prize. He told the Ephesians that he had finished his race with joy.

Let's not quit running our race. Let's run to win a prize. Let's finish with joy.

In a normal race, we know where the finish line is. We know how many miles or laps we have to run to finish the contest. But when it comes to life, you and I don't really know when we will round that last bend or run that last step. Even though we think we have a long ways to go, we might be right at the tape. What an encouragement to live each day for Jesus as though it were our last.

GET UP AND RUN

> *I have fought the good fight, I have finished the race, I have kept the faith.*
> *(2 Timothy 4:7)*

When you are racing, you run to win. And it's not enough simply to start, we have to finish the race, too. And some of us stumble at times.

The main character in the film *Chariots of Fire* fell in his important race. He was hurt and discouraged. But he got up again and continued to run, eventually finishing the race—and even winning it. Even when you stumble, even when you fall, you can still get up and run. You can still win. It's not over 'til it's over.

Some of us may have taken some pretty nasty falls in the race of life. Or maybe we have been discouraged or something has happened to set us back. It's not too late to get up and start running again!

For instance, if you have ever read a passage of Scripture that didn't seem to make any sense to you, or if ever there was a time in your life when it seemed as if God didn't come through for you, or if you have ever been tempted as a Christian to just give up following Jesus, then know this: you are in good company. You have a good idea how Jesus' disciples felt on the day when Jesus laid down some of His hardest teaching yet (see John 6). But instead of giving up on their faith, they deepened in it.

That was a day when the wheat was separated from the chaff, the true disciples from the false ones. In the same way, will we decide to stop, or to keep running?

Tuesday

ETERNAL VALUE

"Most assuredly, I say to you, you seek Me, not because you saw the signs, but because you ate of the loaves and were filled. Do not labor for the food which perishes, but for the food which endures to everlasting life, which the Son of Man will give you, because God the Father has set His seal on Him."
(John 6:26–27)

In John 6, we see a huge crowd following Jesus in Capernaum. Why is this? Because Jesus had performed His most popular miracle ever: the feeding of the 5,000. Jesus had taken the little boy's lunch and blessed it and multiplied it. And everyone was filled. They thought, *This is great. Not only does He teach us, not only does He dazzle us with miracles, but He gives us a free meal.*

When the crowd pursued Him, Jesus told them, essentially, "Let's skip the formality. I know why you are here. Stop laboring for the bread that simply feeds your stomach. I am the bread of life. I want you to focus on spiritual things. I didn't do that miracle to just feed you that day. I was trying to teach you something more. Don't labor for the food that perishes."

Jesus was saying that life is more than the things of this Earth. Life is more than food, more than clothing, more than possessions, more than a career, more than the pursuit of success. Believe in Him, and eat the bread of life.

Feed on Him every day and grow strong. As Jesus promised, this is food "which endures to eternal life."

TOP PRIORITY

"So don't worry at all about having enough food and clothing. Why be like the heathen? For they take pride in all these things and are deeply concerned about them. But your heavenly Father already knows perfectly well that you need them, and he will give them to you if you give him first place in your life and live as he wants you to." (Matthew 6:31-33, TLB)

When Jesus told us not to worry about food and clothing, His emphasis was on the word worry. He didn't say, "Don't think about it." Nor did He imply, "Don't plan ahead for your needs." He said, "Don't worry."

The fact of the matter is that the Bible criticizes the lazy person who lives off the generosity of others and neglects or refuses to work for a living. The Bible says that if you don't work, you shouldn't eat (2 Thessalonians 3:10). Go get a job. Provide for yourself. The Bible even encourages us to plan for the future and learn from the example of the ant, that tiny creature which is always planning ahead (Proverbs 6:6-8).

But there is balance here. The Bible is saying to us, "Yes, do an honest day's work and be financially responsible, but *don't be obsessed with these things*. Jesus said that's how nonbelievers are.

"Therefore do not worry, saying, 'What shall we eat?' or 'What shall we drink?' or 'What shall we wear?' For after all these things the Gentiles seek. For your heavenly Father knows that you need all these things. But seek first the kingdom of God and His righteousness, and all these things shall be added to you."
(Matthew 6:31-33)

Isn't that the emphasis of so many people today—what to eat, what to wear? Their whole lives revolve around materialistic goals. Jesus said this won't satisfy the deepest needs of your heart.

Don't make these things your primary purpose in life. Rather, seek God first and foremost in your life, and everything that you need will be provided for you. God will take care of you. He cares about you. He will supply all of your needs.

NOT ASHAMED

"For I am not ashamed of this Good News about Christ. It is the power of God at work, saving everyone who believes—Jews first and also Gentiles."
(Romans 1:16, NLT)

In his book, *The Devaluing of America*, former Secretary of Education William Bennett made this statement. "During my tenure as U. S. Secretary of Education, nothing I said seemed more unforgivable than my good words about religion. I was attacked as an Ayatollah when I supported voluntary school prayer and the posting of the Ten Commandments in school."

His experience is so typical of our culture today. You can say anything. You can believe anything. But if you stand up and say there are absolutes, if you say there is right and wrong and the Bible says so, then you are accused of hurting our society. You are the worst possible thing that could happen to our culture. Ironically, the very problems that are the result of society's rejection of God are then placed at the feet of the Christian, as though the Christian has brought these troubles on our culture.

But this isn't the first time in history that Christians have become scapegoats for the ills of a culture. Christians were blamed for the burning of Rome when it was Caesar Nero who was largely responsible for its destruction.

We live in a time when people are standing up for all sorts of causes. We have people standing up for the rights of animals, for the environment, for perverse sexual lifestyles. We have people standing up for everything imaginable, even willing to die for their cause.

Isn't it time that we, as Christians, stand up for what we believe? It's time to stand up and be counted.

SAVED SOUL, WASTED LIFE

For no other foundation can anyone lay than that which is laid,
which is Jesus Christ. (1 Corinthians 3:11)

A poll was taken not long ago that asked Americans what they thought was their main purpose in life. The responses were interesting. You would think some might say, "To make a contribution to society," or "To have a meaningful life." But what most people said was, "The main purpose of life is enjoyment and personal fulfillment." It's interesting to note that fifty percent of those polled identified themselves as born-again Christians.

According to the Bible, the purpose of life is not enjoyment and personal fulfillment. The Bible teaches that we are put on this earth to bring glory to God. We need to mark that well in our minds and hearts. Speaking in Isaiah 43:7 (NLT), God said, "All who claim me as their God will come, for I have made them for my glory. It was I who created them." Therefore, we are to glorify God in all that we do with our lives.

Are you using your resources and talents for His glory? Sometimes we think that God has given us this life to do what we will. We will say, "Lord, this is mine. This is my week. Here is Your time on Sunday morning. The rest of it belongs to me." Or, "Here is the plan for my life, Lord. Here is what I want to accomplish." Or, "This is my money. Here is Your ten percent, Lord. I give a waitress more, but ten percent is all you get." We develop a false concept of God.

It's possible to have a saved soul, but a wasted life. If you were asked today, "What is the main purpose of life...of *your* life?" what would you say?

WHO CAN BE AGAINST US?

*"Fear not, for I am with you; be not dismayed, for I am your God.
I will strengthen you, yes, I will help you, I will uphold you
with My righteous right hand." (Isaiah 41:10)*

Have you ever had someone forget an occasion that was important to you? Maybe your spouse forgot your anniversary or your birthday. Or maybe your children forgot you at Christmas. Even when people forget you, you need to know that God never forgets you. You are always on His mind. Romans 8:31 says, "What then shall we say to these things? If God is for us, who can be against us?"

God is thinking about you right now. He isn't thinking about you merely as a member of the human race or as a part of your church. He is thinking about you as an individual. The psalmist wrote, "Your thoughts toward us cannot be recounted to You in order; if I would declare and speak of them, they are more than can be numbered" (Psalm 40:5).

God's thoughts toward you are continual and uncountable. God Almighty, the one who holds the heavens in the span of His hand, the one who spoke creation into being, is thinking about you right now.

Not only is God the Father thinking about you, but God the Son is interceding for you. Hebrews 7:25 says, "Therefore He is also able to save to the uttermost those who come to God through Him, since He always lives to make intercession for them."

God the Father is thinking about you, God the Son is praying for and interceding for you, and God the Holy Spirit is helping you as well: "Now He who searches the hearts knows what the mind of the Spirit is, because He makes intercession for the saints according to the will of God" (Romans 8:27).

God is for you. God is thinking about you. God is on your side!

SPIRITUAL CASUALTIES

Now the Holy Spirit tells us clearly that in the last times some will turn away
from the true faith; they will follow deceptive spirits and teachings
that come from demons. (1 Timothy 4:1, NLT)

I t's clear that we are living in the last days. All around us, we see signs being fulfilled before our very eyes that Jesus and the prophets told us to look for. The Bible warns that in the last days things will go from bad to worse (see 2 Timothy 3:1-13). The Scripture also warns that one of the signs of the last days will be a falling away from the faith, or an apostasy.

The question is, could you or I ever become one of those spiritual casualties? Could you or I ever fall away from the Lord?

In a word, *yes.*

Without question, the potential, even the inclination, to sin is clearly within us. I have the potential to fall. You have it as well. This is why we must give careful attention to the potential pitfalls that Scripture describes. We must be aware of certain things as we are living in the last days. As the apostle Paul wrote to the church in Rome: "The night is far gone, the day of his return will soon be here. So quit the evil deeds of darkness and put on the armor of right living, as we who live in the daylight should! Be decent and true in everything you do so that all can approve your behavior. Don't spend your time in wild parties and getting drunk or in adultery and lust or fighting or jealousy. But ask the Lord Jesus Christ to help you live as you should, and don't make plans to enjoy evil" (Romans 13:12-13, TLB).

This is no time to be playing games with God and living in half-hearted commitment to Him. The only way to survive—and even flourish—as a Christian in these last days, is to be completely committed to Jesus Christ. Otherwise, we will be easy targets for the tactics, strategies, and flaming arrows of the devil.

Tuesday

TRUE SEEKERS

Now after Jesus was born in Bethlehem of Judea in the days of Herod the king,
behold, wise men from the East came to Jerusalem, saying, "Where is He who
has been born King of the Jews? For we have seen His star in the East
and have come to worship Him." (Matthew 2:1-2)

The story of Christ's birth is one of the Bible's most famous and loved
stories, probably one that most people who are not even familiar
with Scripture have heard at one time or another. And certainly a story we
hear repeated every Christmas is the account of the wise men being led by
the star to the place where the King was to be born.

Matthew's Gospel tells us these wise men came from the East (see
Matthew 2:1). Skilled in astronomy and astrology, these men were highly
revered and respected in their culture and were especially noted for their
ability to interpret dreams.

Because of their knowledge of science, mathematics, history, and the
occult, their religious and political influence grew until they became the
most prominent and powerful group of advisors in the Medo-Persian and
Babylonian empires. More than just soothsayers and magicians, they were
dignitaries. And though they weren't kings, they were men of tremendous
importance.

But even with all their knowledge, these wise men still had not found the
answers they had been looking for in life. You might say they were seekers.
We know they were true seekers, because God revealed himself to them
in a special way when the star led them to the place where they could find
Jesus: "When they saw the star, they rejoiced with exceedingly great joy"
(Matthew 2:10). Then they offered Him their gifts of gold, frankincense,
and myrrh.

God tells us in Jeremiah 29:13, "And you will seek Me and find Me,
when you search for Me with all your heart." If you are also a true seeker,
if you want to know the true God, then He will reveal himself to you too.

THE LITTLE THINGS

Don't you realize that you become the slave of whatever you choose to obey?
You can be a slave to sin, which leads to death, or you can choose to
obey God, which leads to righteous living. (Romans 6:16, NLT)

When I was a kid, I collected snakes. I thought they were just great, and I had them in all shapes and sizes.

I once met a man who collected venomous snakes and had worked in some type of zoo. I really admired him. He had been bitten by a tiger snake, which is the most venomous snake on Earth—even worse than a cobra. This man survived the snakebite because he had been taking serum and had developed an immunity to the tiger snake's venom. As a result, this man basically thought he was indestructible, that no snake would ever take him down. He actually had cobras that had not been defanged slithering around loose in his house.

One day in his home, he was bitten by a cobra and didn't realize it until later when his leg began to swell. He was rushed to the hospital and died. This man thought that because he had survived the tiger snake's bite, he didn't need to worry about cobras. That became his downfall.

Many times, it is the little things that bring us down. Some Christians think, "I can handle this. I'm strong. I'll never fall." But we need to be careful.

When we feel the most secure in ourselves, when we think our spiritual lives are the strongest, our doctrine is the most sound, and our morals are the purest, we should be the most on guard and the most dependent on the Lord.

Sometimes the weakest Christian is not in as much danger as the strongest one, because our strongest virtues can become our greatest vulnerabilities.

MAKE THE RIGHT CHOICE

"I have set before you life and death, blessing and cursing; therefore choose life, that both you and your descendants may live." (Deuteronomy 30:19)

When I first became a Christian, I decided that I would somehow find a way to live in two worlds. I was planning to hang out with my old friends and still be a Christian. For a time, it was almost like I was in a state of suspended animation. I wasn't comfortable with my old buddies, but I wasn't quite comfortable with the Christians, either.

So I decided to be Mr. Solo Christian. I even said to my friends, "Don't worry about me. You're thinking I'll become a fanatic and carry a Bible and say, 'Praise the Lord.' It'll never happen. I'm going to be cool about this. I won't embarrass you, but I'm going to believe in God now."

However, as God became more real to me and I began to follow Him more closely, He changed my life and my outlook…and my priorities began to change as well.

There are people who will discourage you from growing spiritually. They'll say, "I think it's good you are a Christian. I go to church, too—at Christmas and Easter, and for weddings. But you're getting a little too fanatical. You actually brought a Bible to work the other day. We were so embarrassed. You're no fun anymore. We're glad you have made changes in your life, but don't become too extreme." There are people like this who will discourage you.

When this happens, you have the choice to either do what God wants you to do or to go with the flow. So here's the question: Are you going to let people hold you back? Are you going to let people discourage you from wholehearted commitment to Jesus Christ?

The path will divide before you at this very point. Take the way of God's blessing and favor! The first step will be the hardest, but He'll be with you all the way.

WHAT CHRISTMAS IS ABOUT

Of the increase of His government and peace there will be no end, upon the throne of David and over His kingdom, to order it and establish it with judgment and justice from that time forward, even forever. The zeal of the Lord of hosts will perform this. (Isaiah 9:7)

As we look at our world today, we realize that part of the promise of Isaiah 9:6-7 has not yet been fulfilled. The Son has been given. The Child has been born. *But He has not yet taken the government upon His shoulders.* Not yet! At this time in our world, we don't have peace with judgment and justice. But the good news is that there will come a day when Christ will return. He will establish His kingdom on this Earth. And it will be the righteous rule of God Himself.

Before Jesus could take the government upon His shoulder, He had to take the cross upon His shoulder. Before He could wear the crown of glory as King of Kings, He had to wear the shameful crown of thorns and give His life as a sacrifice for the sins of the world. The first time, a star marked His arrival. But the next time He comes, the heavens will roll back like a scroll, all of the stars will fall from the sky, and He Himself will light it.

Christ came to this Earth. God came near to you so you can come near to Him—to give your life purpose and meaning, to forgive you of your sins, and to give you the hope of heaven beyond the grave. Christmas is not about tinsel or shopping or presents. Christmas is not about the gifts under the tree. Rather, Christmas is about the gift that was given on the tree when Christ died there for our sins and gave us the gift of eternal life. That is the gift He extends. That is what Christmas is all about.

WHY DID JESUS COME?

"For the bread of God is He who comes down from heaven and gives life to the world....I am the bread of life. He who comes to Me shall never hunger, and he who believes in Me shall never thirst." (John 6:33, 35)

This has been a busy time of year for almost everyone. For us as Christians, it's been a joyful celebration of the birth of Jesus. We marvel at the fact that God humbled Himself and was born in a rustic stable—perhaps even a cave—housing animals. But why did He come?

He came to proclaim good news to the spiritually hurting and broken-hearted. Medical science has found ways to reduce and even remove pain. But there is no cure for a broken heart.

Jesus came to set people free who are bound by sin, to open our spiritual eyes to our spiritual need. He came to lift up those who are crushed by the harsh circumstances and realities of life. And more than that, He came to give us abundant life. Jesus came to lift us from the physical realm of the senses to the spiritual realm to show us that there is more to life.

He came to give His life for us. Jesus said, "For even the Son of Man did not come to be served, but to serve, and to give His life a ransom for many" (Mark 10:45).

Finally, He came to die. Jesus Christ came to this Earth to seek and save those of us who are lost, just as a shepherd seeks a lost sheep.

So in all of this hustle and bustle, wrapping paper, mistletoe, and brightly colored lights, let's get down to the bottom line. Christmas is about God sending His Son to die on a cross. He was born to die, to give us abundant life, to give us a life that is worth living.

WRONGED FOR THE RIGHT REASON

> *Yes, and all who desire to live godly in Christ Jesus will suffer persecution.*
> *(2 Timothy 3:12)*

Before I became a Christian, I was always the one mocking others. So to suddenly become the one who was laughed at because of what I believed, to see people treat me differently when they found out I was a Christian—that wasn't easy.

But this will happen if you decide to follow Jesus Christ. The good news is that you are in good company.

We are so quick to quote the promises of God for His healing, protection, or provision. But when is the last time you heard someone praying, "Lord, You promised that all who live godly lives in You will be persecuted. Lord, I claim that promise"? Who would want to be persecuted?

If you are a true believer, then persecution will not uproot you, but strengthen you. It will strengthen you in your resolve to walk with Christ. I believe God will give us the strength to face persecution, should it come to us. But are we willing to make a stand for Christ?

Some people who claim to be Christians, however, are persecuted not because they are living godly lives, but because they are obnoxious and pushy. They don't know how to share God's Word in a loving, compassionate manner. They come off as condescending, pompous, and arrogant.

Let's be persecuted for the right reasons. If we're going to suffer hardships for belonging to Jesus Christ, let's do it because we are like Him and reflect Him to a dark and needy world.

JUST ONE LIFELINE

Jesus said to him, "I am the way, the truth, and the life. No one comes to the Father except through Me." (John 14:6)

I'm so grateful that the way to God has been made known to us. God has not said to humanity, "Find your own path. If you are really diligent, then you will eventually find it. You may have to climb mountains in Tibet. You may have to explore the teachings of eastern mysticism. You may even have to call the psychic hotline."

Thankfully, God has clearly told us how we can be forgiven of our sins. Only one lifeline has been dropped from heaven, and that is Jesus Christ and knowing Him. There is only one correct answer to the question "What must I do to be saved?" and the answer is coming to God through Jesus Christ. He said, "I am the way, the truth, and the life. No one comes to the Father except through Me" (John 14:6).

Did any other religious leaders die for our sins, and more importantly, rise again from the dead? No, they did not. They are still in their tombs today. But Jesus Christ is alive. He was uniquely qualified to bridge the gap between God and humanity, because He was the only person to ever walk this Earth who was both fully God and fully man. When He died on the cross for the sins of humanity, He became the bridge between a flawless, perfect, and holy God, and flawed, imperfect, and unholy people like us.

Repenting of your sins and putting your faith in Jesus Christ as your Savior and Lord is a decision that only you can make for yourself. He is ready and willing to come into your life, forgive you, and be your Savior, your Lord, your God, and your Friend.

SOMEONE LIKE ME

> *For he understands how weak we are; he knows we are only dust.*
> *(Psalm 103:14, NLT)*

When we look back on the first-century believers and the apostles in particular, we tend to see them on pedestals, as though they walked around carrying pedestals under their arms, and when they were preparing to say something, they would climb up on them. They would speak in King James English. We see them as perfect people in stained glass.

Yet when we read the biblical accounts of their lives, this is certainly not the case. If we were to have had the opportunity to check these guys out back then, the last thing we would have thought was, *I think these men will change their world*. These were common, salt-of-the-earth-type people. They had calloused hands and few social graces. They were uneducated. They had a limited knowledge of the world. They had undefined leadership and no money. We wouldn't have bet too much on their future.

But something happens to a person when he witnesses someone rising from the dead. That has a way of changing your perspective. It dramatically impacted these men.

One of the things I love about the Bible is that it's a thoroughly honest book, presenting us with those whom God used, warts and all, shortcomings and all. That is one of the reasons I am so appreciative of the Bible. It gives hope to people like me...people like me who fail...people like me who fall short. We think, *If God can use someone like that, maybe there is hope for me*. That is precisely the point. God recorded all this for us so we can see that He can work in spite of our weakness.

NO IMAGINARY PLACE

"And do not fear those who kill the body but cannot kill the soul. But rather fear Him who is able to destroy both soul and body in hell." (Matthew 10:28)

The word "hell" makes a lot of people bristle. They don't like the idea of hell, and they don't think it is right or just that God would send anyone there. Others will shrug it off, laugh about it, and say that it will be one big party. Still others envision hell as a cartoonish place with the devil sitting on a throne and holding a pitchfork.

People may try to laugh it off, but hell is no joke.

Most of the biblical teaching on the subject of hell came from Jesus Christ himself. Of the 1,870 verses in Scripture recording the words that Jesus spoke, 13 percent are about judgment and hell. And more than half of the parables Jesus told relate to God's eternal judgment of sinners.

Jesus spoke more about hell than everyone else in the Bible put together. Some wouldn't expect Him to speak about hell, because they think of Him as the personification of love and compassion. And He is! That is exactly why He warned people again and again about the reality of hell. He doesn't want anyone to go there. The same Jesus who tells us about heaven with all of its glories also tells us about hell with all of its horrors. He never would have said these things if they weren't true.

John Lennon sang, "Imagine there's no heaven. It's easy if you try. No hell below us. Above us only sky.... " We can imagine all we want, but hell is a real place. And we need to know what the Bible says about it. For our own sake...and for the sake of everyone we love and care about.

THE DANGEROUS QUESTION

*Therefore, whether you eat or drink, or whatever you do,
do all to the glory of God. (1 Corinthians 10:31)*

What does it mean to test God? It is the mentality that asks the question, "As a Christian, how much can I get away with and still be saved? How far can I go and still be a child of God?" In other words, "How close to the edge can I get without falling off?" It is a dangerous question to ask.

The church at Corinth had developed a similar problem. It was located in the midst of a metropolitan city, with visitors coming from all around the world. The city of Corinth was entrenched in sin. The problem with the believers there was that they thought they could commit certain sins, and still remain acceptable to God.

Paul had to set the record straight. He wrote to the Corinthian believers, "All things are lawful for me, but not all things are helpful; all things are lawful for me, but not all things edify" (1 Corinthians 10:23).

Let's not push the limits and see how much we can get away with as believers. In fact, let's go the other direction! We should be asking, "How much more can I know this One who died for me and forgave me and has done so much on my behalf? How can I become more like Him? How can I make an impact in my world for Him?"

Let's not take for granted all that God has done for us in our lives. May we never see "how far we can go" and be guilty of testing the Lord. Rather, let's stay as close to Him as we possibly can.

CONDITIONAL OBEDIENCE

"Yet they did not obey or incline their ear, but followed the counsels and the dictates of their evil hearts, and went backward and not forward."
(Jeremiah 7:24)

My dog practices selective listening. When he doesn't like what I'm saying, he acts as though he doesn't understand me. If he's in my room at bedtime and I tell him to leave, he looks at me as if to say, "What?" It's as though his hearing is gone. On the other hand, he can be asleep behind closed doors, and if I go downstairs, open the cupboard, and pull out his leash, he suddenly has supersonic hearing. He's right there at my side.

When he likes what I want him to do, my dog hears and obeys me. But when he doesn't like what I want him to do, my dog doesn't hear and doesn't obey.

We can be the same with God. When God tells us to do something we like, we say, "Yes, Lord! Right away, Lord." But when He tells us to stop doing something, we say, "Uh...sorry, God, but I think You're cutting out on me. I'm not hearing you clearly. Must be a bad connection."

Jesus said, "You are My friends if you do whatever I command you" (John 15:14). He didn't say, "You are My friends if you do the things that you personally agree with." God has told us in His Word how we are to live, and it's not for us to pick and choose sections of the Bible we like and toss the rest aside.

If God tells you to do something, He says it for good reason, and you need to obey Him. If God says not to do something, He also says it for good reason. Even if you don't understand it, obey Him.

You'll be glad you did. Blessing always follows obedience.

AFTERWORD

J ust about everything I can think of in this world of ours has its limits: wealth, time, wisdom, opportunities, even physical life itself.

Paul wrote: "For this world in its present form is passing away" (1 Corinthians 7:31). John declared: "And this world is fading away, along with everything that people crave" (1 John 2:17, NLT).

But I'll tell you one thing in my experience that has no limits at all.

It's God's Word. In one Bible paraphrase, the psalmist declares: "I see the limits to everything human, but the horizons can't contain your commands!" (Psalm 119:96, The Message).

No matter how many times I read a passage of Scripture, there's always something new, something I'd never seen or considered before, some fresh Word from the Lord. It's like peeling an onion, finding layer after layer—only the onion never grows smaller. With the Holy Spirit as our Guide and Teacher as we read and study the Word, we will never exhaust its wisdom, beauty, and good counsel. No one will. Not ever.

This devotional is just one more example of that truth. I have dipped into the Word here and there, bringing up questions, insights, and encouragements for life. And the desire of my heart is that these daily pages will simply whet your appetite for more and more and more. Sometimes you may find yourself with limited time and can only read a little. At other times, you'll want to lose yourself in the depths, immersing your heart in truth.

Either way, the Lord will speak to you, help you, sometimes warn you, but always draw you close to Himself.

So the way I see it, you may be finishing a devotional, but the whole Bible still lays before you…infinite in its wisdom, because it was inspired, word for word, by our infinite God.

ABOUT THE AUTHOR

Greg Laurie is the pastor of Harvest Christian Fellowship (one of America's largest churches) in Riverside, California. He is the author of over thirty books, including the Gold Medallion Award winner, *The Upside-Down Church*, as well as *For Every Season, Volumes One and Two*. He also has released his autobiography, *Lost Boy*. You can find his study notes in the *New Believer's Bible* and the *Seeker's Bible*. Host of the "A New Beginning" radio program, Greg Laurie is also the founder and featured speaker for Harvest Crusades—contemporary, large-scale evangelistic outreaches, which local churches organize nationally and internationally.

Greg and his wife Cathe live in Southern California, and have two sons, one on earth and one in heaven. They also have two grandchildren.

OTHER ALLENDAVID BOOKS PUBLISHED BY KERYGMA PUBLISHING

The Great Compromise

For Every Season: Daily Devotions

For Every Season: Volume II

Strengthening Your Marriage

Marriage Connections

Are We Living in the Last Days?

"I'm Going on a Diet Tomorrow"

Strengthening Your Faith

Deepening Your Faith

Living Out Your Faith

Dealing with Giants

Secrets to Spiritual Success

How to Know God

10 Things You Should Know About God and Life

Better Than Happiness

His Christmas Presence

Making God Known

The Greatest Stories Ever Told

The Greatest Stories Ever Told: Volume II

Why God?

Visit: www.kerygmapublishing.com
www.allendavidbooks.com
www.harvest.org

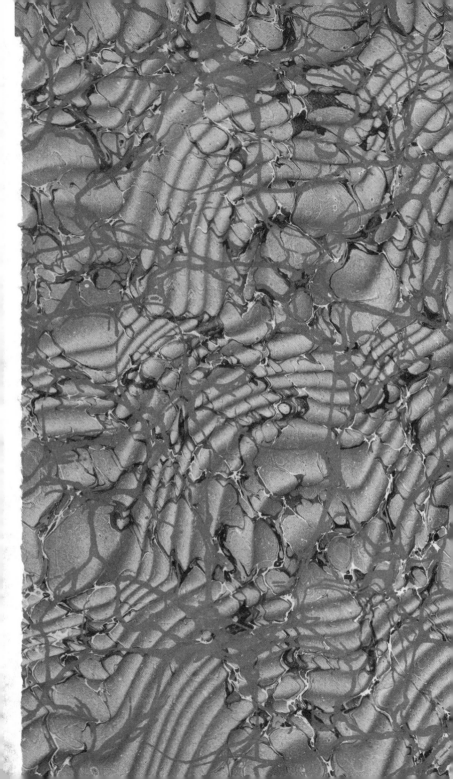

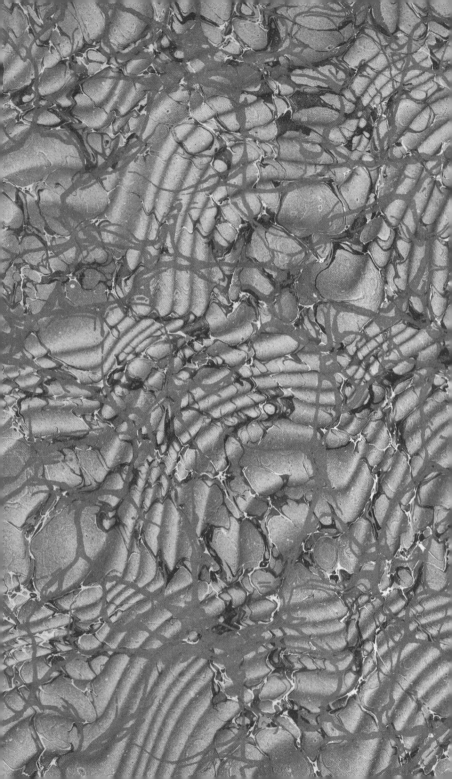